More Voices of The Willows

and the Adoption Hub of America

KelLee Parr

Published by KelLee Parr, 2020.

MORE VOICES OF THE WILLOWS

First edition. October 21, 2020.

ISBN: 978-0997849226

Written by KelLee Parr.

Table of Contents

Acknowledgements 1

Preface 3

Chapter 1 | The Seclusive Willows 6

Chapter 2 | New Information on The Willows 19

Chapter 3 | Kansas City Maternity Homes 36

Chapter 4 | Opal's Story | (1908) 53

Chapter 5 | Robert's Story | (1927) 62

Chapter 6 | Johnny's Story | (1928) 69

Chapter 7 | Steven's Story | (1943) 96

Chapter 8 | Jan's Story | (1949) 105

Chapter 9 | Janet's Story | (1949) 112

Chapter 10 | Judi's Story | (1950) 130

Chapter 11 | Patty's Story | (1951) 137

Chapter 12 | Linda's Story | (1951) 150

Chapter 13 | Barbara's Story | (1952) 158

Chapter 14 | Cynthia's Story | (1955) 177

Chapter 15 | Joni and Susan's Story | (1955–1958) 184

Chapter 16 | Sally's Story | (1958) 198

Chapter 17 | Amie's Story | (1961) 212

Chapter 18 | Norma and Dan's Story | (1962) 221

Chapter 19 | Kathy's Story | (1964) 237

Chapter 20 | Peggy's Story | (1965) 247

Chapter 21 | Jane and Peter's Story | (1966) 253

Chapter 22 | Carol's Story | (1969) 285

Chapter 23 | Letters to the Social Worker 295

Author's Notes 303

Acknowledgements

I would like to thank all the wonderful people I have gotten to know in the past two years since *Mansion on a Hill* was published. It has been a joy to meet so many great people and hear your stories. Not all of these stories were shared to be in this book but each is special in its own right.

To Margaret Heisserer, my friend and editor. Thank you for your patience, endurance and continued pushing to get this book completed.

To Trista Bieberle, my graphic designer. Thank you for once again coming up with a beautiful cover for the book.

To Karen Amos, my friend and Veil expert. Thank you for sharing your knowledge and all the hard work and dedication you have put in over ten years to help adoptees to find answers.

To Rachelle Mengarelli and LeAnn Harmon, my friends who keep me grounded. Thank you for your continued support and feedback to make the book better.

To Carol Haworth Price, my Willows' connection. Thank you for your friendship and helping me to learn more about The Willows.

To Joni Wilson, my newest Willows' friend. Thank you for contributing your story and for making yourself available to support this project by sharing your editorial skills.

To Grandma Leona, Grandma Emma and Mother. Thank you because it was your lives and inspiration that made this all happen.

Finally, I would like to thank all of you who shared a piece of yourselves in your stories. Thank you for giving inspiration and hope to many others.

Preface

When I started writing *My Little Valentine* in 2014, I had no idea where it would lead. Basically, I was wanting to document my mother and my grandmother's story for our family after finding my grandmother's letters. I could never have imagined that I would write a third book and meet so many incredible people. Friendships have been made that will last a lifetime and would never have happened if I hadn't been encouraged by family and friends to share our story. As my wonderful editor and friend, Margaret Heisserer, has said to me, "You were destined to share your story and look at where it has led you."

My Little Valentine raised so many questions about The Willows. I became intrigued by its history and the huge number of women and families (just like mine) it served over so many years. However, the more I talked to people about my book, the more I realized just how few actually had ever heard of the facility or the role Kansas City played in the adoption world. It was definitely a well-kept secret and the seclusion hospitals did a darn good job of hiding from society and the history books.

As more and more people read my mother's story, I started to hear from other Willows' patients and adoptees. They shared reunion stories and asked questions about The Willows I couldn't answer. Just as I had been curious to know more, these "alums" had a need to learn more about the facility and the people behind The Willows who played such a huge role in shaping so many lives. As

I began to research The Willows, I realized a second book was necessary.

I am grateful to all those who have reached out to me and told me they appreciated *Mansion on a Hill*. It means a great deal to know it helped others to learn more facts about The Willows and to uncover some of the falsehoods that have circulated for years. Several have told me how my book encouraged them to search and they found answers they have wanted to know all their lives. That means a great deal to me and I hope others will find the answers they are seeking.

I will be forever grateful to Carol Haworth Price (granddaughter of the founders of The Willows) for accepting my friend request on Facebook and sharing her family's history with me. She was understandably hesitant at first, but when I expressed that I wanted to thank her and her family for what she had done for my family, we started on a journey that has led to a special friendship. I just wish my mother could have met Carol, her mother Garnet, and her grandmother Cora May. I know my mother would have thanked Cora May for helping her to have had the family that raised her and blessed her life.

To this day, I am still learning more and more about my mother's birthplace. In the past two years I have given dozens of presentations and spoken to hundreds of people. Giving presentations about The Willows is something I never imagined I would be doing. But every time I have spoken, someone new approaches me to share their connection to The Willows and often gives me some tidbit of information that I never knew. The desire of Willows adoptees to know more about their birthplace is real and I am glad I have been able to try and help fill a little of that void.

There are those who judge or question the Haworths' motive for operating a home for unwed mothers, but I truly believe it provided a service that was heartfelt and for the right reason. After learning about other maternity homes, I am even more grateful that my mother was born there and her adoption was made through The Willows. I do know there are those not as fortunate as my mother in their placement.

Adoption from those days sometimes led to an unpleasant and, on occasion, a horrible homelife. However, at one of my presentations, an adoptee who hadn't had the best adoptive homelife shared with me this statement. "We can't control the cards we are dealt in life. Unfortunately, there are many more children raised in terrible home situations with their biological parents and have no choice. I know many more adoptees who were blessed to have good homes where they were raised than bad like mine."

A lot has improved since my first book in regard to laws changing in Missouri to allow adoptees to get their original birth certificates (OBC). Many new connections and reunions of adoptees with their biological parents have been made after the OBC door was opened in 2018 and adoptees went charging through. After reading the "Voices of The Willows" stories that were shared in the second half of *Mansion on a Hill*, dozens have contacted me, asking if I was going to write another book. They wanted to share their stories.

Knowing how much documenting Wanda and Leona's story has meant to my family, I want to help others document their stories. *More Voices of The Willows* is a collection of additional search and reunion stories shared by Willows mothers, adoptees, and children of Willows alumni. There are a few additional reunion stories shared by some who spent time at other Kansas City maternity homes. Their stories also need to be heard. Some of the storytellers have changed the names to protect the identity of those in their stories. I have enjoyed getting to know each person who has shared and I know you will enjoy each unique story.

Chapter 1
The Seclusive Willows

It is amazing how many people are unaware or never even heard of The Willows. After asking if they have ever heard that Kansas City was the "Adoption Hub of America," I can probably count on one hand those who responded yes. A good example of this was when I traveled to Kansas City to meet Carol Haworth Price, the granddaughter of Edwin P. and Cora May Haworth, for the first time. We had a nice lunch and I shared my idea of writing my book. She offered to help in any way.

After our lunch, I thought it would be fun to drive by 2929 Main Street again. It is always fascinating to me to see the location even though the building is long gone. I then wanted to stop and see the Union Station train depot while I was in town. I had never been and I wanted to see where my grandmother arrived when she came to Kansas City for the first time.

Union Station was closed in the late 1980s and sat idle for many years. Close to being demolished, a bistate (Kansas and Missouri) initiative was passed in 1996 to restore it. The building's majestic architecture now includes a planetarium, science center (called Science City), a theater, a post office, restaurants, and shopping. Amtrak trains with daily arrivals and departures have been in operation again since 2002. It was surreal entering the huge building for the first time and imagining my scared grandmother and her brother walking down these mammoth corridors.

I stopped at the information booth to see if there was any information about Kansas City being the "Adoption Hub of America" and Union Station's role. The nice information lady had never heard of this. She was fascinated with what I shared about The Willows and women traveling by train to Kansas City. She suggested I go ask one of the docents who was at the entrance to the Union Station history museum. As she put it, "If anyone would know about The Willows, it would be Charlie. He knows everything about the history of Union Station."

Following her advice, I found Charlie. He was in his seventies and greeting people at the entrance to the exhibit, making sure all food and drink were disposed of before entering. I could tell from his smile, he loved his job and sharing about the history of this special building. I told him that the information booth lady suggested I chat with him because he knew so much about the history of Union Station. That brought an even bigger smile to his face.

Charlie asked me to join him and to sit on the bench outside the museum. He told me about his working at Union Station, dating back to when it was a train depot. He reminisced about the hustle and bustle of people coming and going. He was so glad this beautiful old building had not been demolished and was now open to the public to enjoy. It was obvious he loved volunteering and sharing his knowledge about this special place.

After receiving my brief history lesson, my first question received an inquisitive look. Had he ever heard of Kansas City being called the Adoption Hub of America and the role the train and Union Station had played in bringing over 100,000 women to Kansas City to have babies and give them up for adoption? He was astonished. He had never heard this. I asked him if he had ever heard of The Willows Maternity Sanitarium that had been located on Main Street just a few blocks up the hill from Union Station. He had some recollection of this. He said he remembered there being a hospital on

Main Street that sat up on a hill with lots of steps. His parents had pointed it out to him as a kid and had said it was a home for unwed mothers. That was really all he remembered though.

He was shocked when I told him there were between 25,000 and 35,000 (some documents say over 35,000) young women who stayed at The Willows and most gave their babies up for adoption though there were a few who kept their babies. He had no knowledge of the connection of The Willows to Union Station and was intrigued at what I shared. I told him I was working on a book about this Kansas City distinction. He suggested I might want to include photos of Union Station in my book. He told me how to get to the main office to inquire about them.

About that time a family with lots of little kids full of energy (and what looked like handfuls of cotton candy) was headed our way down the long corridor that led to the museum. Charlie needed to wrap this up and get back to his station. We thanked each other for our history lessons. I left Charlie to his task to welcome and disarm the new group before they entered the museum.

During my presentations, one of the first questions I often get asked is how did the Haworths get started running The Willows. As told to their granddaughter Carol, Edwin and Cora May brought the first girl into their home to help friends in 1905. These friends had a daughter who was unmarried and pregnant. They must have been extremely close to the Haworths and trusted them implicitly to have shared such a scandalous situation. The couple planned to send their daughter off to some relatives to have the baby, out of sight of Kansas City friends and relatives. They wanted to avoid the embarrassment and ostracism that would be placed on their young daughter and family.

In those days, it was not acceptable for a young woman to be in such a situation let alone have had sexual relations out of wedlock. The Haworths opened their arms and home to their friends, inviting the girl to come stay with them. After the baby was born, they helped find a home for the baby to be placed for adoption. Edwin would say later in his writings that there was no reason for these girls' lives to be ruined from one bad decision. They were still decent young women who made mistakes and needed help. Thus, began The Willows.

The first Willows was located in the residence of the Haworths. The first documented ads appear to have been placed in medical journals starting in 1906 and 1907. These ads for The Willows Maternity Sanitarium showed two different locations for the facility. The first address given was 217 Park Avenue in Kansas City, Missouri. The second location included two houses at 1215 and 1217 Park Avenue in Kansas City. Carol was not familiar with these locations and neither of the addresses were homes she knew that her grandparents had lived. As stated in *Mansion on a Hill*, she figured her grandparents just wanted to keep their location a secret and used fake addresses. However, I recently discovered these were legitimate ads and the Haworths lived at both of these addresses and operated The Willows there.

Ad for The Willows in medical journals in 1906
217 Park Avenue., Kansas City, MO

Ad for The Willows in medical journals in 1907
1215/1217 Park Avenue., Kansas City, MO

I was invited to give a class in Olathe, Kansas, for the University of Kansas Osher Lifelong Learning Institute lecture series about The Willows and Kansas City being the Adoption Hub of America. During my presentation, I shared these advertisements and the address of these two early locations associated with The Willows. One of my Osher students Googled the addresses of these two homes. To our amazement, she said that both of those houses are still standing and there were photos. Technology today, right? It was amazing to see current photos of these early Willows locations.

Wanting to see these houses for myself, I headed back to Kansas City a few weeks later. My first stop was at the historic Jackson County Courthouse now known as the Truman Courthouse in Independence, Missouri. In the early 1900s Jackson County had two courthouses, one downtown and this one in Independence. When Truman was a judge in the 1920s, he would travel back and forth between the two courthouses. The Truman Courthouse no longer holds any county offices but houses the Jackson County Historical Society office and archives. I wanted to look in the city directories from 1903 through 1908 and see if they had anything listed about these Willows locations and where the Haworths lived. From the only records I was able to find, it appears the Haworths must have rented these houses.

Edwin and Cora May were married October 6, 1903. They weren't listed in the city directory until 1904 and lived at 217 Park Avenue. In 1906, The Willows Maternity Sanitarium showed up for the first time and at the 217 address. Edwin was listed as superintendent. The city directories in 1907 and 1908 had them living at 1217 Park Avenue and The Willows at 1215 Park Avenue.

After leaving the courthouse with my new information, I set my GPS for 217 Park Avenue and headed from Independence toward Kansas City. It was exciting to hear the directions and to be getting closer and closer to Park Avenue. My GPS announced, "You have reached your destination." I couldn't help but sit in amazement as I stared at the building that had been the first Willows. What stories we might hear if only those walls could talk. I doubted anyone currently living at this residence had any idea how the home had been used over 100 years ago.

The house at 217 Park Avenue has seen a lot of changes when compared to the advertisement from 1906. The wraparound porch is gone and a balcony has been added, but the main structure of the house is the same as in the old photo. The advertisement photo cuts off the front yard of the house, so the steps leading up to the home aren't showing. They reminded me of the limestone wall and steps leading up to 2929 Main Street location but on a smaller scale.

The Willows 1906 and 2019
217 Park Avenue, Kansas City, Missouri

After taking photos, I entered 1215 Park Avenue into my GPS. The first thing I noticed was the 1217 Park Avenue house shown in the 1907 ad was gone and only an empty lot remained next to the house at 1215. A tree that was in the original photo at 1215 Park Avenue was even still there, just much larger. I took several photos and could just imagine the Haworths living here and hosting in their home the young women in need of help. One of these women had a baby in 1908 and gave the baby up for adoption. This baby was given the name Opal by her adoptive parents. Chapter 4, "Opal's Story," is shared by my friend Laura. Her mother Opal was that baby born at the 1215 Park Avenue facility.

The Willows 1907 and 2019
1215 Park Avenue, Kansas City, Missouri
In 1909, The Willows showed up in the city directory listed at 2929 Main Street. This would make sense because in December 1908,

the Haworths purchased the mansion and five acres that included a couple of other houses next door. The mansion was built in 1873 by Colonel Asa Maddox. He was a pioneer lumber dealer and prominent citizen of Kansas City for over forty years. He was an active Mason for many years and helped establish Temple Lodge. He died in 1897.

Asa Maddox's widow and her family are listed as the residents in the 1908 city directory. They remained in the mansion until December 14, 1908. The mansion became The Willows shortly thereafter. Newspaper records show that there was a fire in the attic on Christmas Eve morning, December 24. Six women and infants were living at the hospital and moved to an annex building. An interesting note, Carol shared that her father was born on December 23, 1908, and he was probably one of the six babies in the nursery who were carried out of the burning building.

Union Hill, Kansas City, Missouri
X shows The Willows' approximate location
Google and the Google logo are registered trademarks
of Google LLC, used with permission

The Willows was located in an area originally called Dutch Hill but today is called Union Hill. It overlooks downtown Kansas City. Union Hill is about a four-block area south of Crown Center and

Union Station. It is an area between Main Street and Gillham Road. Within Union Hill is the oldest public cemetery in Kansas City, Missouri, called the Union Cemetery founded in 1857. It is located just north of where The Willows stood. It is listed on the National Register of Historic Places and many of the early founders and prominent citizens of Kansas City, including Colonel Asa Maddox, are buried there with a majestic view north over downtown. One of the most famous people buried in the cemetery is George Caleb Bingham, known in his lifetime as "the Missouri Artist." He was a soldier, politician and an artist. He was a member of the Missouri legislature and fought the extension of slavery westward.

With the Union Cemetery being so close to The Willows, one would wonder if there might be stillborn infants buried in the cemetery. Kevin Fewell, President of Union Cemetery Historical Society, shared that there is a section of the cemetery that has markers for stillborn infants and children up to two years of age. There also is an area of the cemetery called Potter's Field for impoverished people where some infants are buried. It seems logical that this could be the resting place for infants who were lost in childbirth at The Willows. There is record of one child who was one year and three months old who died from lobe pneumonia and congenital debility in 1910. The address on the death certificate record shows 2929 Main Street. However, no other records have been found to date that show stillborn infants from The Willows buried there.

The Union Hill area was serviced by Kansas City's large streetcar system that included running along Main Street from Union Station past The Willows. The first streetcars (horse-powered) began operation in 1870. By 1908, at the opening of The Willows, the streetcar on Main had been converted to electrical power. Young women or families could have traveled by streetcar or taxi from

Union Station to The Willows. The streetcars remained in service until the last one was shut down in 1957.

The Willows is no longer standing as it was torn down shortly after closing in 1969. The steps leading up to an empty lot where the building stood were there for many years. Peter—who is Jane's son from Chapter 20, "Jane's Story," in this book—remembers many years when he was growing up in Kansas City going down Main Street to Crown Center with his parents. They would point out the location where he was born. He recalled during the late 1980s when he was in college at University of Missouri–Kansas City (UMKC) that he went down there, parked, walked up the steps, and just stood on the empty lot, taking it all in.

In the early 1990s, after searching and finding my grandmother, I drove to Kansas City from Topeka. I wanted to see the place where my mother was born. I didn't know anything about The Willows other than that was where my mother was born. I thought it might still be there. I was quite disappointed to see that in its place stood a Residence Inn hotel. I remember thinking there was something ironic about it being a "Residence" Inn with the history of the location. I took photos and shared them with my mother.

Today there are condominiums in its place. Recently a man named Phil Samuell contacted me and shared that he was born at The Willows in 1950. His sister was born there in 1945. He was passing through Kansas City on his way home from Colorado and drove by 2929 Main Street to see the location where he had been born. Of course, to his disappointment, the building and long climb of steps were no longer there. He suggested it would be nice if there was a historical marker placed to show where so many were brought into this world.

With an estimated 30,000 babies born there, Willows alumni and relatives are scattered all across America. Who knows how many others have gone to 2929 Main Street in search of a peek of their history.

2929 Main Street, 2020
Photo courtesy of Phil Samuell

A historical marker would be a good way to educate Kansas Citians unfamiliar with the history of The Willows and Kansas City's distinction as the Adoption Hub of America. The Jackson County Historical Society has given their full support to the project, as has the granddaughter of the Haworth family, Carol Haworth Price. Through Phil and Carol's perseverance and dedication to this project, the marker is being made as I write this. Willows alums and friends have contributed to help bring the historical marker to fruition. They are working on getting permission to erect the marker at the corner of 2929 Main Street and Walnut Street, hopefully in November 2020.

The following is a mockup of what the historical marker will look like.

THE WILLOWS MATERNITY SANITARIUM
Home for Unwed Mothers

At this location, 2929 Main Street, stood The Willows Maternity Sanitarium. It was a home for pregnant unwed mothers in a time when the situation was unacceptable by society for mother or child. Established by Edwin P. and Cora May Haworth in 1905, The Willows was moved to this location in 1908 after the Haworths purchased the mansion from the Asa Maddox family. The home was established for the benefit of the unfortunate young woman and her child facing social and moral ostracism. The Willows was known as the "Ritz" or "Waldorf" of the many such facilities in Kansas City, helping Kansas City to be named the Adoption Hub of America in the early- to mid-1900s. At capacity, The Willows could hold as many as 100 young women and 125 infants. Often the young unmarried women traveled by train to Kansas City Union Station and then took a taxi to The Willows to remain in seclusion until giving birth. The women would return home heartbroken and empty-handed as each left her child to be adopted by another family. An estimated 30,000 babies were born here and placed for adoption. The Haworth family owned and operated the facility until it closed in 1969.

"The pergola covering the walk up to the front yard of the Sanitarium is rose- and vine-clad, forming a sheltering shade from the glaring sun and light of summer's days and offering a windbreak from storm and wintry blasts. And so its soft shadow and protection break the view of the outside glaring world from her who passes under its sheltering panoply. She walks with a sigh of relief and may draw the deep breath of relaxation and comfort that has failed her for some time previous to her coming. Quiet, peace and rest find her who enters here."

– E. P. Haworth, 1925

Chapter 2
New Information on The Willows

It is important when reflecting on the history of The Willows to understand and grasp how different times are today compared to when The Willows opened one hundred fifteen years ago. Much changed during the sixty-four years The Willows was in operation until it closed in 1969, but even fifty years ago, the negative perception society placed on the unmarried, pregnant woman remained. The way women were treated in those days was deplorable and women's rights were few when it came to a choice of keeping their babies. The stigma of being unmarried and pregnant was horrific, an abomination for the girl, family, and child born out of wedlock.

Thankfully today that perception has changed but it took a long time. If one reads all the documentation that E. P. Haworth wrote over the years about this subject, it is pretty apparent that the Haworths were ahead of their time as far as their compassion and empathy for the plight of these women in this situation. Today one might believe the philosophy of The Willows was misguided in the push for secrecy, seclusion, and placement of babies for adoption. After reading hundreds of pages of documents, I truly believe E. P. and Cora May's hearts were in the right place and believed faithfully in their mission as Christians.

A thirty-two-page document called *Who Will Help—How to Get Help* published in 1927 goes into great detail, sharing the philosophy of The Willows. It gives a clear image of the era and societal attitude. Mr. Haworth explained his beliefs and why they wanted to help these women and their babies. Here is just one passage that shows a little insight into his thinking:

"She knows that she has made a mistake. It had already occurred and she cannot avoid the misfortune that follows in the wake of this mistake. And in any case, she cannot provide the child with freedom from the stigma of conception that society places on cases like hers.

The double standard as set by society has forced womankind to undertake every conceivable means to cover up her mistakes from society, knowing full well the catastrophe which would befall her once her secret became known. With her brother flaunting his mistakes in the face of the world and receiving little or no condemnation, can she then be blamed for seeking to protect herself from injustice and suffering from which until recently she had had little or no recourse?" – E. P. Haworth

Recently my friend Kathy Dayberry, whose story is found in Chapter 17 of this book, shared with me a Willows document I had never seen before. It is titled *Troubled Waters* and is from 1919.

Troubled Waters document
Photo courtesy of Kathy Dayberry

In this document, Mr. Haworth shared information that is the most detailed about The Willows I have seen. Known as a seclusion hospital to protect the patient's identity, The Willows prided itself in helping keep each young woman's secret. The 1919 document addresses the question "How do you guard the respectability and identity of the patients?" This is the response given.

"In the first place we impress upon the young lady that because she has made a misstep, is no reason for her to lose her own self-respect or the respect of others. In The Willows all of the patients are living in glass houses. They cannot throw stones. To preserve this condition, the married woman is denied admittance.

The unfortunate young woman's mistake is not thrown in her face. She is not 'preached' to. Rather she is inspired with the thought that her future can be just the same as any girl's if she lives right and her secret has not been public knowledge.

Our records, including all of the correspondence with the physician, are kept in locked files available to no one except those in the office whose business it is to look after it. No matter how old these records are, even when they are placed in transfer cases, they are kept locked. When the patient enters The Willows, her identity is lost. She is known to the nurses, other patients and those about the institution only by her first name. She is Dorothy, Charlotte, Mary or Rose to everyone here through her entire stay, and need not be otherwise known unless she herself tells more.

While the unfortunate young woman is in seclusion at the Sanitarium, she need not be seen by anyone outside the home, unless she so desires. However, provisions are made that friends and relatives may visit her on occasions, with her consent."

Over the years, much had changed, but this *Troubled Waters* document shines an early light into the day-to-day operations of the facility after just fourteen years of being in existence. It is written for practitioners to give them specific details of commonly asked questions. It is in a dialogue format as if writing answers to a Dr.

J. W. Williams, who is inquiring about The Willows for one of his patients.

Let me share a few of the tidbits of information I have gleaned from this document. One of the first things that jumped out was the statement *"The Willows is the largest exclusively seclusion maternity hospital in the country."* The maximum capacity at this time was seventy-five patients. By 1919, The Willows had already had over 2,000 women stay at their facility. I have often been asked how long did the women stay at The Willows. Again, this changed over the years and was adjusted case by case, but this document answered the question for this time period.

"We take every care to hasten the convalescence of the patient, but their physical condition requires that they remain at least two weeks after confinement [delivery] *that they may be well and strong upon their discharge and that the baby may be given a start in life at the mother's breast as nature intended it should."*

Arrival

Dr. Williams asked, *"Should a physician accompany his patients to The Willows?"* Mr. Haworth's answer was that it was preferable for the personal physician to accompany the young woman for the patient's peace of mind. It would also provide the physician an opportunity to see the facilities where his patient would be living while in seclusion.

"The practicing physician of today is almost as much of an advisor as he is a practitioner. The patient, when she comes accompanied by her physician, will feel that she has at least one outside friend to whom she can turn for advice and counsel should she wish. While it is not necessary for a patient to be accompanied by her physician, we believe in its advisability."

The Willows gave the doctor directions to take a taxi and come to the back entrance at 2926 Walnut Street. The other option was to take the trolley car, which ran from Union Station past The Willows, and get off at 29th Street and walk the half block south.

Dr. Williams also asked what would happen if he was unable to accompany a girl by train. Mr. Haworth's reply was someone would be at the train depot to greet and escort the girl to The Willows if given forty-eight hours' notice.

"Should necessity require, she can come here alone and be assured of just the same treatment as though you brought her."

Living Quarters

Another new piece of information was the level of care provided the women. There were three departments. First was the **New Addition**. This was the most upscale and expensive section of the home. It had capacity for fourteen patients.

"These rooms are attractively and tastefully furnished with two single metal beds finished in white enamel or Vemis Martin [a type of gold effect]. *The beds have comfortable steel springs, good mattresses and are dressed in white linens. Each room is equipped with a lavatory with hot and cold water and a white enameled wardrobe."*

Previously, all documentation shared that the women were moved to a convalescent section after confinement, away from the girls still waiting to deliver their babies. This was not the case for the New Addition as stated in this document.

"The rooms and furnishings have been so arranged and designed that after the patient has been delivered in the confinement chamber, she is returned to her own room for recovery."

The second department was the **Main Building**. This was an intermediate grade of service, though the document states the rooms were constructed under the same plans as the New Addition but not furnished as elegantly. The same quality service is provided. The Main Building had accommodations for thirty-six patients.

"This building is only a few years old and the rooms are constructed on a similar plan to that in the New Addition although not furnished

and equipped as elegantly as in the New Addition. The rooms are as neat and home-like as is consistent with Hospital sanitation. Each floor has a parlor-lobby the same as the New Addition, only, of course, not so elaborately furnished. The patients in the Main Building have their own bathrooms which open off the parlor-lobby on each floor."

The last department was **The Cottages**, which provided accommodations for women with limited means. Two adjacent Cottages, on the back end of the lots, connected by an areaway with each other and the front buildings, formed two of the general divisions of The Willows. These were not really cottages but two-story residence buildings constructed of brick and frame and slate roofs. Like the rest of the locations, they were heated by steam. One of these cottages was the Nurses' Cottage or home. The Cottage residents' babies were delivered in one of the confinement chambers in the main building and then moved to one of the convalescing rooms on the second floor of what was once the administration building. Small ward service was rendered there. The Cottages had rooms for twenty-five additional patients.

"The rooms in The Cottage are clean and substantially furnished although not as elaborately as the appointments in the other buildings. They are light and airy with north, east and south exposure. The building is modern in every way, oak finished on the first floor, steam heated, has a tub bath and hot and cold water. The Cottage department offers the services upon which The Willows Maternity Sanitarium first established its reputation, only the services are better now than they were then."

Kitchen and Dining Room

Imagine what it must have been like to have a kitchen to feed seventy-five women in 1919 and up to a hundred women at The Willows highest capacity. Dr. Williams asked, *"And the kitchen? Have you any special diet service? What about food supply?"* There was a general kitchen where all meals were prepared for serving in the dining room. The cook had a double range, large cook's table, racks for cooking vessels and a bain-marie system (a type of heated bath) for keeping the food warm.

"While our kitchen is large and of hotel size, still our menu and service are of the 'home' variety and the meals made home-like."

The Willows had a diet kitchen connected to the main kitchen to provide high-grade diet service during convalescence. The staff wanted to provide the best meals possible to make sure the mother and baby would have the best results possible. Diet kitchen meals were served on dainty china with glassware for beverages to make meals more attractive and enhance the tastiness of the meals.

The facilities included a temporary storage room for supplies used on a daily basis and then large storage rooms in the basements, including the basement of one of the Cottages. They could store huge quantities of food (canned goods, vegetables and fresh fruits). Items purchased in bulk were priced much lower than when bought in small amounts. In addition to food, a large quantity of milk was required and cared for properly.

"The basis of the babies' foods is pure, high-grade cow's milk modified to meet the requirements of each individual child. We patronize a high-class dairy that keeps a herd of choice inspected cows for this purpose. Extra care is taken in the handling of this milk. It is double strained and put into glass bottles and immediately placed on ice. A few hours later it is delivered to the Nursery, and the only time it is off ice is when it is taken from the wagon."

Nurseries

I was also quite intrigued by the information and photos given in other documents about the nursery for the infants at The Willows. These documents often mention a roof garden nursery and the name fascinated me. But not much description was ever given. *Trouble Waters* gives a much better understanding of the infant nurseries and sheds light on how the infants were cared for in 1919. There were actually four nurseries. First was the **Main Roof-Garden Nursery**, located on the third floor of the New Addition. This was where the older babies were kept whose mothers had already left.

"In it we have built one of the most complete and comfortable of nurseries. This Roof-Garden Nursery is cut off by a closed stairway which deadens the sound of the crying babies. It has an all-window feature, which gives it a flood of sunshine from the east, south and west. In summer these windows are thrown open and make as airy a room as any sleeping porch, while even on the coldest days of winter, by means of the excessive heating radiation, we have no difficulty in keeping the Nursery as warm as toast."

There was a **Smaller Roof-Garden Nursery**, also located on the third floor. No specifics are given as to the use of this room. In the photo it appears to be much smaller but next to the larger nursery. About this nursery the document states the following.

"Careful attention to the needs of their little charges is the constant endeavor of The Willows' nurses."

The Roof-Garden Nursery was floored with battleship linoleum (a heavy gauge of flooring known for its gray color and used on US Navy ships). It was laid on concrete. There was a small elevator that provided for carrying babies from the nursery to the office floor. Next to the nursery was a **Nursery Service Room** that was advertised as being modern. It included porcelain bath slabs and bathtubs for bathing the infants.

"Built in above them is a large water tank with a thermometer and valves for regulating the temperature of the water prior to bathing the infants. By means of a spray attached to a rubber pipe, the babies are given needle-spray baths which assure a quick bath under the most hygienic and sanitary condition."

On the roof of the New Addition was a **Roof-Garden Nursery Tent**. It was open on all four sides, enclosed in fine screen wire, and had a double canvas roof, permitting an air space between.

"Through a sprinkling system the canvas is moistened. The sun on the wet canvas evaporates the moisture, cooling the tent so that even on the hottest days a Willows' baby finds some comfort in our Roof-Garden Nursery Tent."

The Willows also had a **Creche or Nursery** which was for smaller and younger babies. This was adjacent to the confinement and sterilizing room on the second floor.

"Its convenience to the sick patients [women in labor] *delegates it to the services of the new-born babies and is used exclusively for them. It is large, light, and well ventilated."*

Additional rooms included: Milk Room, Milk Refrigeration Room, Massage Room, Sterilization Room, and Drug Room

Laundry Facilities

With such a large number of young women and infants in the facility, I assumed the laundry room in the basement had to be a huge daily operation. It is stated in some brochures that some of the young women would work in the kitchen, laundry or office to help defray the cost of their stay. Dr. Williams asked, *"You have considerable laundry work. How do you handle it all?"* The *Troubled Waters* document states how the laundry was handled in 1919.

"Our laundry goes outside to a commercial laundry, but we have a large room in the new basement which is equipped to do such laundry as is done at the hospital. This room is connected with the floors above with linen chutes. There are ironing boards, drying racks, stationary laundry tubs and cupboards; also, tables and racks for counting the laundry in and out."

I often wondered what the women brought with them to The Willows. This question of Dr. Williams I found interesting, *"What clothing should the girl bring?"* The answer was quite detailed and even offered a solution when young women didn't have the time to gather the belongings required.

"Patients only wear loose clothing during their stay at The Willows and usually wear very simple garments. It is advisable to bring as little streetwear as possible, as it will not be needed and will only be in the way. A patient requires the following articles of clothing and toilet sundries for use while in waiting and convalescence: Three wrappers or kimonos, two petticoats, six night gowns, three suits of underwear, perhaps three tight underwaists, four pairs of hose, one pair loose shoes, six handkerchiefs, twelve sanitary squares, six washcloths, one toothbrush, one comb, one hair brush, one three-quart rapid-flowing fountain syringe. Such of the above articles as the patient does not have may be purchased after she enters."

I was told by a friend, who was a patient during the 1960s, there were clothes stored in the basement for the women to use if needed. As their bodies grew and larger clothes were needed, the women could go through and pick out something to wear that they liked. The clothes would be left and washed for the next patients to arrive. My friend said there was one blouse she really liked and took it home with her. Unfortunately, her mother was not thrilled with anything that was a reminder of the experience with The Willows and got rid of the blouse.

Fire Safety

After the fire that occurred in 1908, the Haworths took things very seriously to provide safety for their patients. Dr. Williams asked this question, *"Have you any fire protection?"* I found the response quite amazing. For the time period, the sophisticated system put in place was way ahead of its time. This is the answer given by Mr. Haworth:

"Hand extinguishers are provided and distributed over the entire building. In building the Main Building and New Addition of brick, precaution was taken to protect it from damage of fire. All the windows in the rooms facing and near any of the frame structures are equipped with metal sashes and frames, together with wire glass window panes.

These would prevent or delay fire from getting through the windows from one building to another. Insurance labeled metal fire doors that automatically and instantaneously close when a temperature reaches 160 degrees through the melting of a metal link have been installed between all connections of the brick with the frame building."

The Women

So, who were the clientele of The Willows? Some say The Willows was just a place for the social elite, which to some extent it was, but the Haworths never denied or misled people about their clientele. They were usually middle-class to upper-class white women. In the earlier years, they came mostly from rural or small communities. Mr. Haworth stated in the advertisements that The Willows was not a charity. It was a private institution and none of the operating expenses came from churches, philanthropic organizations, foundations, or endowment funds.

The Willows took no government money. It operated solely on the funds they received from the women and their families. They were thus able to be selective in who they brought into their facility. It was not inexpensive to stay at The Willows, which led to the label as "The Ritz" or "The Waldorf" of the Kansas City maternity homes, which seemed quite fitting. There were many high society and wealthier families who were provided service at The Willows, which guaranteed their privacy. However, the vast majority was middle-class young white women who stayed there.

They came from all over the United States and even other countries. A Willows document, *True Facts 1937 to 1946*, shows the states represented and the number of women who were patients over a ten-year period.

THESE STATISTICS COVER WILLOWS' ADOPTIONS FOR THE
PAST TEN YEARS, BY STATES, 1937 TO 1946 INCLUSIVE

State	Count	State	Count
Illinois	299	Arkansas	8
Indiana	200	South Dakota	6
Missouri	161	Pennsylvania	6
Kansas	152	New York	6
Wisconsin	100	Louisiana	5
Oklahoma	99	Florida	3
Iowa	97	Maryland	2
Ohio	97	West Virginia	2
Michigan	71	Nevada	2
Nebraska	48	Washington	2
Minnesota	44	New Jersey	2
New Mexico	28	Dist. of Col.	2
Texas	21	Idaho	1
Wyoming	19	Oregon	1
California	18	Tennessee	1
Colorado	10	Connecticut	1
Arizona	10	Hawaii	1
Kentucky	8		

*The Willows Maternity Sanitarium is an
ethical institution offering seclusion and
protection to the unmarried mother and
her baby.*

APPROVED BY

The American Medical Association

American Hospital Association

Missouri Hospital Association

Mid-West Hospital Association

The Jackson County Medical Society

True Facts 1937 to 1946
Document courtesy of Carol Haworth Price

The document shows that 1,533 Willow's adoptions occurred in these ten years. The adoptions were all made to families who had been investigated and approved by the Adoption Department of the Juvenile Court of Jackson County, Missouri. The reputation of The Willows as a highly regarded institution was noted by the endorsement of The American Medical Association, among others.

The majority of the young women who stayed at The Willows were unmarried but not all. In *Trouble Waters,* it stated that married women were not allowed. This policy changed at some point. There are documented cases of married women staying at The Willows. Most placed their babies for adoption and some kept their babies, just as unmarried women did. As you will read in Janet's Story, Chapter 9, a young married couple was not allowed by the wife's mother to keep their baby, which had been conceived out of wedlock.

Another known case was a couple with several children who could not afford a sixth child during the 1930s Great Depression. A baby was born in 1936 and given up for adoption. How difficult this must have been for the couple. They carried their secret to the grave. The son of this adoptee did a tremendous amount of searching to help his mother find her biological family. DNA testing and Facebook were the keys that unlocked the mystery. A connection was made with relatives of his mother's siblings. These siblings had no idea they had a long-lost sister. Nobody in the family had known there was a child given up for adoption. It made sense though, because there was a child born every two years until the four-year gap from twins born in 1934 until the last child was born in 1938. After eighty years, the siblings were introduced to their lost sister and a loving bond was formed.

Another interesting fact is how many adoptees born to unwed mothers have found out their biological parents eventually got married. I have heard of several such cases. This seems to have occurred often when a young woman became pregnant and the boyfriend went off to war or the couple was in college. The only solution seemed to be to place the baby for adoption because being unmarried and with child was not acceptable.

My friend Esther, born in 1929, is a great example. After getting her OBC, we were able to determine her parents got married after she was born. They never had any other children. We could not find any history of what their circumstance was, but they did marry and move to Hollywood, California, shortly after Esther was born.

Another friend found out that her parents were a couple during World War II. The boyfriend went off to serve his country and left behind his girlfriend, who later discovered she was pregnant. Though the couple was in love, marriage was not an option at that time. The only thing the young woman could do was hide her pregnancy and give the baby up for adoption. Once her boyfriend returned home from the war, they married and raised their children without ever knowing where their first baby was located.

The stories and rumors of the clientele are endless with the thousands of women who were at The Willows. One story includes a Playboy bunny from Chicago. One woman was a flight attendant who was based out of Kansas City. One of the more fascinating stories is of a woman who was sent to The Willows and assumed to be paid not to disclose an affair with a wealthy, married man from an affluent New England family. Even after being located by her child given up for adoption, the biological mother would not disclose the name of the birth father and went to the grave without sharing.

Once I was asked if famous people stayed at The Willows. There is no indication of anybody of notoriety. Mr. Haworth noted in his early writings that "The facility was not a haven for the debauchery of Hollywood and the big cities with loose morals. Instead they focused on helping the young women, mostly rural country girls who were of higher standards but who succumbed to temptation or were forced upon without consent."

The Willows was not riddled with lawsuits and scandals, as several other facilities were in the day. There were rumors and speculation that The Willows "sold" babies. In the early years, The Willows did not receive money from the adoption families except for court costs. In 1925, when my mother was adopted, my grandparents' letter from The Willows with the bill stated the court fees were $21. The cost of the Wasserman blood tests, given to check that mother and baby did not have social disease, was $10. This was a total of $31, which was a lot of money back then. This would equate to $454 in 2020.

Over time, laws changed regarding adoption and the courts and social workers became more involved. One change was a requirement for adoptive families to wait a period of time to receive their baby they had chosen. The Willows began charging for care of a child once the baby was spoken for by adoptive parents. In a letter from Mrs. Haworth to prospective parents, it stated it could take up to four weeks for the adoptive couple to have the infant released into their custody by the courts. A minimum of $100 was charged the adoptive couple for the care of an infant once spoken for until taken to the new home.

It has been asked if the Haworths were wealthy socialites in Kansas City. In 1928, Mr. Haworth relinquished his role as superintendent of The Willows to his wife Cora May. He pursued other business ventures, including owning a trailer park. One would consider the Haworths as an upper middle-class family who lived a modest but good life. They were not part of the highest society of Kansas City. They poured their hearts and souls into The Willows and strived to make it the best facility they could.

The devotion to their mission is quite apparent in the fact that Cora May had an apartment at The Willows where she lived most of the time. Though she and E. P. owned a house, she wanted to be close to "her girls" and make sure they were taken care of properly. She passed away alone in her apartment on Christmas morning, 1953. The Haworth's son Don and his wife Garnet (Peggy) Haworth purchased The Willows from the estate and kept it operating until 1969. They had a special bond to The Willows not only because of E. P. and Cora May running it for so long, but because their daughter Carol was a Willows baby adopted in 1944.

Cora May and Garnet were often asked for advice from adoptive parents on how to communicate with the adoptees about being adopted. It was difficult for adoptive parents to know how to handle sharing information about adoption. Societal attitudes not only shamed the unwed mothers but also adoptive parents in the early years. These parents often wanted to protect their adopted children from the stigma of being born out of wedlock. They sometimes would hide the adoption from society. More often than not, parents kept the secret from their child as well. What a shock for many adoptees to find out, later in life, they were adopted. The only parents they have known aren't their biological parents. This revealed secret has caused much heartache, anger, and sadness in many adoptees' lives.

Early on, The Willows encouraged parents to keep this secret, thinking this was best for the child, the birth mother, and the adoptive parents. At that time, it might have been sage advice. But secrets almost always come out. In later years, The Willows began suggesting adoptive parents share with their adopted child from an early age that they were chosen to be a part of their family.

An adoptee shared with me a letter written by Cora May Haworth to the adoptee's mother. The mother had asked how to tell her daughter she was adopted. Cora May suggested the book *The Chosen Baby* (by Valentina Pavlovna Wasson, originally published in

1939) to the mother and encouraged her to share that her daughter was chosen.

Today, with DNA testing and social media, honesty is the only answer for adoption. Thankfully, my mother, born in 1925, was one of the children whose adoptive parents thought it best to be open and honest with her. She knew from an early age she was adopted, or chosen as she would say. She truly was blessed to have wonderful parents who raised her. Still, as with many adoptees, she had this unrelenting desire to know about her biological parents.

As has been noted before, The Willows was just one of many maternity homes in Kansas City. Sadly, some of these facilities were shady and less-than-honorable facilities. One could also easily assume The Willows was shady. However, The Willows was in operation for sixty-four years and owned by the same family. The Willows wouldn't have survived if it wasn't a reputable facility. Women who shared with me about their experiences at The Willows, though a harrowing time in their lives, have stated over and over they were well taken care of and treated with respect. My niece shared that she has read books detailing women's horrible experiences regarding maternity homes and adoption agencies from around the country. She said, "I am so thankful Grandma Leona was at The Willows and Granny was born there."

Chapter 3
Kansas City Maternity Homes

In 2019 my friend Charlene Brownson, who had read my books, asked me if I would be interested in taking part in the Osher Lifelong Learning Institute lecture series that she helped organize in Manhattan, Kansas. She thought my mother's story and Kansas City's being known as the Adoption Hub of America would make for an interesting topic people would enjoy. She shared that the lectures were geared for adults fifty and older and each was a two-hour lecture, one night a week for three weeks.

Holy cow, I didn't think I could talk for six hours about The Willows. I had given several one-hour presentations by this time—but six hours! She encouraged me to share my mother's search and reunion story, and then share all I had learned through research about The Willows and Kansas City. This sounded good but I knew it still wasn't enough. I would need to learn more about the other maternity homes that helped Kansas City earn its title. This led to more research and opened the door to some incredible discoveries.

In *Mansion on a Hill*, I shared about several of the maternity homes that I had read about in newspaper articles and other documents. Those included the Fairmount Maternity Hospital, East Side Maternity Hospital, Kansas City Cradle, St. Vincent's Hospital and the Florence Crittenton Homes. This seemed like an incredible list. Little did I know just how shortsighted and often incorrect this information was. Once I began delving deeper, I was astonished at the number of homes and the dynamics behind their existence. Oh my, this really piqued my interest and I dove into more research.

First, let me say I have just touched the tip of the iceberg in learning about these other maternity homes. Unfortunately, much of the information about them may be lost forever due to secrecy and lack of records. But with a little sleuthing, some details emerged. In all honesty, a book could and should be written about each of these facilities. I know one maternity home, The Veil, which I didn't mention in my previous book, is being documented in a future book that I can't wait to read.

One of the first things I noticed when researching the maternity homes was how the homes opened and relocated several times over their years of operation. In addition, some of the buildings were utilized by several different maternity homes, just in different years. Sort of a "musical chairs" of the homes for unwed mothers. The Willows was one of the few facilities that was stationary. It remained in the same location from 1908 until it closed sixty-one years later in 1969.

Let's take a look at some of the homes I listed in *Mansion on a Hill* and information I have gleaned through research and information shared by friends. In addition, we'll investigate several other homes that are not as well documented and almost obscure in the history of Kansas City's role as the Adoption Hub of America.

The Fairmount Maternity Hospital

The Fairmount Maternity Hospital was one of the larger homes in Kansas City and opened about 1911. In a 1913 city directory, the Long's Nurses Directory and The Fairmount Maternity Hospital were both located at 809 Troost. Mrs. T. Long was the manager listed in advertisements for the home, though it appears her husband was actively involved as well. The Long's home address was 2030 Montgall Avenue. In 1914 ads, The Fairmount Maternity Hospital's address was shown as 2024 Montgall Avenue, just down the street from the Longs' home. Documentation shows The Fairmount to have been located there until 1916.

A custody battle embroiled The Fairmont in 1915 over a baby that apparently was placed for adoption by Mr. Long without the birth mother's consent. When the adoptive parents received the baby, it had sores on its head and needed their doctor's care. After a period of time, the birth mother returned for her child, thinking the baby was just being kept until her return. It was determined the signature on the release for adoption was forged. The judge awarded the baby back to the birth mother as the adoptive mother cried out in anguish, having had the child in the adoptive couple's care for six months.

By 1917, The Fairmount Maternity Hospital was moved to 4911 E. 27th Street and appears to have been there until 1934. The records show that a group (possibly doctors) then took over The Fairmount at some point. This group leased from the Neurological Hospital the three-story building plus basement at 1414 E. 27th Street from 1934 until 1951.

Ad in *Wichita Daily Eagle* newspaper May 18, 1919
A group of private doctors, headed by Dr. Fred R. Kyger, purchased the Brighton Hospital property at 4911 E. 27th Street in 1951. This was the previous location of The Fairmount from 1914 to 1916. Records show that The Fairmount remained in operation until August 1963 when it closed.

The Fairmount Maternity Hospital (1931–1952)
1414 E. 27th Street, Kansas City, Missouri

There appears to have been some cooperation between the maternity homes in finding adoptive parents. Several adoptees have original birth certificates that show they were born at The Fairmount, but their adoptive parents actually adopted from The Willows. In later years, social workers handled the adoptions at multiple maternity homes, and it would be easy to understand how this could have happened.

Florence Crittenton Homes

The Kansas City Florence Crittenton Home for Girls was one of the first homes for women opened in Kansas City in 1896. It was located in the City Market area and originally began as a home for prostitutes but later focused on unwed mothers. Florence Crittenton was relocated to 225 W. 43rd Street at Wornall Road. This was a non-profit organization as compared to The Willows, which was a family-owned, for-profit business.

Their original mission was to help the young women keep their babies and only place them for adoption when absolutely necessary.

This was true until around the 1940s when the Florence Crittenton leadership philosophy and societal pressures changed. Birth mothers at Crittenton were strongly encouraged to place their babies for adoption. Some have stated they weren't really even given an option. Crittenton stressed that a single mother would have extreme difficulty in raising a child on her own. They said it would be best for mother and child to go the adoption route. It was a complete shift in ideology from the original intent of the founders of the organization.

There was a second Florence Crittenton opened in 1925, which was the Florence Home for Colored Girls. a four-bedroom home. Elizabeth Bruce Crogman was instrumental in getting the home open with a donation from philanthropist William Volker, a wealthy Kansas City businessman. His Volker Foundation and anonymous donations, led him to be nicknamed "Mr. Anonymous of Bell Street." Volker lived in a modest house at 3711 Bell.

Later, in 1930, he donated an additional $10,000 and Mrs. William N. Marty donated land for a new facility at 2228 Campbell Avenue. This facility provided shelter, medical care, education, and counseling for thirty women and their children. In 1958, it was renamed Florence Home. This facility operated until the 1970s when it merged with the Florence Crittenton Home and became racially integrated. Florence Crittenton evolved into a 156-acre mental health facility for children and their parents.

St. Anthony's/St. Vincent's

The Catholic Charities of Kansas City and St. Joseph opened the St. Anthony's Home for Infants in 1899. They were located at 3210 E. 23rd Street between Walrond and College Avenue. A sixty-room building was added in 1906 and called St. Vincent's Hospital. Children were kept at St. Anthony's until age five before being sent to orphanages. In 1915, a new wing was added to accommodate 235 children. The new wing was St. Anthony's and the old wing became known as St. Vincent's Maternity Hospital. Babies were often left on their doorstep.

In 1954, the hospital became a general hospital and was named Queen of the World Hospital. The maternity home was relocated in the former Fairmount Maternity Home at 1414 E. 27th Street, which previously had been the Neurological Hospital. At this location, there was residency for twenty-five women and the rest were outpatients. The babies were most often born at St. Mary's Hospital.

In 1964, the home was changed once again. At this time, infants were not cared for at St. Anthony's but instead placed in foster care homes until adopted. It was felt that personal contact and sensory stimulation were important. Additional space for unwed mothers was expanded into the rooms once used for infants. The name was changed to St. Anthony's Home. Medical attention was provided most often through St. Mary's Hospital where the babies were usually born.

St. Anthony's was closed in 1969 due to lack of personnel. This is often where confusion comes into play regarding its role with adoption in Kansas City. St. Anthony's originally was just for infants and St. Vincent's was the maternity home. Then in 1954 after the move, the name St. Anthony's was used for the maternity home.

East Side Maternity Hospital
Harry M. Evans Children's Home Finding Society
Kansas City Cradle

In many documents, East Side Maternity Hospital and Kansas City Cradle are often listed as the same facility. Toss in the Harry M. Evans Children's Home Finding Society and it is really confusing. City directories and a couple of timelines helped reveal the details a little bit clearer in my research. First, East Side Maternity Hospital and Kansas City Cradle were different facilities and operated by different groups. The two facilities did have a close working relationship. East Side delivered the babies. The infants born to unwed mothers at East Side were sent to other facilities, primarily the Kansas City Cradle, which was a home for infants being placed for adoption.

The name for East Side is confusing. Some documents show the name as East Side Maternity Hospital and other places list it as East Side Hospital. Still others spell Eastside as one word. Whether it was a seclusion hospital similar to The Willows, I have yet to determine. The maternity hospital was started in 1914 with Alva B. Mulvany as the manager. It was located at 6800 Independence Avenue. According to the 1924 city directory, it was moved to 920 Newton Avenue and Mulvany was still manager. However, in 1945, East Side Hospital was relocated to the site of the old Fairmount at 4911 E. 27th Avenue. I have not been able to find information about when East Side Hospital was closed.

The Kansas City Cradle actually began as the Children's Home Finding Society about 1916 with R. C. Riley as the superintendent. The Children's Home Finding Society was just a name and not a residence for babies. The staff helped locate homes for infants. Mrs. T. W. Hill conceived of the idea of a home for infants and found a location near Mercy Hospital. In 1920, the Harry M. Evans Children's Home Finding Society began, thanks to donations from Harry M. Evans, a wealthy philanthropist, and Kansas City socialites. It was not a maternity home but considered an adoption agency. It opened on June 23, 1920 at 520 Woodland Avenue with Mrs. Hill as the superintendent.

Soon after opening, the home got off to a rough start. A baby was sent to them who was sick with whooping cough. All of the babies in the home were sent to private homes until safe for them to return. The Evans Children's Home was supported by local organizations, including the Harmony Chapter of Eastern Star. By the end of 1920, the capacity of the home was increased to forty babies and between fifteen and twenty babies were placed for adoption per month. Things went well until the end of 1921. Suddenly babies started becoming ill from malnutrition. Eight babies died from December until January. It was found the formula being used to feed the infants was being miscalculated. The board members changed their policies to ensure better care was given to the infants. Mrs. Hill retired and Mrs. Mary J. Weaver took over as superintendent.

In 1935, the name was changed to the Kansas City Cradle. Mrs. Pearl S. Matthews became the new superintendent. Money was raised to build in a new location at 4321 Wornall Road. It wasn't without protest from the neighbors, not wanting such a facility in their neighborhood. The new facility opened January 15, 1937. Adopting parents came from as far away as Texas and California to adopt from the prestigious Kansas City Cradle. At an open house in 1944, there were over 200 people in attendance. Babies wore white dresses with blue or pink booties. The boys' hair was combed to regulation and the girls wore bows. The facility closed in 1945 and became part of Saint Luke's Hospital.

The Veil

One maternity home I hadn't heard of when I wrote *Mansion on a Hill* was The Veil. This maternity home was not mentioned in any documents I had read about The Willows and the other Kansas City maternity homes. I was contacted by someone who had read my book and asked if I had ever heard of The Veil. This person was born there and couldn't find any information. Since I hadn't heard of it, I decided to look on Facebook and there was a group for The Veil. I wrote a question on the group page, asking if anyone could tell me about The Veil. Someone answered and told me I should contact Karen, saying she was the authority on The Veil. I sent her a message and she wrote me back.

We began to share and I learned Karen is an adoptee. She researched and found information about her biological parents. During her search, she began connecting to adoptees from The Veil though she herself was not a Veil baby. After learning there just wasn't much information about The Veil, Karen wanted to help these Veil adoptees. Her adventure began, gathering information and helping Veil adoptees for over ten years. She has a database with over 900 adult Veil adoptees whose birth families and siblings are looking for information about their biological family. There just isn't much information, but Karen is doing tremendous work to help make connections. She continues to turn over new stones and uncover new information.

We swapped information back and forth about The Willows and The Veil. Karen shared there was a Kansas City Veil and three Veil hospitals in Pennsylvania towns. The owners were Charles and Irene Janes. Karen shares that Mrs. Janes was a midwife. She believes they started receiving girls in about 1908 (and maybe as early as 1904, according to some obscure advertisements she found in archived newspapers). The Kansas City Veil, or one of its alternative names, was in operation from about 1908 until 1929 in different locations around Kansas City, Missouri. The records are quite ambiguous. They might have even had more than one location under different names at the same time.

The Janes opened their Corry Veil maternity home in Corry, Pennsylvania, in 1921 and it was open until 1927. The Langhorne Veil was open from 1927 until 1929. It appears the Janes sold their Kansas City facility at a loss in 1929 to purchase a building in West Chester, Pennsylvania, to start a new West Chester Veil maternity home that remained open until 1937.

Charles and Irene Janes
Photo courtesy of Karen Amos

When Karen first told me about Mr. Janes, she said he was born in Pennsylvania but moved to Kansas as a child. He lived near Willard, Kansas. Now I am sure my jaw must have dropped as I heard this. My parents lived on a farm that was just a few miles from Willard. Later as I researched, I found Charles Janes' family listed in the 1905 census and he was two years old. It showed his family living at Maple Hill, Kansas. They had lived on a farm that was between Willard and Maple Hill. Our farm would have been on the other side of the Kansas River from where he had lived. Small world, right?

Karen believes the Janes originally started The Veil with good intentions but seem to have gotten sideways along the way. The few documents available show they had unethical practices, if not illegal, and "shady" adoptions and several lawsuits occurred.

One thing I have found quite interesting in comparing The Veil to The Willows is that The Veil moved from location to location and changed names often, seemingly trying to stay one step ahead of health inspectors looking into their questionable practices. The first address for a Janes' maternity home that has been found is 625

Arlington Avenue in Independence, Missouri. The home was called Fair Park Maternity Home.

Fair Park Maternity Home, 1913
625 Arlington Avenue, Independence, Missouri
Advertisement courtesy of Karen Amos

It isn't clear when they began their operation but there are ads for this location from 1913 until 1918 often with a different name. On my trip to Kansas City to locate the first two Willows houses, I also went in search of 625 Arlington. Much to my amazement, the building is still standing and looks almost identical as it did in advertisements from 1913.

625 Arlington Avenue, Independence, Missouri
January 2020

Uncovered through newspaper ads and city directories, this is a list of the names used by the Janes for their maternity home in Kansas City. There are probably even more not discovered.

Arlington Hotel
Arlington Infant Home
Arlington Inn
Fair Park Maternity Home
Kansas City Maternity Hospital
Kansas City Women and Children's Hospital
Missouri Baby Home
Missouri Maternity Home
Mount Washington Infant Home
Mt. Washington Hospital
Mt. Washington Maternity Home
Mt. Washington Private Maternity Home
Mt. Washington Sanitarium
Private Confinement Home
Veil Babies' Home
Veil Baby Hospital
Veil Baby Hospital and Home
Veil Nursery
Veil Sanitarium

PERSONAL

VEIL MATERNITY HOSPITAL—OFFERS efficient medical and hospital care supplementing congenial homelike surroundings for young women during confinement. Private, reasonable. Babies for adoption. 512 E. Main St., Corry, Pa., 15 W. 31st Street, Kansas City, Mo.

Example of ad for The Veil Maternity Hospital posted by Mrs. C. M. Janes in local newspapers

```
                              10--10-10-A

FAIR PARK MATERNITY HOME—
  Strictly private, adoption free. Prices
  reasonable.  Mrs. C. M.  Janes,  625
  Arlington, Mt. Washington Station,
  Kansas City, Mo.          16—80-1tm
```

**Example of ad with different name posted
by Mrs. C. M. Janes in local newspapers**

It is interesting that at one point, the Janes opened up an office at 2828 Main Street, just down the street from The Willows. It doesn't appear that they lived at this address or had a maternity home in this location. It was just listed as the office address in their newspaper ads and doesn't show up in the city directory. Locating at such a similar address as The Willows at 2929 Main Street makes me wonder what the Janes were doing. Was it just happenstance? Were they trying to keep an eye on what was going on at The Willows? Could they confuse potential patients and steal clients? We'll never know.

The Janes also appear to have figured out the saying, "Why reinvent the wheel?" It is quite apparent that they stole ideas from advertisements created by The Willows. As mentioned before, Mr. Haworth was a prolific writer and advertiser. Catalogs created and written by Mr. Haworth in the 1910s showed photographs of the facility, staff, and the operation. They had pages describing the office, patient rooms, kitchen, dining room, nursery, and delivery rooms. It was all very elaborately laid out and new brochures were created almost every year. They could be as long as ninety pages. Very similar documents for The Veil from the 1920s have been found with almost exactly the same layout and description.

Check out the following two postcards that were included in the mailers sent to doctors across the country.

Card sent in The Willows catalog to doctors in 1910s

Card sent in The Veils information to doctors in 1920s

The cards were for doctors to use to send back for more information. Notice how similar the wording and format is in both documents. The Willows is from the 1910s and The Veil from the 1920s. Do you think it's a coincidence?

There are many stories Karen has shared about The Veil and the Janes that make me thankful that my grandmother was sent to The Willows and not The Veil. So many people have sought information about The Willows and there is quite a bit of information thanks to Mr. Haworth's documenting details in his ten-year survey accounts.

The Janes family migrated back to Kansas City after years of operating The Veil facilities in Pennsylvania. Karen told me she thought they were buried at the Mt. Washington Cemetery in Independence, Missouri. On my trip to the Truman Courthouse, I stopped at the cemetery and found their burial plot.

**The Janes' burial plot, Mt. Washington Cemetery
Independence, Missouri**

Karen is writing a book about The Veil maternity homes and the Janes. She will provide many answers for Veil babies where there just hasn't been any information. It will be a true eye-opener and maybe will help us to know more about the shadier side of at least one maternity home in the Adoption Hub of America.

Known Kansas City Maternity Homes/Hospitals

This is a list of maternity homes that were in Kansas City at one time or another based on advertisements in newspapers and other documentation.

Conley Maternity Hospital
Dr. Dunn's Maternity Home
Dr. Hartman's Sanitarium
Dr. Mathis Maternity Home
East Side Maternity Hospital
Evan Children's Finding Home Society
Fairland Heights Maternity Home
Fairland Maternity Home
Florence Crittenton Home for Girls
Florence Home for Colored Girls
Hughes Maternity Home
Kansas City Cradle
Rest Cottage
St. Anthony's Home
St. Anthony's Home for Children
St. Vincent's Maternity Home
The Veil/Mt. Washington (and other names)
The Fairmount Maternity Hospital
The Willows Maternity Sanitarium
Washington Sanitarium

The Willows would have been the premiere facility of all these listed and yet it has kept its secret for many years. As more and more people seek information about their ancestries and birth places, use

DNA testing, and search the internet, the secrets kept all these years by the seclusion hospitals in this country are coming into the light.

There is a documentary that was released in 2020 called *Unintended* by Colleen Bradford Krantz. It is a three-part series that shares the struggles of three different women who were pregnant and unmarried in the early 1900s. It depicts the embarrassment and shame society placed on the young women and families in this era and how even today those old secrets are buried very deep. It shares to what extent the families would go to hide the secret to avoid being humiliated and made outcasts by their communities.

The first episode is about a young woman who was forced by her parents to have an abortion and subsequently dies. The second episode reveals the history of seclusion maternity homes that were available for young women in the early 1900s. It shares the story of a young woman who was sent to The Willows in Kansas City to have her baby and give her daughter up for adoption. This adoptee shares her experience and search for answers. The last episode is about a lawsuit related to another woman named Maude who died during an abortion. The doctor who performed the abortion was sent to jail and the young man who was the baby's father was put on trial but not convicted. It is a very informative documentary about a topic that was not discussed with secrets buried very deep.

The rest of this book includes stories of those who have been a part of these secrets and the uncovering of them. The stories include searches and reunions, along with connections to The Willows and other Kansas City facilities. Some of the stories express the pain that birth mothers experienced by giving up their babies and the agony felt their entire lives. Other stories show the struggle adoptees have in needing to find answers. And though not all the stories have the fairy tale ending, they all share answers and healing. Enjoy!

Chapter 4
Opal's Story
(1908)

L *aura shared her mother's adoption story with me. Her mother, Opal, was one of the earliest babies born at The Willows. She was born August 11, 1908. The 2929 Main Street location wasn't purchased until December of that year. According to advertisements in early medical journals from 1905 to 1908, there were two locations (217 Park Avenue and 1215/1217 Park Avenue) where the Haworth family lived and operated The Willows before moving to their final destination. Laura's mother would have been born at one of these locations and most likely at 1215/1217 Park Avenue. The houses at 217 Park Avenue and 1215 Park Avenue were still standing in 2020.*

Searching

In 1932, my mother, Opal, was twenty-four years old with four children. Standing at her adopted mother's gravesite, Opal was handed her adoption documents by the only father she had ever known. I am not sure when she was told about her adoption. Definitely not in her childhood. I am guessing around 1926 when she got married. But she had never been given the documents.

My mother had only good memories of the life her adopted parents, William Richard and Dora Sample Farmer, had provided for her. My grandfather had been a loving father—as fine a man as he knew how to be. In his old age, his wife long-dead, my mother took him into her home and cared for him through his last years, just as he had cared for her.

But she wanted to know who she was. Where she came from. She seemed to have a great emptiness. Some need that I, her daughter, never was able to fully understand. Because I had her and my dad and a family, I knew where my place was. I knew who I was and to whom I belonged. I was surrounded by people who "looked like me." But Mother did not. And so, she began to search.

I don't know how my mother actually knew she was born at The Willows before she received her adoption papers, but in 1931, the year before her adopted mother's death, my mother had begun writing letters. She wrote to The Willows asking for any information about her birth mother.

She received a letter in response that firmly rejected any inquiry and reminded her that she should consider herself lucky and not do anything that could interrupt the life of the person who had given her birth and walked away. It was stated unequivocally that the interests of The Willows, as articulated by Mrs. Haworth, were solidly aligned with the person who had purchased their services when Mother was brought into the world. It was not a kind letter and hurt her deeply.

Letter from The Willows in 1931
Letter courtesy of Laura Redford

MORE VOICES OF THE WILLOWS

January 19, 1931

Dear Mrs. Stock:

We have your letter of January 15th and in reply will say we do not give out information of a confidential nature to strangers, have we any information to give. Our patrons, both patients and foster parents must be protected against people who make it a practice of finding out all they can about other people's affairs, hence you can appreciate how very careful we must be to protect our patrons.

Since your adoption, by Mr. and Mrs. W. R. Farmer, as you mentioned in your letter, you doubtless were well reared by them and are now married. You will probably have a family of your own, and in rearing them and caring for your household duties, you will find happiness and contentment, therefore I should let the past remain dead, if I were you. Perhaps your mother, wherever she is, is married and has a family, consequently she might be greatly disturbed and worried were you to break in upon her home life with your presence.

We usually make it a point with our patients that in the future should they wish to know something of their child's whereabouts, and provided it is satisfactory to the foster parents of the child, that we, The Willows, act as go-between and deliver any message from mother to child or from child to mother. Practically all patients, however, leave their babies for adoption and wish the incident of their having been a Willows' patient closed for all time, as soon as their baby is adopted.

I trust this information is satisfactory, and wishing you the best success in life, I am

Very truly yours,

Mrs. E. P. Haworth, Supt.

THE WILLOWS

My mother's adoption documents she received at her mother's death said that Opal was born at The Willows in Kansas City, Missouri, in 1908. Her date of birth seemed somewhat fluid. Different documents signed on different occasions gave her birthdate differently. Dr. John Kepner was listed as the attending physician. Hers was a single birth. The phrase in the document that declared her birth mother to be a "single woman" had a line struck through it.

Mother wrote again in 1938, the year before I was born. The response was less harsh but lay down requirements impossible for Mother to meet. Her adopted mother was dead. She could not get permission from her or from a birth mother whose identity she did not know. She requested an appointment to meet with someone at The Willows. They agreed to see her.

Letter from The Willows in 1938
Letter courtesy of Laura Redford

MORE VOICES OF THE WILLOWS

January 6, 1938

Dear Miss Stock:

We have your letter of January 4, and note that you wish information relative to your birth and mother. Without more information and the proper credentials, we are unable to say at this time whether or not you were born at The Willows. We, therefore, suggest that you bring your adoption record and have your foster parents come along if possible and we shall see what can be done. Any day except Sunday will be satisfactory.

Very truly yours,

Mrs. E. P. Haworth, Supt.

THE WILLOWS

At The Willows, she was directed to the office and sat in a chair across from a desk almost covered with papers and supplies. A lady came in with a folder that held all the information, all the personal knowledge that Mother sought. But it was not shared. The folder was opened and lay on the desk for the lady to review. She told Mother she could only share "unidentifying" information. It was sparse. Her mother was over twenty-one. She had a sandy complexion and she came from a town on the river. The lady got up and left the room.

She left the folder open on the desk. Mother could have reached out and read its contents easily. I would have. Probably you would have. Mother did not. She would no more have read their written records, unsanctioned, than she would have read the neighbors' mail or listened in on their phone calls—or any other act that was opposed to her rather rigid code of behavior. But she did try to read the open page—upside down—and saw beside the word "Husband," a handwritten word that she thought to be "Shidler" or something like that. Her adoption paper indicated that her mother "was not a single woman" but no other person had any claim on the child. However, Mother clearly understood when she spoke to the lady at The Willows that her mother "planned to marry" but the birth father had no claim on the child. She was told the father was not named or involved in any way.

Mother kept searching for answers through the years. She contacted an attorney that she could ill-afford. He told her she needed a private investigator for that kind of work. She really couldn't afford that either.

So the mystery lay unsolved, unspoken until one August evening in the early 1980s when Mother and I sat alone before a campfire at the lake where our family gathered for summers. The night was beginning to be chilly and she crossed her arms across her breasts for warmth. "I just want to know," she said.

"Let me try, Momma."

I didn't think she would agree. As the youngest and most frivolous, I had little credibility for such a task. But I wanted to do it for her. I said, "When we get back home, give me what you have and what you can remember and I will try."

One of my first tasks was to write to the Kansas City, Missouri, Department of Health, Bureau of Vital Statistics to get a certified copy of my mother's birth record. It gave my mother's name as Opal May Farmer, a white female. She was born on August 11, 1908. It listed her adopted parents' names and matched the previous documents showing Dr. J. W. Kepner having reported the birth.

KANSAS CITY, MISSOURI
DEPARTMENT OF HEALTH
A- 24311   Bureau of Vital Statistics

Certified Copy of Birth Record

Surname _____ FARMER, Opal May _____ Sex _Female_ Color _White_

Date of Birth _____ August 11, 1906 _____ Place of Birth _____ N/A _____

Name of Father ___ Farmer, William Richard ___ Birthplace _____ N/A _____

Name of Mother ___ Dora Florence ___ Birthplace _____ N/A _____

Birth reported by _J. W. Kepner_

File Number _____ 0-438 _____ Date of Filing _____ August, 1906 _____

State of Missouri,
City of Kansas City

I hereby certify that the above is a true and correct copy of the certificate of birth of ___ Opal May Farmer ___ filed in the office of Vital Statistics of Kansas City, Missouri; that the above certificate is filed in said office and is a part of the permanent records of the Bureau of Vital Statistics of Kansas City, Missouri.

Witness my hand as Director of Health, Kansas City, Missouri this _2nd_

day of _____ December _____ 19 _85_

_____ Richard M. Bing, MD _____
DIRECTOR OF HEALTH

An affidavit filed in this office states that this child was named ___ Opal May Farmer ___

Certified copy of birth certificate
Letter courtesy of Laura Redford

During my subsequent search in the mid-1980s, I attended meetings of an organization of adoptees seeking birth parents. I heard the stories of many adoptees who were seeking and grieving their own losses. In the earliest of my search, I met an adoptee from the Orphan Trains. The Orphan Trains provided a weirdly inhumane salvation for children snatched from the dangerous and filthy city streets of the East. They were brought to the Midwest and portioned out to any taker willing to come to the train station. A child was often carried home as a new servant or field hand—and sometimes, miraculously, simply a child to love.

I also met men adopted out from religious children's homes. The only requirement of the institution was that prospective parents belong to that specific religion. These were the angriest of men. Still seeking answers. Still loathing the people and process that determined their life in their helplessness and, too often, had delivered them into abuse and suffering.

And I met many, who like my own mother, seemingly came from nowhere, bred from nothing, claimed by no one.

My grandfather said that they "chose" mother. He and my grandmother, whom I never met, were taken into a large room at The Willows with several small cots. All the cots held babies. He said they chose Mother because of her "head full of beautiful red curls." And he loved her from that day on.

I am glad my mother was adopted by good people. I am glad her childhood was as happy as they could make it.

Opal's Parents—Dora Florence and William Richard Farmer
Christmas postcard with Opal in 1908
Photo courtesy of Laura Redford

Ten years after Mother's death, my DNA told the true parentage of my mother. I so wish I could have shared the information with her. The father's—and her mother's—last name was not Shidler, but a name when read upside down, must have looked like "Shidler." DNA has certainly proved the facts of her biological parents and they were married! I discovered that family's long trail of family secrets and sorrows.

Laura's mother Opal
Photo courtesy of Laura Redford

I would hope that those ugly days of not knowing are long gone—secrets buried in the dust of all those hidden records that would prevent another human from knowing who they really are.

Chapter 5
Robert's Story
(1927)

G inny Bennett Hesler wrote to me after attending one of my classes.
She shared that her father and her husband both had been
adopted. One doesn't hear of that situation often. Even more
astonishing, they both had been adopted from The Willows! Ginny
shared that her father had been the governor of Kansas. She sent a story
her father wrote for a friend's book about his adoption from The
Willows. I asked Ginny if she would want to share her father's anecdote,
along with her memories of her father, and share about her husband's
search for his birth parents. I am so pleased she said yes. I know you will
enjoy Ginny's sharing about her father's and her husband's adoption
and her father's heart-warming short story.

I doubt there are many out there who can say both their father
and their husband were adopted and possibly from the same place,
The Willows, but many years apart. With the pandemic these days,
I now have so much time I have been running across items of my
father's that I had forgotten. My dad was the thirty-ninth governor
of Kansas back in the 1970s—Robert F. Bennett. He served from
1975 until 1979. There is a wealth of documents written by him but
the most precious is a brief piece he wrote at the request of his friend
who was compiling a book: *I Am Loved: True Stories of True Love
from People Like You.* Dad wrote about his adoption at The Willows.

I would like to share it with you, but first let me tell you a little about my dad and my husband's stories.

As I write this, we are in such a difficult time with the coronavirus and changes that have happened in our lives. I wish there was a way to benefit from others' experiences dealing with quarantine, sheltering in place, and social distancing. It keeps me up at night and sad, confused as well as quite angry during the long days! I'm so missing my grandchildren and wondering how my grandparents would have handled this—which brings me to my dad. I wonder how he would have come to handle his leadership responsibilities in this difficult world in which we now find ourselves. I'll never know; however, he probably would have dug through all the "bs" that surrounds our life and times and found some version of truth, such as putting my children—and everyone's children—first and foremost beyond anything else.

My father's love for his children and his children's children was most important to him. I believe he learned to value little ones from his parents. And though he knew he was adopted, he also never doubted who his parents were—and knew that he was lucky to have them as his mother and father. He never tried to find his biological parents. Yet he did tell his own four kids that we had his permission to search for his biological parents and that he completely understood if any of us was curious.

I was his oldest daughter and second child after his first and only son. My father was never fond of any of the boys I dated—that is until he met the guy who I would end up marrying. Although he did not like that this guy was four years older than me, he got over that when he found out that not only was this guy's name the same as his but this new Bob was also adopted. My future husband at that time was under the impression that he was also adopted from The Willows. Later he became convinced he was adopted from Florence Crittenton. Yet after he attended an adoptees' search group at the

Kansas City Public Library, he was told that the doctor whose name was on his (edited) birth certificate was mainly the doctor known for delivery of babies at The Willows. So, he was back to believing he was born at The Willows.

My husband Bob's interest in finding his biological parents ebbed and flowed while his adoptive parents were still alive. While my father understood Bob's curiosity, he was of no help in this search but was a good listener. Unlike most people at that time, my husband felt comfortable discussing his adoption with my father. Others looked down on his curiosity and interest in discovering his genetics and heritage and saw this desire as ungrateful and hurtful.

After four years of marriage, it appeared that I was not going to be getting pregnant. My father began recommending adoption. I don't know how many times he would say how much he would love a grandchild and an adopted child would be wonderful! His law firm would occasionally handle private adoptions and we gave him our permission to let us know of any babies who might be placed for adoption through his law firm.

Dad really urged us to adopt. He loved the idea of having an adopted grandchild. He began to sing the praises of being adopted. Then wonder of wonders—I became pregnant. Well, Dad also loved the idea of having a grandchild—period. Yet he couldn't hide his disappointment of being unable to raise a lucky grandchild, adopted such as he was, who was chosen by parents just as he was. He settled for having a son-in-law, who not only was adopted but had the same first name and might have also been adopted from The Willows.

My father had no desire to search for his birth parents. He also was under the impression that his birth records were destroyed in a fire at the daughter of The Willows owners' house. (Recently I've come to find out that was not true and the records were not burned but taken to the Federal Reserve where they were probably destroyed.) Later my father told me that there might be records available through the state of Missouri, and he was going to sign some form that gave his permission for his kids and grandchildren to search if they desired.

Dad was aware that my daughters were trying to create family trees for an assignment when each was in the fifth grade. His first grandchild, my daughter Brooke, was stumped at first as she tried to tackle the assignment. She only knew who her grandparents and ancestors were on her mom's side and then only about my mother's ancestry. Brooke eventually just created the tree using the adopted parents and ancestry.

However, her little sister Erynn saw an opportunity to cut time that most required when drawing the family tree. She just drew it as she knew it. Her tree ancestry ended on one branch with just her dad. On her mom's side, one branch ended with my dad. She had a very lopsided tree that was traced back to Scotland in the 1700s—with only about a fourth of her relatives. I did have to verify for the teacher that indeed my youngest daughter had a father and a grandfather who were adopted.

My husband stopped searching for birth parents while his parents were alive. Eventually he found his original birth certificate in his father's documents. So, he found out his birth mother's name and his original name. He did not find out where he was adopted from. Brooke eventually jumped through all the hoops that Missouri required and presented her father with all of the info concerning his birth and heritage.

He discovered that his birth mother died two years after his birth. She had been shot by her husband, who then turned the gun on himself. We read all about that from the *Kansas City Times* where it was front page news. Eventually we discovered that her husband was not Bob's birth father. Unfortunately, his real birth father had recently died. However, it was quite an unexpected discovery that Bob had a half-sister! His sister was left an orphan at the age of four. They did the DNA tests and confirmed their relationship. They spoke on the phone and were in the process of making plans to meet when Bob unexpectedly died.

Brooke broke the news to her new aunt. Devastation. Bob's newly discovered blood relative—his half-sister—met the family of her newly discovered half-brother at his funeral. She has kept in touch with us and has visited us and dined with us in Lawrence. So sad. Yet my daughters also have had the remarkable experience of discovering this new aunt who very much reminds us all of Bob.

That is the story of our relatives and some we did not even know existed. Perhaps I should fill out the forms and try to see if I can find out more about my father's birth parents. I always thought that it was impossible to dig up information from the 1927 birth of my father. And maybe I should at least try before I kick the bucket, just in case.

This is my father's story he wrote about his adoption. He was so proud of his parents and being chosen. I hope you enjoy.

The Brass Button

It was a cool November day about 70 years ago. A baby boy born six months earlier was in his crib in a place called The Willows, a home for unwed mothers. He's spent the first six months of his life trying to find a mom and a dad, but he wasn't having much luck. From time to time people would come and peer, pinch and pat, but so far there had been no takers. Time was running out. He couldn't be a sweet loveable and cuddly little baby forever.

On this particular day, a man and a woman had come to The Willows looking for a baby girl, a sweet beguiling female child who would endear herself to them as only a baby girl could do. "No boys for us," the man told the nurse. Their hearts were set on finding "that special little girl." They wouldn't be looking at boys that day.

The man and the woman moved from crib to crib checking out each baby girl with great care and giving barely a glance to the boys who were also available. They wanted their chosen child to be a blonde just like the woman and to have the woman's blue eyes. There were three candidates that fit that requirement to a "T" and the couple moved back and forth between the three to decide. Each time they had to pass by one little boy's crib. He must have sensed the urgency of the situation because he grew more animated and vocal.

Finally, the man who was dressed in a suit and wore a vest adorned with brass buttons, stopped at the boy's crib to see what the ruckus was all about. Trying to calm the little tyke, he bent over the crib and gave the boy a loving pat.

That was all it took. In a split second, the child grabbed a brass button on the man's vest and held on for dear life. The man looked helplessly at the woman.

"He won't let go," he said.

The woman smiled and said, "Maybe he's choosing us."

"But he's a boy," the man protested.

"I like little boys," the woman responded.

"But he has brown eyes," the man demurred.

"I know, and right now those eyes tell me that he wants to go with us," said the woman. "I'll tell you what," whispered the woman, "if you can uncurl that little hand from your button and walk away, we'll find a blonde, blue-eyed girl, but personally, I'd rather have a brown-eyed boy to raise as my son."

So, I chose and I was chosen. I left The Willows with my parents and was the lifetime beneficiary of their love, with due credit to a little brass button.

Otto and Dorothy Bennett with Robert
Photo courtesy of Ginny Bennett Hesler

This photo shows my "Nanny" and "Grandpa" Bennett holding their one and only special son Robert. It appears to have been taken shortly after his adoption. I can even make myself believe that this newly adopted baby is staring at his new father's brass button!

Chapter 6
Johnny's Story
(1928)

John's daughter Teri (or Theresa as John informed me) wrote to me and shared that her father was born at The Willows and might like to share his story. She told me that her father was 91 years young and had lived an amazing life. Little did I know just how amazing. His story truly is incredible and filled with highs and lows but told with wit, humor, and love. Most people would be filled with anger and despair if they had his upbringing. Everything he went through in his life, and to have survived, is amazing in itself, but to become a man with such love for life and others gives me nothing but admiration for him.

I spoke to John shortly after his 92nd birthday and what a delightful person. I'm amazed at the people he has met along his journey in life. In this book, I have included just the experiences John told about his adoption and search for his ancestry. He shared more of his life story with me and this needs to be written in a book all to itself. Who knows, I just might try to make that happen. You can find "John's Life Story" on my website at www.mylittlevalentinebook.com[1]. I promise you will be amazed, shed a few tears, and grin from ear to ear. Anyone struggling with their life can read John's story and know they too can overcome any obstacle.

---

1. http://www.mylittlevalentinebook.com

Let me introduce myself, I'm Johnny. Around the later part of the year of 1927, I was conceived by a mysterious union of two people that were enjoying themselves and let things get out of control. About eight months later, I was growing into a small baby in what I found out later was a woman that I was to call mother.

My mother, Bessie, kept a big secret that she did not want anyone to know about. That secret was that she was going to have a baby, me. She was upset, as could be expected, because she was not married at the time.

She did not know what to do but a friend came to her rescue and offered to pay her way to Kansas City, Missouri, and enrolled her in The Willows Maternity Hospital. All the time I was getting excited that I was going to see the world for the first time, but I was also getting anxious for my mom to hurry up. I would like to know who the friend was that befriended my mother so that I can thank him.

I was wanting out to see the world but for some reason the exit door would not open. About a month later, there was a lot of motion going on and that was when I noticed that the exit door was opening, and I got really excited. The time was drawing near for my great entrance and I could hear my mom saying some very loud words that I could not understand as I didn't even know how to talk yet.

There was a lot of pressure against me to slide out the exit door but for a while I was holding on as I was scared as to what was happening. The pressure got too great for me and I started to slide out into the world.

Then, all of a sudden, there was a very loud scream and there was a lot of excitement as I was finally out in the world. I guess the excitement was due to me but again I did not understand why they were cheering for me, but I guess it is done for every newborn. Darn it, I thought it was only for me.

The next thing that I remember was that there was a person with a beard who was holding me, and then he gave me a strong slap on my butt, which made me start crying. I was told that the person with a beard was called a doctor, whatever that means. People were sticking things in my nose and covering me up with a really nice blanket. I guessed that I was special as I was alive. My mother was hurting now, and she was being taken care of by several people. I found out later they were called nurses. Now that I was out in the world, what do I do with myself? I was on my own.

The doctor gave me to a pretty woman who started to put something in my mouth and then gave me a warm bath because I was sorta dirty. The pretty woman put a warm blanket around me and put me in a bed so that I could get some rest as I was tired from the long trip that I just took. Because this pretty woman was called a "nurse," I thought that she was the one to nurse me but instead she put a nippled bottle filled with milk in my mouth to feed me.

Oh, by the way, my birth was on July 2, 1928. There were a lot of people out of work at this time and some were begging for a handout just to be able to survive. I guess that I was lucky to be where I was at. I had a bed to sleep in even though there were a lot of crying babies. There was always someone sticking a bottle in my mouth and then cleaning me up, as what goes in has to come out. You should have seen the look on the face of the person cleaning me. I enjoyed that very much.

After I was born, I was called **John Doe**. About seven days later, someone started calling me **John Thurmond**. I am not sure why they changed my name to John Thurmond. I was excited to be in good health and surrounded by several crying new births. At that same time, I found out that my mother was nowhere around, and I got upset as I had a feeling of attachment toward her. I was disappointed to find out that my mother had left the hospital and was headed back to her home without me.

One day a person, who the pretty nurse called a superintendent, came and picked me up and placed me in the hands of another person that I assumed to be a nurse. It was not a nurse but a person by the name of Mildred Leake. I heard people talking that she was now going to be my mother. How can that happen? I already had a mother and I got a little scared. Mrs. Leake would be taking me to her home in Missouri to raise me as her son. I was to call her Mother. In a very short time, I had had two mothers and I remember that I had only strong feelings for the first mother. This was very confusing to me and still is.

There was a procedure called "adoption" that I had to go through. Not knowing just what to expect, I got a little bit scared again. I found out later that the only thing that would affect me was that I would be leaving The Willows Hospital and traveling to Missouri, whatever that is, with Mr. and Mrs. Leake. They also told me that they were going to change my name again, this time to **Charles Louis Leake**.

Not sure what ever happened to my name of John Thurmond but I guessed that I would find out later in my life. Wow, John Doe, John Thurmond and now Charles Louis Leake.

We finally arrived at that Missouri place and they took me into their home. There is not much that I can recall about living with the Leakes. I have heard that they were loving people, but they had serious health problems. Shortly after I came there, Mr. Leake passed away and Mrs. Leake was not in the best of health. Based on her health problems, she decided to put me up for adoption again. At this time, I was only two months old and did not really understand what was going on around me.

Mrs. Leake got in touch with her niece, Mittie Barry, and asked her if she could raise Charles (me) as she (Mrs. Leake) could not do it properly. Mrs. Barry talked to her husband, Dr. Richard Barry. They wanted a boy in their life. Since I was available, they decided that they would adopt me and raise me as a good Christian boy. After the adoption, they decided to change my name again. This time it was changed to **Charles Louis Barry**. I started out my life as John Doe, then John Thurmond, then Charles Louis Leake and now Charles Louis Barry and I am only about two months old. Wow!

Baby Charles Louis Leake (Johnny)
Photo courtesy of John Thurmond

Dr. Barry was a veterinarian and Mrs. Barry was a homemaker. It took me a while to get used to calling them Mom and Dad but after so long I got the hang of it. Dr. Barry, or Dad, was a very likeable person and helped several of his neighbors with their animal problems, even though some of them had no money at the time. He would accept whatever they would offer him, such as eggs or vegetables.

Charles Louis Barry on tricycle (Johnny)
Photo courtesy of John Thurmond

There were many times that I went with my dad on some of his trips to see the farmers about a sick animal. I got a big kick out of this, as well as being able to get out of the house. There was a time when I was chased by an unfriendly goose and I wound up on top of our truck.

One time I remember getting into big trouble. I was playing with matches and somehow, I got the adjoining field on fire. The firemen came and put it out. They told my parents how it started and then I was called into the house, but I never showed up because I was hiding under the house. When they finally located me, I was told not to do that again as someone could have gotten hurt. Speaking of hurt, after our talk I was not able to sit down for a while. I wouldn't do that again.

Charles Louis Barry at an early age (Johnny)
Photo courtesy of John Thurmond

I was with Dr. Barry for about six years. During that time things started to happen in my life. Dr. Barry contracted cancer and passed away. Mrs. Barry was at a loss at what to do with me as I was becoming a burden to her. She decided that rather to keep me with her, she would place me in an orphanage.

The orphanage was the Saint Joseph's Orphanage located in St. Joseph, Missouri. I was there for about two long years. At this time in my life, things were starting to happen that I did not understand. For example, why was I in an orphanage when my mother was living about two miles away? On the weekends, she would pick me up but always returned me the following Monday. This was very rough for me.

I have found out by searching several legal documents that Dr. Barry left me a small amount of money as well as part ownership of their house. The money was to be used toward my future education. That did not sit too well with Mrs. Barry so she had herself appointed as my guardian, thereby, she would be in control of my inheritance. Mrs. Barry spent my inheritance on things that she thought that I needed as well as loaning some to her friend. Now I know why I was placed in the orphanage. There was a small amount of money left for my future use.

Life for me at the orphanage was not the best. The sisters were very strict toward us and I also believe that I was not the best angel. So, I had several problems. The sisters would whip us with a belt if we made too much noise after we were sent to bed. But to get even with the sisters, we would make a lot of noise late at night just to be able to wake the sisters up. They would whip me, but I was determined not to cry and I didn't.

There were girls at the orphanage as well as boys, but the girls were in another building downhill from us. So, boys being boys, we decided to put on our roller skates and crouch down and coast down the hill. That was a great idea but with one exception, we had to stand up to get back up the hill and that is when we got caught. Caught again!

There was not much to do so we decided to make up our own games. One of our so-called games was rolling small rocks down the hill into the traffic just to see how far they would travel when they were hit by a car or truck. Caught again! I do not want to imply that all the sisters were cruel, they were not, just a few.

When I was about nine years old, Mrs. Barry had me placed in a boys' home named Boys Town. Boys Town was a home that took boys who needed guidance in everyday life. It was a home that was founded by a priest named Father Flanagan. I was the youngest boy at Boys Town when I was there. Being so young caused me a few problems just trying to blend in, but after a while I did ok.

The home is still in operation today and located just eleven miles out of Omaha, Nebraska. Boys Town is a home that I am very proud of. I believe that even though I was there for a very short time, I learned a lot about what life is all about as well as the true meaning of respect and honesty.

There were times that I did get in trouble and had to go before the Boys Town court, which by the way are fellow boys that have been voted into different town offices. Court was one of the offices. For example, there was one time when I was out by the lake when I came upon a duck egg. I picked it up and went to a close-by shed where I was going to cook it. As I was looking for a match, I looked around behind me and there stood someone. I was caught again!

For that mistake, the Boys Town court gave me a sentence of not being able to have any dessert for a week. That was not too bad, but the bad part was that I had to stand up as everyone enjoyed their dessert. The lesson that I learned was to be honest and not selfish as that duck egg did actually belong to all the boys and just not me.

My job at Boys Town was to be a visitor guide to all of the visitors that arrived from different states. Once my guiding was finished and the visitors were roaming around, I would sneak out to their cars and touch the license plates and in my mind, I felt like I just traveled to that state.

One time I recall that I was asked to be an altar boy for Father Flanagan. I was thrilled to do it, but I did not exactly know how. With the guidance of Father Flanagan, I was doing ok, so I thought. But there was one time I was supposed to move an altar book to the opposite side of the altar. Everything was going ok until I tripped and dropped the book. The pages went everywhere. I knew that I probably would be in trouble, but it never turned out that way. After Mass was completed, Father Flanagan came over to me and patted me on the head and never said anything about the accident. I was surprised but grateful.

Father Flanagan
Photo courtesy of John Thurmond

While at Boys Town, I got to do some acting. I was in the background scene of the movie titled *Boys Town* with the main actors being Spencer Tracy, Mickey Rooney and of course me. Someone's acting must have been exceptional because the movie received an Academy Award. I assumed it was my acting.

Another activity I was involved in for a while was the band, but I was not musically talented. Just to make sure that I had something to play, I was given the bird whistle, triangle and blocks.

I was given a chance to live a respectable life and I did just that. Maybe not just while I was at Boys Town but in my later life. If it was not for a duck egg, I would have had a perfect life at Boys Town.

I was hoping that I would get to go to school and start getting some smarts, however, that never happened. I was placed up for adoption again to a family that was living in Malad City, Idaho. The adoption was not to take place until the family decided if I was the kind of boy that they wanted. The people's names were Mr. and Mrs. Edell. I was with them for about a year, and they did adopt me. They also changed my name, this time to **Jack Edell**.

John Doe, John Thurmond, Charles Louis Leake, Charles Louis Barry and now Jack Edell. This is starting to get out of hand.

Mr. Edell worked as a station master for a railroad company, and there were many times I would go to his work area and just sit around and watch the trains go by. When at home, Mr. Edell enjoyed himself by watching me jump from being shocked when he used a cattle prod on me.

The Edells enrolled me in school. I was thrilled to be going and I met a lot of new friends. They took away my glasses and that made it hard for me to see the school blackboard. But things didn't work out as the Edells had hoped. Mr. and Mrs. Edell were upset with me as they accused me of stealing and being dishonest. Technically I probably did steal, but what I did was I was given some money to buy school supplies and instead of bringing back the change, I purchased candy for my new school friends. The worst part about the time with Mr. and Mrs. Edell was that I never again got to go to school full time. This adoption was never finalized as I was taken back to Boys Town.

I was back at Boys Town a very short time before Mrs. Barry decided to take me out of Boys Town and placed me with a farm family, Mr. and Mrs. Levi Waggoner of Chanute, Kansas. They were going to adopt me and did change my name to **Dick Waggoner**.

Here we go again, John Doe, John Thurmond, Charles Louis Leake, Charles Louis Barry, Jack Edell, Dick Waggoner.

I have located a notarized document that states that I was adopted, but I cannot locate any legal adoption records yet. The Waggoners were farmers but Mrs. Waggoner was a school teacher. They also had a son by the name of Sylvan. He was four years younger than me. Sylvan and I got along well. He was like a brother to me.

Sylvan and Dick (Johnny)
Photo courtesy of John Thurmond

With a lot of effort on my part, I tried to get along with Mr. and Mrs. Waggoner. The Waggoners had their standards that were extremely difficult for me to understand. When I first arrived at the farm, everything was nice. But after a few days there, Mrs. Waggoner took my glasses away from me and then told me that if God had wanted me to wear the glasses, God would provide them.

This is the second time my glasses were taken away. I was not allowed to leave the farm for over a year other than to go to school, which was just a mile away, or to go to work for the neighbors to earn money for the family.

Dick Waggoner, age 14 or 15 (Johnny)
Photo courtesy of John Thurmond

79

My life on the farm was terrible. I was at the farm for about a year and during that time I do not recall my bed sheets ever being changed. Also, the food that I was given was terrible. There was fried mush every day and if I wanted any dessert (when it was available), it was banana pudding. I never want to see those items again.

The school that I went to was a one-room school and had about twenty students. I was the only one in my eighth-grade class and also the largest student in school. I am not sure why I was in the eighth grade as I still did not know how to read and write very well. The name of the school was the Little Friend School but today it has been destroyed by Mother Nature.

The most terrible thing that I can remember was that in order to go to school, I had to wear old hand-me-down shoes that had soles made by Mr. Waggoner from soup cans. I guess that was their way to save money, but it was a problem for me as the kids in school always had something to say about my shoes.

Dick (Johnny) and Sylvan
Photo courtesy of John Thurmond

I used to work for the local farmers and one time I remember when I was working for my Uncle Silas putting hay up in the barn, I was approached by a visiting person that just happened to be very pretty and was a female airline stewardess. She came over to where I was and wanted me to show her just what I was doing. So, I took her up to the dirty, old hay loft to show her when she approached me about playing doctor. Not knowing just what she was talking about, she showed me the facts of life.

Sylvan and I were always doing something that would annoy his parents, especially his mother. One of the things that we did was to make tunnels in the barn hayloft and pretend that we were in caves. That was fun if only the cats would not use the tunnel for a place to go crap. We had so many cats that Sylvan and I decided on a plan to get rid of them. The plan was for Sylvan to gather up as many cats as he could and I would go to the hayloft and get the hay ready to feed the cows. So, as I dropped the hay, Sylvan would place a cat in the manger hoping the cows would eat them along with the hay.

Well, that plan did not work so we had to come up with something else to get rid of them. Only before we could come up with a plan, one day Mr. Waggoner gathered up the cats and put them in a bag and tossed them in the pond. I remember hearing the cats meowing even after they were under water. We would have never done that. He made us stand by and watch the situation.

Sylvan and I were always doing something together. We raised a calf to get ready to show at the fair. We taught it to join us in our walks to the pond and things like that. One day one of us did something wrong and Mrs. Waggoner came out of the house with a rifle and shot our pet cow and told us to get back to work. That was terrible for both of us.

I was always hoping something horrible would happen to Mr. and Mrs. Waggoner. Part of my wish came true as Mr. Waggoner got real sick and passed away. I shed no tears. There were times that I wanted to do bodily harm to Mrs. Waggoner. For example, Sylvan and I just came back from hunting on the farm when a very strong wind came up. Mrs. Waggoner wanted me to stop what I was doing and close some barn doors. I guess that I did not move fast enough, and she located a bicycle chain and started beating me with it. I reached down and picked up my rifle and pointed it at her and said, "Bang." If I had pulled the trigger, I would not be here writing this story from where I am now. This is when I said goodbye to Sylvan and left the Waggoner farm. I was just thirteen at the time. Mrs. Waggoner gave me a dollar and a sack full of old clothes and bid me farewell and not to come back.

Sylvan and I were very close, and it was hard to leave him behind. I did stay in touch with Sylvan over the years. He got married and he and his wife, Marilyn, raised a wonderful family. They are great people and I love them very much. They had three children and I never got to really associate with them as I had moved away from Sylvan. They had two sons and a daughter that now have their own families.

There were a lot of medical problems that Sylvan and his wife had to endure. Sylvan passed away a few years ago and is missed by many. Before he passed away, he asked me to watch after his daughter and wife as they were having a tough life at that time. I told him that I would do my best, but it seemed to me that she had everything under control. Sylvan's wife passed away in 2014 and will be missed by many. Their daughter, Michelle, and I do correspond by email and we keep in touch. Even though I was not officially Sylvan's brother, I was his brother.

So, after I left the Waggoner's, I was fourteen years old and never had a full year of schooling. It just dawned on me that I never had a chance to go to school as I was placed with so many families during my younger years. The longest time that I was in school was when I was with the Waggoner family in Chanute, Kansas. I was placed in the eighth grade hoping that I would absorb something pertaining to the lessons taught. I was able to graduate from the eighth grade even though I really never knew how to read or write. I believe that I outgrew the school desk.

After a while on my own, I went to work for a farmer that traveled the country harvesting wheat during the summer months. After we got finished with work for the day, we spent the evening and night sleeping in the field. The last job that we harvested was in northern Nebraska. When they finished harvesting for the season, most everyone went to town to cash their checks and to have a good time. They never came back to the field where I was, and I was left to make it on my own. I did not get my check, but I did have a small amount of money to tide me over. After the harvest season was over, I migrated to Wichita, Kansas, hoping to find a job. But being only fourteen years old, it was rough.

The reason I went to Wichita was that I wanted to get my paycheck as I knew where the person with my money lived. I approached this person and was able to collect the money that was owed me without any problem, but later I found out that this person claimed that I had robbed him of the money. The police contacted me but nothing came of it. I never heard any more about it after they questioned me.

For two weeks after I arrived in Wichita, I had to live the best way I knew how. I was literally a homeless street person and only about fourteen at the time. I found out that I could live in the gas station restrooms, but I had to put a board against the door to keep people from opening it. This was not the best idea, but it was my idea at the time. I also slept under road bridges just to be able to get out of the bad weather.

When the weather was good, I would climb up the ladder fire escapes to get to the building roof and that was where I spent many nights. I had to come up with a plan to survive the best way possible. I would get food in the grocery stores and go to their restroom and eat it. I would also follow the milk men on their routes to get a bottle of milk just to survive. I was sorry for creating problems for other people, but I had to survive.

I finally located a job with a taxi company washing their taxis. One night after finishing up washing the taxis, I noticed that here was a back door to a cafe that opened into the garage and I was getting hungry. I decided that I would climb through a window that was over the door and get me a slice of their pie. I did just that but as I was eating the pie, I heard a siren. I knew that it was time for me to leave, so I tried to go back through that window but it seemed like the window got smaller. I did get through the window and fell on the garage floor hurting myself. I then knew that being a crook was not for me.

There was a time when I did get in trouble with the police. I was caught selling some hubcaps that I didn't know were stolen. By not knowing they were stolen and no money was exchanged at that time, it got me out of the problem with the police. It was during this time I was befriended by a detective named Mike Gunter of the Wichita police, and he became like a father figure to me. It was with his guidance and the knowledge I picked up at Boys Town that I believe kept me out of any serious trouble.

Detective Mike Gunter would let me sit in his office and watch what goes on in a police station. That was very informative. He was tough as nails. I had been trying to locate Mr. Gunter's family to let them know just what a big part he was in my younger life. I was told by the Wichita police department they never had a Mike Gunter working for them. Now I just wondered who he was. Could he have been my angel? Later I found out that his real name was Detective Preston Albert Gunter and Mike was just a nickname.

Around the first of 1945, I decided to be able to stay out of trouble I would sign up for the Navy, even though I was only sixteen at the time. The Navy was needing good men and I believed that I was a good man as I was large for my age. The recruiter that interviewed me was very nice. He explained to me that it was nice for me to want to join, but I was too young and also, I never had a birth certificate. So, I had to change my plans. As I was leaving the recruiter, I noticed that the Merchant Marine were also wanting good men. I then went to see their recruiter. The recruiter was also nice, but he also kept telling me that I had to have a birth certificate in order to sign up.

My next step was to try and obtain my birth certificate as soon as possible. I did not have any extra money to hire someone to help me, but I took a chance that maybe I could get some free help. I did contact a lawyer in Wichita, Kansas, who just happened to be an ex-governor of Kansas at the time. His name was Payne Ratner. He was governor from 1939 until 1943. He was able to get my original birth certificate from my sealed files in Kansas City, Missouri. How he was able to do that I never understood, but I am thankful for his effort.

Merchant Mariner John Thurmond
Photo courtesy of John Thurmond

Merchant Mariner John Thurmond (second from right)
Photo courtesy of John Thurmond

I presented the birth certificate to the Merchant Marine recruiter, which made everything okay and I was accepted to become a merchant mariner. This time I had to change my name back to **John Thurmond** to match my birth certificate. I did not do this through the courts but on my own.

John Doe, John Thurmond, Charles Louis Leake, Charles Louis Barry, Jack Edell, Dick Waggoner and finally John Thurmond.

There is much to be shared about my experience in the Merchant Marine, but I will save that for another time. When I returned to Wichita from Korea, I met and fell in love with a wonderful girl named Mary Louise Connor. The way that I met her was just a little unusual. I had purchased a bottle of beer and was trying to open it on a street corner crossing push button when Mary and her girlfriend came walking down the street toward me. I stopped them and asked them if either had a church key (bottle cap remover) in their purses. It just happened that Mary had one and then I asked her for a date.

Mary and John in 1946
Photo courtesy of John Thurmond

After a few months seeing her, I knew in my heart that she was to be my soulmate forever. We got married on May 30, 1946. I was sweating out our wedding day as I needed my unemployment check for $18.00 so that I could pay the preacher. The check finally came and as the saying goes, "Let the show begin."

At the time Mary was only fifteen and I was seventeen years of age. We were married in Wichita, Kansas, by a justice of the peace. The reason I believe that Mary's parents let her get married at such a young age was that they just wanted her to be happy, and in their minds, getting married to me was a way to keep her happy. Her parents were really nice and her mother was a great cook.

Mary and John's wedding day
Photo courtesy of John Thurmond

87

Mary and I had our ups and downs as all marriages do but we shared a great love and were together for 63 wonderful years. Life was not always easy but I believe my early years prepared me for so many situations that I faced. There are many more stories to tell but for now I will share about my search for my birth mother and my lost identity.

Many years ago, I realized that a lot of my friends had a mother and father, but I didn't since I was adopted so young, lost my adoptive parents, and lived in so many different situations. Mary and I decided to try to locate my own family, even if it took us a lifetime. We started to try and locate my mother and father. I started checking for leads to my parents, not realizing that I already had my mother's name, which was on the original birth certificate I had gotten when I joined the Merchant Marine. The name of my mother was Bessie Thurmond. She had lived in Iowa. Mary and I put out questions to people who could have known a Bessie Thurmond that lived in Iowa.

John's birth mother Bessie
Photo courtesy of John Thurmond

A person from the Catholic Welfare Bureau of Kansas City, Missouri, sent me a copy of a letter dated July 27, 1938, stating that the Bureau had contacted my mother requesting information on Charles (me). The reply from my mother was not to contact her again as she was now married and had three children of her own, and her husband did not know of the existence of Charles (me). That note on the letter stating that, in 1938, Bessie had three children at the time confused my search. I knew that by 1938, she only had two children, not counting me. Was there a mistake stating that she only had three children by 1938?

However, Bessie did acknowledge me as being her child. Did she mean that I was one of the three children she had by 1938? These things had to be sorted out. In my mind, I was not really sure that I had located my true family. I felt like my newfound mother's older sister could have been my mother, and the older sister's youngest sister could be my sister. This was just a thought.

Because I did know the name of my mother, I thought that it would be easy to locate her but was I ever surprised. After approximately twenty-plus years and with the help of the internet, we did gather a lot of information, not only on my family but Mary's family as well. My search stopped for a while as we decided to try to locate information on both families. We were able to connect to approximately 10,000 people that were related to both of us. But I was never able to locate my father.

A person in Iowa wrote to us stating that she knew Bessie Thurmond, but she had just passed away. We located the area that Bessie had lived and found out through several birth records that were available to us that she was my mother. We also found out that she was a great lady and loved by so many. As the old saying goes, "She would give you the shirt off her back if necessary." That was my mother. I don't know why she gave me up for adoption and I don't care to know because she had her reason at the time.

John and his half siblings
Photo courtesy of John Thurmond

I have met with Bessie's children and they are a great bunch. I now have brothers and sisters and I am very proud of them. They have their own families and I got to meet most of them over time.

One of the strangest things that was uncovered in our search for my family line happened while we were living in Florida. I came across a photo posted in the local paper about the opening of the local swimming pool. It showed the two people chosen to be the first to jump in the pool. One was my son. The other boy turned out to be his unknown cousin at the time. My brother and his family lived in the general area close by, but we never met at that time. Small world.

My son Richard helped track down a lot of my information and was able to get copies of letters from Boys Town. One letter is dated July 19, 1938, and appears to be written by someone from Kansas City who was contacted by a Father Demers from Boys Town. It is not signed but it is sent from this person who is searching for a home for me when I was "Charles Barry" and living at Boys Town.

In the letter it described me as:

Ten years old, of Irish American stock, has blue eyes and blond hair and fair complexion, is of a lively and gay disposition. Mentally he is normal, being in the fifth grade in school. Physically he has no imperfections. Wasserman and Schick texts taken June 2, 1938 were negative and he has been immunized against Diphtheria and Smallpox. He is 4 feet 5 inches tall and weighs about sixty-five pounds. He is a well-bred child and should make a childless couple happy. I will try to get a Kodak picture to send to you.

The letter explained how I ended up at the Catholic orphanage.

Father Demers at that place [Boys Town] wrote us asking to see if we could find a home for him. The boy has had a rather odd experience for one so young. The boy was adopted from a maternity home here. The man died and the woman had him re-adopted to the Barry's. Mr. Barry had requested on his deathbed that I be raised Catholic. Mrs. Barry had remarried and does not want to keep the boy. She is not Catholic and I suppose her new husband also does not want the boy. She placed him at the Catholic Orphan Home at St. Joseph, MO, and they sent him to Father Flanagan's Home. He is a trifle too young for Boys Town; usually they do not take them till they are twelve. The boy has been baptized Catholic and I feel he has something good in store for him. He lost both of his homes through no fault of his own, and as Father Demers describes him to me, he is an attractive, smart, likeable little fellow. In fifteen years, this boy ought to be a fine young man. The home you could give him would guarantee that. At that time of your life it would be nice to have a big son like that. What do you think of it?

Unfortunately, this Doctor Smith from Texas did not adopt me. Maybe Father Demers saw something in me though. I do feel Boys Town is what helped me to become the person I am today.

My wife and I had gone back to visit Mrs. Barry after we got married and a couple of other times. One time when we went, we found her in the bathtub. She had fallen and broken her arm. We got her to the hospital and helped take care of all her medical expenses.

We really liked her a great deal and thought she was the greatest thing since apple pie. It wasn't until after she had passed, we found this information out about her not wanting me, all she had done to me and why she gave me up for adoption.

John, son Rick, and Mrs. Barry
Photo courtesy of John Thurmond

There were still some loose ends that needed to be taken care of. One of the most important ones was to try to locate my father. Information was hard to come by on this subject, but I was determined to not give up until I succeeded or passed on.

DNA testing showed without a doubt that Bessie was my mother. My son, one of my half siblings, and I all did the DNA test. My sibling's father was German but I was not, so we definitely had different fathers. My tests showed I was from Scandinavian descent and we were able to locate my father's family. We are down to two brothers who could be my father. Neither of the brothers had children, well, except for me. So, DNA tests aren't available to figure out which one. My daughter joked with me that she wondered why we couldn't drill a hole down through the casket and get a DNA sample to find out. One of these brothers is buried in the same cemetery in Dows, Iowa, as Bessie.

My birth father's last name is Erickson. Turns out on the DNA testing I'm related to Norwegian royalty and Leif Erickson. I have to laugh because some of my friends are now calling me Sir John. I guess I could have been **John Erickson.**

John Doe, John Thurmond, Charles Louis Leake, Charles Louis Barry, Jack Edell, Dick Waggoner, John Thurmond, John Erickson. Nah, I think I will stay with **John Thurmond.**

May 28, 2009, Mary got really sick. I took her to the local hospital to find out what was bothering her. Once in her hospital room, our doctor started running tests on her. But she slipped into a coma and on June 3, 2009, Mary passed away. She has taken up residence with God. I have been trying to get my life together, but it has been hard as I am still missing my companion of many years. This was something that I never counted on, so I started taking small steps at a time, trying to get on with my life alone. I miss her dearly as she was a very great person.

Mary and John
Photo courtesy of John Thurmond

As I stated above, there were several people who helped me but the ones that really deserve credit are my children. They were there whenever I needed them. I am thankful for them as they are the best.

John's children Teri, Rick and Scott
Photo courtesy of John Thurmond

Looking back on my life, a lot of people say to me, "What a rough life you have had." Maybe so by some people's standards, but for me, it was a life-learning experience.

I feel that the lesson that I did absorb was that if you have the ability to get ahead, then go for it. But if you do not have that ability, then you need some help and guidance to set you on the right path of your life. As for me, I did a lot of jobs in order to cope with living in my early younger days. Some were honest and some were not. When I finally retired, I had the work title of mechanical and electronic tech and was making a very good wage. But the most important part of my life has to do with my family. In my mind, God gave me a great family and I believe that is the best part of my life.

John and his 92nd birthday
Photo courtesy of John Thurmond

Chapter 7
Steven's Story
(1943)

*I*t was through my website that Steve reached out to me shortly after Mansion on a Hill *came out. We wrote back and forth and got to know one another. He shared that he had a reunion story and asked if I would be interested in reading it. Of course, I was excited to read his story and told him I was thinking about writing another book if he wanted to include it. I am so glad Steve agreed to share it. His is a great story that has grown over the time we have known each other. It is so joyful when lost relatives do get to meet and learn to love one another. Not everyone is so lucky as Steve's family and mine. We are very thankful. Enjoy "My Duck Hill, Mississippi, Family."*

My Duck Hill, Mississippi, Family
By Steven M. Barney

For many years, my wonderful adoptive parents diluted any intense interest for finding my birth roots.

But as you age, you spend more and more time in doctors' offices where you get asked about your parents' health. For me, I never had an answer.

My wonderful parents, Robert and Katherine Barney
Photos courtesy of Steven M. Barney

Thanks to Missouri's allowing me to get an original birth certificate (OBC) and the magic of DNA testing, I have located my maternal roots. So, I have a little more information to share with my physician. But being welcomed into a whole new family experience tops everything!

My OBC arrived in December 2018, indicating my mother was Beatrice Watkins from Duck Hill, Mississippi. DNA connected me with Ada Dyer, a first cousin of my mother. Ada's daughter Stacey Wheeler relayed messages between us. It was quickly discovered "Watkins" was not my mother's maiden name; it was Wilkins—Ada Beatrice "Cee" Wilkins, who had been twenty-three when I was born in 1943. As was usually the custom, no father was listed.

Ada Beatrice "Cee" Wilkins
Photo courtesy of Steven M. Barney

I was adopted at eight days old from The Willows where my birth mother was staying and doing some work (she had medical training). However, I was actually born at Fairmount Maternity Hospital. My adoptive parents picked me up at The Willows and took me by train to Wisconsin where I would grow up.

**My mother Kathryn P. Barney and me
back to Wisconsin from Kansas City**
Photo courtesy of Steven M. Barney

My sister was also adopted at The Willows six years later.

My sister Sue (one year old) and me (seven years old)
Photo courtesy of Steven M. Barney

It was just a couple of days before Christmas 2018 that Ada helped me uncover the mystery. The last name had been altered, which was not unusual. The history provided by The Willows (like the crib card given to the adoptive parents) was fairly accurate in helping Ada, who is in her mid-eighties, identify my mother as her first cousin. She added, "You have a brother and sister who still live in Duck Hill."

Christmas was only a few days off at this point, and Stacey said that she and Ada would contact my brother, John Frederick "Rick" Swanson, Sr., 74, and my sister, Dorothy Dee "Dee Dee" Swanson Sims, 71, to tell them about my interest in connecting with them. They wanted to wait until after the holiday. We had no idea whether they knew their mother had had a child before they were born. They did not.

On December 28, I received an email from Carolyn Haddon Swanson, my sister-in-law, which said, "Recently you were matched with a relative of my husband (Ada Dyer) as being blood related. If you are interested in meeting my husband and his sister, let me know."

Interested? I sure was. The next day, Rick and his wife were on the phone with my wife Karen and me. Their warm Southern accents and our more clipped Northern sounds quickly came together. The first words I recall from Rick were "Hello, brother!"

They had no prior knowledge I existed but enthusiastically and graciously invited us to visit Mississippi and meet family. Suddenly I had many nieces and nephews and their families as part of this growing family circle. We had a great grandmother who had seventeen children, which means lots of second cousins too.

In late January 2019, we drove south from St. Louis, Missouri, on Interstate 55 to Duck Hill, Mississippi, to meet the family. It had only been five weeks since we had discovered each other.

My brother still lives just outside of Duck Hill where our mother had grown up. My sister, Dee Dee, lives not far away in Grenada.

Rick and Carolyn's home was filled with relatives that last weekend in January with adult children, grandchildren, and cousins. A son (my nephew) flew in from Denver. A cousin drove in from Birmingham, Alabama, and some drove for several hours to be there.

**Newly found brother John "Rick" Swanson (left) and me
and sister Dorothy Dee Swanson Sims
at Rick's house, January 2019**
Photo courtesy of Steven M. Barney

They seemed as interested in meeting the mystery brother-uncle-cousin as I was in meeting them.

Scrapbooks, framed pictures, news clips, and memorabilia were piled on the dining room table and sideboard. They told a fascinating family history. Our mother's original ancestor from England was George Eskridge. He had an adopted daughter named Mary Ball, who married an Augustine Washington. Mary named her son for her adoptive father. Yes, his name was George Washington!

It took several generations of Eskridges before descendent Richard arrived in Duck Hill and founded a plantation, bringing with him his slaves. Many of these slaves from the very early days also carried the name Eskridge, as was the custom before the Civil War.

Coincidentally, a descendant of the slaves, Stephen Hanks and an Eskridge as well, wrote a book tracing both his black history and the parallel history of our white ancestors. His book, originally published in 2005, is *Akee Tree—A Descendant's Search for His Ancestors on the Eskridge Plantations.* The author met our mother in Duck Hill; she helped him locate plantation sites and even relatives. Unfortunately, she died a year after the book was published and a dozen years before I realized I had roots in Duck Hill.

The Duck Hill family no longer lives in the home in which both of my siblings and our mother had grown up, but my brother contacted the current owners who made it possible for us to tour the stately home.

Me, Dorothy Dee, and Rick at the home
the two younger siblings grew up in
Photo courtesy of Steven M. Barney

I was born in the World War II years. After my mother gave birth to me in June 1943 in Kansas City, Missouri, she returned to Duck Hill and soon met John Swanson. He was serving as an officer at a large Army base just outside of her hometown. They married in October 1943. My brother, born in November of 1944, is quite close to me in age. Our sister Dee Dee came along in 1947. My sister by adoption Sue, who I've known for seventy years, was born in 1948 at The Willows.

What an astonishing history I was learning. Our four grown children include our biological son with a European heritage, and two adopted daughters and a son, all of whom have African American ancestry.

Our children's new relatives reached out to the whole family, and they reached right back. Everyone seems thrilled with the unexpected family explosion.

Rick and his wife Carolyn are both retired educators and school administrators. Dee Dee married after college and devoted her time to family. She is very creative and artistic; perhaps we share some creativity through my writing interests.

One of their first questions to me: Do I sneeze a lot? Indeed, I do! Obviously, it's an inherited trait. I've had a lot of treatment for allergies, and now I know why.

My brother is an extraordinarily skilled craftsman, good with tools of all kinds. He has built two of his homes, knows car mechanics, and has expertise in things like solar energy. That is not one of my inherited traits—I can use a screwdriver if I have to.

After knowing our new family for only a couple of days, we were delighted to have brother Rick and sister-in-law Carolyn agree to join a family cruise that had been planned for June 2019. Dee Dee had a prior commitment, and we were all sorry she couldn't be there to meet more family and friends. My sister by adoption was also on that cruise and met part of the new family. Official or not, we all felt like family.

We have all been curious about my biological father. Who was the man our mother knew before she met Rick and Dee Dee's dad? My adoptive parents were told my biological father was a pilot killed in the war. An older relative of ours in Mississippi acknowledged to Rick that he had heard that our mother had had a baby and that the father had been killed before I was born. (The relatives who "knew" about my birth had been sworn not to tell!)

Through Ancestry.com, I was able to identify my biological father. It turns out that my biological father was an Army Air Corps pilot killed in a training exercise in 1942. The death of John Edward "Johnny" Hayden took place in Louisiana when my mother was about two and a half months pregnant with me. Because Johnny had no other children, it took some time for me to locate a first cousin. This cousin I found was the daughter of Johnny's brother.

My father John Edward "Johnny" Hayden
Photo courtesy of Steven M. Barney

What made the research more confusing was that their family name was Barbaria, but both parents had died when the children were very young. My father and his brother were raised by different sisters of their mother. The boys each took his foster family's last name. There are no immediate relatives, unlike with my mother where I have a brother and sister. The death of my father early in my mother's pregnancy preempted any plans of marriage and may explain the placement of me for adoption. These were turbulent and anxious times of World War II.

My father John Edward "Johnny" Hayden's headstone
Photo courtesy of Steven M. Barney

The loving parents who adopted me in 1943 both died when I was in my mid-twenties and my sister was eighteen. They never made a secret of our adoptions, and I like to think they would approve of the connections we have now made. And we also think my birth mother, "Cee," would as well.

Chapter 8
Jan's Story
(1949)

Facebook has been a great medium for me to meet new people. Jan reached out to me in 2019 and shared that she was born at The Willows. She did an internet search and learned about my book and ordered it. She said it helped in her search for her birth family and thanked me. That made my day! Her story is another "made for TV" movie. I'm so glad she reached out to me recently to share about finding her sister. This is her story. I hope you enjoy.

From as young as I can remember, I knew I was adopted. It was my favorite bedtime story told by my mama and my daddy, Naomi and Glenn Howrey. They had been a forty-year-old childless couple, living on a farm north of Coin, Iowa, when they adopted me. The story they told me included a long ride in the car to Kansas City, Missouri, and how they picked me out of all the babies.

I was born at The Willows on August 7, 1949, and adopted on September 30, 1949. I had the perfect life on the farm with the most loving parents I could ever have. My mama played dress up with me and also beauty shop on the back porch, pretending the milk separator bowl was for washing hair. Daddy put me on his lap to drive his John Deere tractor, and we played in the rain with our swimsuits on. I had dogs and cats to pet and dress up. My parents had lots of fun neighbor kids come visit because I was an only child.

Janet Sue with adoptive parents, Glenn and Naomi (1954)
Photo courtesy of Jan Burnison

Tragedy struck in January 1957 when my mama got sick and died five weeks later of cancer. I was in second grade and devastated. To make matters worse, my daddy married a widow with four older boys in November that same year. He later told me he only married her because he didn't think he could raise me himself ... trust me, he could have. My perfect life turned into a Cinderella story with a mean stepmother and two of four stepbrothers being degenerates. With God's help, I survived the next thirteen years but it was not easy.

My stepmom was very jealous of my close relationship with Daddy. Everyone thought after having four sons, she would welcome a daughter, but that didn't happen. If Daddy and I were visiting in the living room, she would accuse us of talking behind her back. She would leave early for school and expect me to do the dishes, clean the counters and floors in the kitchen and bathroom before walking one mile to school. I remember running many times to not be late.

I didn't date a lot but when I did, she would often make me call and cancel at the last minute for no reason. One of the most traumatic things my stepmom did was forbid me to shave my legs in high school. I had dark hair, which made it even worse. I remember one Easter putting on hose, applying powder all over them and putting on a second pair, trying to camouflage the hair. She could think of the most bizarre things to make my life miserable and embarrassing.

I graduated from high school in 1967 and couldn't wait to attend college in Maryville, Missouri, mainly to get away from home. I wanted to major in physical education, but my stepmom said I couldn't go unless I majored in music. I loved to sing and had taken piano lessons, but I was not talented enough to major in it. I lasted two years but they were two of the best years of my life. I still keep in touch with my roommate and another dear friend.

In1969, my future sister-in-law worked in Omaha, Nebraska, and I moved in with her and worked at the same bank with her until I got married. My husband and I were married on May 2, 1970. We celebrated our 50th anniversary this year. We were blessed with our son in 1971 and our daughter in 1973. We now have a son-in-law and three grandchildren, all of whom we love dearly.

My daddy died of a fatal heart attack while mowing the yard in 1994, two weeks after our daughter's wedding. That's when I started to wonder about my birth parents. I waited until 1999, the year I turned fifty, to call Jefferson City and the Missouri Department of Vital Statistics about my original birth certificate. I found out it was in a sealed file. I was told I could obtain a four-page social history about my parents and their families with all the names and places omitted so I couldn't track them down.

A week later I received some very interesting details about my birth parents. The document stated that the birth father was thirty-one, separated from his wife, had been in the military on active sea duty, and was a junior in college majoring in physics. The mother was twenty-four, had some business schooling, and was doing clerical work in a department store. They met at a roller-skating rink in November 1948. (They must have done more than just skate!) They dated until she was sent to The Willows in April. There was no talk of him getting a divorce, so the girl's mother thought adoption was the best solution. The father paid half of her confinement expenses. The baby was born in August 1949.

Jefferson City officials also told me I could hire an investigator for $200 to find the parents to answer any questions I had but could not meet them unless they agreed. I told them I had no intention of meeting them but only wanted medical history and to know if I had any siblings. I hired an investigator from Minnesota. She found out my birth father had died in 1972 at age fifty-four of kidney cancer, so his search stopped there. She found my birth mother, who denied she had a baby. After the investigator told my birth mother that she had my original birth certificate and proof right in front of her, my birth mother admitted she had given birth to me. She said the only people who knew about her pregnancy were her parents and older sister. She told the investigator she had not even told her husband or two children—BINGO—I had siblings!

I will fast forward to 2019 for the rest of my incredible journey. Since my adoptive birth certificate had The Willows listed as my place of birth, I Googled it several times during the thirty-seven years I worked in an elementary media center. I had seen old pictures of the hospital and read up on the owners. In the fall of 2019, across my cell phone on Amazon came a picture of KelLee's book, *Mansion on a Hill*. I read the subtitle and about died! I ordered and received the book in four days. I was thumbing through it when I magically landed on the Author's Note and read that the Missouri laws had changed about getting one's original birth certificate. I called Jefferson City to get my OBC.

I was shocked with the news! Vicki McKinney was my birth name and my mother was from Des Moines, Iowa, two hours from my home. I now had her maiden name and an address. For the next few weeks, my family and I searched the internet. With the help of funeral homes, cemeteries, the *Des Moines Register*, the Des Moines Public Library, and White Pages, we were able to find the information I had been hoping for.

My mother died in 1999 of a heart attack at age seventy-four. I have been to her grave as well as my grandparents' graves in Des Moines. On my mother's death certificate, it listed her son's name as informant. I was so excited to have a name, I decided to call him. He understandably hung up on me. Using my mother's obituary and the White Pages, my son-in-law found my sister. I decided to take a different approach and send her copies of all the evidence to show we were related.

On Halloween Eve, she called and we talked for over two hours. She was shocked to get my packet of information and called four relatives to see if they knew anything about her mother being taken to Kansas City to have a baby and give the baby up for adoption. To my sister's surprise, they all knew about me but were sworn to secrecy in their youth. She and I sent pictures and letters back and forth and made plans to meet in the future.

My sister and brother are five and eight years younger than I am. They both reside in Des Moines in the homes my birth mother and grandparents lived in. My sister Janet and her husband have three sons. One of her sons has three children so I instantly became an aunt and great aunt. My brother and my son have almost identical education and job backgrounds. Both have bachelor's degrees in accounting, received their master's at Drake University, are CPAs, and worked at Pioneer—now known as Corteva where my son still works. Our families have met twice in the past few months and each time it seems like we were meant to find each other. We talk every few weeks and send each other cards on special occasions.

Janet Sue (born 1949) and Janet Sue (born 1954)
Photo courtesy of Jan Burnison

My sister loves to cook and do handiwork. She sends me recipes and sometimes includes our mother's. My favorite things from her are dishrags, towels, doilies and Bible bookmarks she made for my women's church group. My favorite gifts to her were a palm cross made in Seward, Nebraska, where our daughter lives, and two Willow Tree® Sisters angels, whose hands interlock when close together. My sister's birthday is August 9 and mine is August 7. She goes by Janet and I go by Jan but the coolest thing about us is we both have the exact same name, Janet Sue!

My own children have always told me my story should be made into a movie. I was blessed with wonderful adoptive parents, blessed to survive the traumatic years with a stepfamily, blessed with a great husband, children, and grandchildren, and now blessed to find out the rest of my story. I am eternally grateful to KelLee for writing *Mansion on a Hill* honoring his grandmother, mother, me, and thousands of women and babies who entered and left The Willows Maternity Sanitarium over a period of sixty-four years. If it wasn't for him, I would never have met my wonderful birth family or had the opportunity to share my story in his touching sequel, *More Voices of The Willows*. God Bless all of your stories and each of your lives.

Chapter 9
Janet's Story
(1949)

*J*anet *attended my presentation at the Kansas City Public Library in January 2020. She wrote to me after meeting at the book signing and asked if I would be interested in including her story in my next book. I am so happy she contacted me and I have gotten to know her. Janet has started an adoption support group in Overland Park, Kansas, for birth mothers and adoptees. She has a wealth of experience to share and it is heartwarming how she is helping others. Hers is a beautiful story and one I know people will enjoy as much as I did.*

My adoptive parents told me that I was born in Kansas City. For some reason, I always thought I was born at Saint Luke's Hospital near the Country Club Plaza shopping center. When I requested my original birth certificate (OBC) in 2018, that is when I found out I was born at The Willows. My brother is two years older than me and he also was born at The Willows. Because my parents are deceased, I am not able to ask for more information about The Willows and my adoption there. My parents actually adopted five children but only my brother and me from The Willows. My other three younger siblings were all private adoptions.

My father was John Dukewits. He was a Ford dealer in Springfield, Missouri. My mother was Jane. My parents met in Abilene, Texas, when my father was in the Air Force in the 1940s.

They were married and their first child was stillborn. My mother was hemorrhaging after the birth and the doctor had to do a hysterectomy. My father told her if she could survive this, she could adopt as many children as she wanted. He held true to this promise and they adopted the five of us.

They moved to Independence, Kansas, after the service and then moved to Springfield, Missouri, where my father opened up his car dealership. They had been married about five years when they adopted their first child. My parents were pretty well established and a little older in their thirties compared to most couples starting families in their twenties. They adopted my brother first and then two years later me. Two years after me, they did a private adoption of my next brother who was born in Texas. My mother being from Texas, I am thinking there was some connection she had there to how they adopted my brother.

After him, my sister was adopted from Florida. My father's older brother lived in Florida. They had some kind of connection where they were able to do a private adoption. We had just received my sister and she was about six weeks old. The pediatrician called and said, "We have a baby boy. Do you want him?" We said yes and so my little sister and brother were raised as twins because they were just six weeks apart in age. After "twins" my mother was done.

I never was curious about my birth family. My parents did everything the way The Willows coached people in dealing with adoptions. From about age three, I remember them telling me my adoption story. They told me all the time growing up, "You know, we got to choose you and you are our child." They made it sound like there was a whole room of babies that they got to pick from and took me home. I never had a sense of being an outsider or less than because of being adopted. If kids would bring it up about me being adopted, I would just say that their parents were stuck with them but mine got to choose me. I'd feel pretty good about that and just go on about my business.

My husband and I met in college. We got married in 1970. When we were ready to have children, it was at the time when Oprah was on TV and often talking about adoption and finding a person's birth family. I never had really thought about it before. Deep down I know I felt it would hurt my parents' feelings if I were to look. I never really talked to them about it and I'd never seen any of my adoption paperwork. My parents were really private people. The stories they would tell were only things they wanted to share. If you asked about something they didn't want to talk about, they weren't willing to open up. In fact, I didn't even know how to go about looking for my biological parents if I wanted.

Once I had my children, I was just hoping there weren't any medical issues. We had known what medical issues were related to my husband's side of the family but not mine. That was the one thing that was hard, every time I had to go to the doctor. I had to say I was adopted and had no medical history. It was a huge void. When I eventually found out about my medical history, it was interesting to see how some of my children's issues were related to my biological family history. We never had learning disabilities in my family, but my son's children both have dyslexia and my birth mother also has dyslexia, so that sort of cleared up some things for us.

In 2018 the laws changed in Missouri so adoptees could get their OBC. My older brother had already received his and shared it with me. This is when we found out about his being born at The Willows. Then he found his birth family, who all lived in Colorado, and all the information such as his social and medical history. He kept telling me I should get my OBC too. Now I have to laugh because I did it mostly to just get him off my back. "Just leave me alone, I'm going to send this in."

I sent the request in February 2018 right after the law changed and it took about nine months to get my OBC back. I got it in November about five days before my birthday. My story is a little different from most people I have met. Most people only have the mom's name and not the dad's name on the birth certificate. Often the birth mother then marries someone else and hasn't told the family or anyone she had a baby or who the birth father was. The surprising shocker for me was that it had my birth mother's name on it, my birth father's name was on it, and it said they were married! I thought, *Why would a married couple give up their baby?* That was really weird.

The OBC stated that I was born at The Willows and my birth parents were from Pecatonica, Illinois, in Winnebago County. I didn't know anything about Illinois other than Chicago and Springfield, that was about it. So, I went on line and started Googling stuff. All on my own I was able to find my birth parents' wedding certificate dated April 15, 1949. I was born in November 1949. What to do next?

My brother had me contact a lady named Sharon Fieker who founded the Adoption Triad of the Ozark. She had access to websites that I didn't know anything about. She was coming to Kansas City to speak and said she would meet me for dinner. We met and she took a photo of my birth certificate. I only had the certificate for about three days at this point when I met Sharon. She was optimistic because my OBC had so much information. Two days later, she contacted me that she had found my parents. It was crazy. She told me they were still alive at the ages of about eighty-seven and eighty-eight years old.

I asked Sharon if she would call them. I really didn't want to be messing in their lives if they didn't want to meet me. I wasn't going to do that to them. I hoped to at least get my medical history and find out my story. I would leave them alone if they didn't want to have a relationship.

The first time Sharon called, she actually dialed and reached their youngest son, Brian. Sharon didn't know at that time who she was talking to but said she had a birth certificate with November 11, 1949, as the birth date and the parents were Allen and Joanne Thompson. She asked if he knew anything about it. Now my birth parents had never told a soul. It was a huge secret that they had this baby and had given it away.

So, their kids had no idea I even existed. Their son just freaked out. I guess not too long before her call, there was a phone scam that had happened in the family. He was reacting from that experience. Sharon didn't know if she was talking to Allen. At this point, we didn't know anything about who she had talked to on that call. He immediately got off the phone and called Allen and Joanne.

Sharon had another phone number for Allen and Joanne and she decided to give it a try. She called this number and Joanne answered the phone. As soon as Sharon asked about the birth certificate and date, Joanne started crying and Allen got on the phone too. Joanne then told Sharon my story and they had wondered if I would ever find them. She wanted to know about me, how I was, if I had any kids, and lots of questions. But Sharon really didn't know enough about me to answer any of her questions.

Sharon relayed to me the story Joanne shared. They were in high school their freshman and sophomore years when they met. They sort of hung out throughout high school. My birth father, Allen, had graduated and my birth mother, Joanne, was a senior in high school. He asked her to go with him as his date to a wedding on Valentine's Day in February 1949, and I was conceived that night.

Six weeks later, after realizing she was pregnant, she went to him and told him. They decided to elope. They went to a city called Morrison, Illinois, about thirty minutes away to a Methodist

Church. The pastor said he would marry them if they would meet with him first. They met with him and then he married them. They thought they had solved the problem. When they went home and announced to my maternal grandmother, named Beatrice, that Joanne was pregnant and they had eloped, it did not go well. Beatrice was like, "You are not having that baby."

Sharon found out more about my biological family. I had three full-blood siblings, two brothers and a sister. I was born in November, and two years later they had my brother named Craig. Then twenty-two months later, my sister named Kim was born. There was a big gap and six years later they had my other brother Brian, who was the one Sharon had contacted first.

I now had my story. Before Sharon made her calls, I had given her my contact information to give to Allen and Joanne. I sort of left the ball in their court then if they wanted to contact me. I figured I would hear from them pretty quick but I didn't.

At Thanksgiving when my children came over, I told them the story Sharon shared to give them an understanding that there were all these new people who might be in their lives. My children had known their whole lives that I was adopted but my grandchildren didn't really register with that. It was fun because my grandchildren were like, "You were adopted, GG?!" And I told them I was. We were laughing about it at Thanksgiving dinner and saying could you imagine them all sitting around their table and saying, "This turkey is really good. By the way, I had a baby you didn't know about." But it didn't go that way.

Right after Thanksgiving, my husband and I went to New York with our son and his family. I called Sharon and asked her what she thought of the idea that I send Allen and Joanne a Christmas card and introduce myself to them by letter. She thought that was a great idea so I wrote them a long letter. I told them about my adoptive family and that my parents had passed away. My father had died in

2000 and my mom in 2012. I shared about the siblings I had grown up with and what I did. Just really wanted to introduce myself to them. I shared that I wanted to thank them for giving me life and the opportunity to have such a wonderful life. I ended by telling them that I loved them as my birth parents and I would love to have the opportunity to meet.

Christmas went by and I still hadn't heard from them. It was so hard. I figured they weren't interested and so I was trying to let it go and just be okay. With social media, I found out a little about them. I didn't find much as far as medical history, but it looked like they were a pretty healthy bunch. I work as a marriage and family therapist and my office is about a mile and a half from our house. I came home on January 3 and in the mail was a letter from Joanne. She didn't give me very much information.

After Joanne introduced herself by letter, I started writing to her and we exchanged about three letters. I learned more about their story. My grandmother Beatrice was a school teacher. I believe she might have had more information being a school teacher about others who were unwed mothers, how difficult it could be, and what others had done. The Willows had marketed in the community, sending information to their doctor. The doctor told them about this place where Joanne could go, have her baby, and place it for adoption. Right after graduation, and my birth mother being about four-and-a-half months pregnant, she was sent to The Willows. Beatrice put Joanne on the train and sent her to Kansas City by herself.

Joanne doesn't have a lot of memory of The Willows. I don't know if she pushed those memories down deep inside herself, but she doesn't recall much about her experience there. It might have been so traumatic for her that she just doesn't want to remember it. She does remember getting on the train and traveling at night. She had to change trains in St. Louis, Missouri, and it was scary. There wasn't anybody there to direct her. She was afraid she would get on the wrong train.

She did make it to Union Station in Kansas City. There was someone there to meet her and take her to The Willows. Her family had made the arrangements for her to live in an area at The Willows where the girls helped with the daily work. This might have been in a part called The Cottages that was next to the main building. She was in a room with four girls and they all worked in the kitchen. She liked this because it helped the time go faster.

She doesn't remember the names of her roommates. She was sort of a rule follower, which I am as well. If they had said, "Don't use your real name," she probably didn't. If they said, "Forget about all this," she just did. Whatever they told her to do, she would be thinking this was the right thing to do. While Joanne was at The Willows from June until November, Allen came down twice and took her out to dinner. They were allowed to do that as a married couple.

Joanne did not have any real recollections about when she went into labor. She was anesthetized and really drugged. She remembers holding me and counting my fingers and toes. That was the only time she remembers holding or even seeing me. She wasn't allowed to give me a bottle or feed me. She believes that it was because she was married and they were afraid she would change her mind. The records I found stated that my adoptive parents had taken me home when I was two weeks old, which I believe was before Joanne went home. She said she was home by Thanksgiving. When it was time to go back to Pecatonica after Joanne gave birth, her mother came to get her to make sure she didn't bring me home with her.

Joanne had said that one of the things she shared with the people at The Willows was that Beatrice felt like this baby would never have a chance in their small community. The baby would always be known as the child that wasn't wanted or something like that. Joanne said that they wanted me and they tried to figure out every way they could to keep me, but Beatrice wouldn't let them do it. Allen and Joanne even talked about staying in Kansas City and thinking if they just left their families and the farm, they could start a new life there. But they realized neither of them could get jobs because they were both just so young.

Her family told people that Joanne was going to Kansas City to attend school to learn how to be an interior decorator. She told me as soon as she got back to Pecatonica after having me, she went to work in the local A&P grocery store. She and Allen didn't live together as a married couple at all. They lived like they weren't married. They each lived with their own parents. They had to lie about their marriage and kept that a secret their entire lives.

The next year on April 15, the very same day they got married the first time, they had a wedding and moved into his father's farmhouse. They have lived there ever since. Allen and Joanne farmed for many years and then they went into a snowmobile business. They also loved to go antiquing and became collectors. When I found them, everybody thought they had been married sixty-nine years when they had actually been married seventy years.

Then she gave me her phone number and asked me to call her. I was really nervous about it and I don't know why because I talk to strangers all the time with my work. But when Joanne and I talked on the phone, it was so easy as soon as she said hello. She said I sounded like her other daughter Kim. We would talk for an hour without taking a breath and we would exchange information. We probably called two or three times a week. She would ask me questions like "Well, did you ride a bicycle?" She wanted to know all about my childhood. One day when I was talking to her, I said, "I know I wasn't planned and I bet Brian wasn't planned since he was six years younger than Kim, but did you plan Craig and Kim?" I still laugh when I think of my mother saying, "I didn't plan any of them."

After about a month of phone conversations, I asked her if I could come up and meet them. She said yes but she didn't want me to come to Pecatonica. It was still a big secret. I understood and suggested we meet in Rockford, Illinois, which was about thirty minutes from their house. I stayed in a hotel and suggested we meet there. They were late. We were supposed to meet at 1:00 p.m. and I waited for like an hour in the lobby. I thought they weren't going to come and they had changed their minds. The phone number I had for them was a landline. They hadn't given me their cellphone number so I didn't know how to reach them.

Finally, they called the hotel front desk and they told the lady they were lost. She came out and told me the people I was waiting for were lost but she had given them directions. "They should be here in about fifteen minutes," she said. When Allen and Joanne showed up, the first words they said to me were, "You probably thought we had abandoned you again." I gave them a big hug and we went up to my hotel room. They were extremely nervous too. I thought, *Well, I am nervous but I know how to help people who are nervous so I'll help calm them down.*

When we got to the hotel room, a beautiful thing happened. I was seated and Allen was standing. Almost the first thing out of Allen's mouth was, "I just really want to apologize to you for not fighting for you. I didn't know I could. I didn't know legally what my rights were. I always regretted that I didn't stand up to my mother-in-law and tell her we would figure it out. She would just have to get over it." That was so precious to me. I don't know how long he had thought about what he would say, but it was really beautiful that he did.

It was amazing to hear their story from their own mouths and in person. We exchanged a lot of pictures and memories. They were really nervous that somebody would see me with them and wonder who I was. They said they didn't want to have to lie about it because they had lied about me their whole lives. I decided I would just leave the rest of what this whole journey would look like in their hands. If they wanted to do more, that was fine and if they didn't, that was fine too.

Janet and her parents, Joanne and Allen
Photo courtesy of Janet Byars

We went out to dinner and nobody came up to Joanne and Allen and asked who I was. They let me take a picture with them.

They still didn't know if they were going to tell their kids or not. However, my brother Brian, whom Sharon had contacted, had called Allen and Joanne about the birth certificate. They did come clean telling him. Understandably a stranger calling out of the blue, he was really worried that I was a scammer or wanting the farm. I found out months later that was the reason for the delay when I contacted them in December. They wanted to get the farm in a trust so there was no way I could get it. I assured them I didn't want the farm. My parents had been very generous to me and there was nothing about the farm I wanted. My brother Brian kept their secret and didn't tell anyone about me.

After dinner they asked me, "Why don't you come out to the farm?" It was a thirty-minute drive so I suggested I just follow them in my car so they didn't have to bring me back. I followed them to the farm and they took me all over their farmhouse. We went into the barns and saw all their antiques that were amazing. We sat around and talked. I wanted to put my hand up against their hands. I have really big hands that nobody else in my family has. My hands were just like theirs and that was pretty neat to see. Allen wrote out a map on how to get back to the hotel. I could have used GPS but my thought was, *Oh, I have something he has written for me now.* I have saved that map he drew.

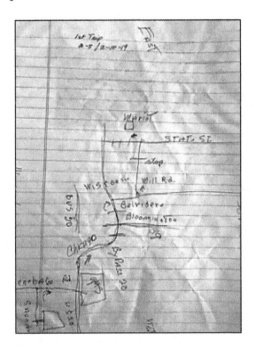

Allen's handwritten map
Courtesy of Janet Byars

I had planned to just go up and then go back to Kansas City the next day. In the back of my mind I know I was wishing that they had asked me to stay longer and afraid they were looking at their watches, wondering when I was going to leave. The next morning, I got up early to drive back home. I was in Des Moines, Iowa, about five hours into the trip and half way back, when they called. Joanne was on the phone crying and apologizing to me. "I'm so sorry. I wished we had raised you. I just can't believe we missed out on your life." So, they both apologized to me, which I think was really healing for them as well as for me. Just to hear they could have cared for me, but they just didn't get the chance to do so.

So now the ball was in their court. On that phone call when I was in Des Moines, they told me they had decided they were going to call their daughter Kim and tell her that she has a sister. I said, "Okay!" They then said though they felt they should tell Kim and my other brother Craig in person rather than over the phone. Kim lived in Manson, Iowa. Craig and Brian both live in Peoria, Illinois. Since it was winter and they received so much snow, it was difficult to get them to come to the farm.

It probably was a month before they could get their kids to come and to tell them about me. They told Craig first. And the thing was, it was his birthday. I couldn't believe they did that. It was like, "Happy Birthday! Oh, and by the way, you have a sister and you really aren't the firstborn." He found me on Facebook and friended me. I was at work when I saw he had sent the request and I thought, *Well, he knows about me and he wants to be friends so I guess that is a good sign.* After about two days, he called me on the phone and we talked for about two hours. I asked Craig if Brian had told him. He said that Brian hadn't said anything and he hadn't known until his folks told him.

It took a little longer to get Kim and her family up to the farm. Kim had always wanted a sister, and it was almost like she had this sixth sense that she knew she had one. She said her childhood makes so much more sense now that she knew about me. She was very close to Grandma Beatrice. She told me that she felt there were many times that Grandma Beatrice wanted to tell her about me. That never happened though.

After Kim knew about me, we made arrangements to meet in Des Moines for lunch. We spent the whole afternoon in this restaurant. When we sat down, we asked the server if it would be okay if we stayed for two or three hours to talk. He said that would be fine. I asked the server if he would take a photo of Kim and me. He said, "How long has it been since you sisters have been together?" We looked at each other and said this is the first time we had met and we laughed. Well, come to find out, the server had been adopted too. He had just found his birth mother. He sat down with us and we had this long talk about our stories.

I met Brian last. After meeting Kim, we arranged to go to Rockford, Illinois, for lunch with Joanne, Allen, Craig, and Brian. Craig and Brian's wives joined us, too. That was the first time Brian and I met and talked.

It is interesting to learn, as I have gotten to know my siblings, they really loved Grandma Beatrice. They have a really hard time thinking she told Joanne she couldn't keep me. Of course, nobody at the time knew anything about Joanne being pregnant. It was a well-kept secret. Joanne and Allen never really talked to me about it, but Joanne did share some things with my sister's daughter, my niece. Joanne told her the possibility of an abortion was brought up and Beatrice made her sit in hot water with Epsom salt to see if she would miscarry. Because she was made to do this, Joanne feared maybe something would be wrong with me.

After I found Allen and JoAnn, I started going up monthly to visit them. At their ages, I don't know how much time I have with them and have wanted to spend as much time with them as possible. I now know all about their farm and I really love it. I have some wonderful memories of visiting. I've seen home movies that they had taken at Christmas and Easter times over the years. So fun to see movies of them all out snowmobiling and seeing what their lives were like growing up there. That's been neat to know. I told Joanne,

"I think I would have liked life on the farm," but I added laughing, "but I really am a city girl. I took ballet and piano lessons. I really liked the life I had." I think this helped ease the guilt of giving me away, knowing I had a good life growing up.

Once Allen and Joanne had told their kids, they went public with all their friends and all their extended family. They were just having a ball, telling everybody because their kids had accepted it so well. They decide to go public too with their wedding anniversary. That it really was in 1949 when they got married instead of 1950. Last year we had a 69th/70th wedding anniversary party for them. All of my family went and we met every one of my biological family. Allen and Joanne met all of their newest grandkids. It was really special. In November 2019, they had a party or open house for all of my extended family on my father's side. Their last names are Hilton. I met about twenty-five first cousins. I walked into this room and it was hilarious because we all looked alike. It was so much fun.

Craig, Janet, Allen, Joanne, Kim and Brian
Photo courtesy of Janet Byars

One relative I met at the 70th anniversary party was someone I had been in contact with way before I found Allen and Joanne. Before I received my OBC, I did the 23andMe DNA test. It came back with a first cousin named Larry who lived in Canada. Larry was on 23andMe looking for his birth father's family. The birth father had left when he was little and his father who raised him was his stepfather. We had chatted online but we couldn't figure out any way we were connected. Come to find out, Larry was Allen's sister's son. But of course, nobody knew that Allen and Joanne had been married or had a baby earlier so we couldn't figure it out.

After I met and started talking to Joanne on the phone, she would mention her nephew Larry. I told her I did this 23andMe test and it had shown I had a first cousin named Larry, but we couldn't make the connection. I said, "I bet when he was talking to you, he was trying to get you to tell him who I was." When Joanne finally did tell Larry about me, we laughed that it finally made sense. After I met Larry for the first time at the 70th wedding anniversary, we went out for breakfast. He shared his story about searching for his birth father's family so we have developed a special bond.

The year 2019 was a huge year in my life. I turned seventy in November and I had all these firsts in my life. Usually a person of my age doesn't have all that many firsts in his or her life. But I had one first after another. It was a very special year for me. At the anniversary party last year in April, Kim's two daughters and two sons were there and my daughter and son were there. The cousins just connected and hit it off. They had so much in common and they didn't want to leave. We kept talking and talking and stayed up almost all night. The next day everybody just hung out in the lobby of the hotel. We talked and talked and talked. It just went on forever. I said to Kim, "Let's plan a girls' trip and take our daughters and do something." She said, "Sure if we can figure it out."

It took some planning but in July last year we went to Hilton Head Island, South Carolina, for a whole week—Kim, her two daughters, her two daughters-in-law, my daughter and my daughter-in-law. We just sat on the beach and talked every day. We played cards and talked at night. They had a ton of questions for me about my life.

The main thing they had to work through was that they couldn't think of Grandma Beatrice as someone who could give away a grandchild. They needed to work through it. I didn't need to work through it but I tried to help them. I kept saying I felt so loved in my adopted family, I don't have any resentment toward her at all. For that time and how society was back then, I understand why that choice was made. I said, "You are having a harder time because you know her and don't think that becomes her."

We worked that out during the vacation and Kim and I became very close. When we were at the beach, Kim asked me if I would give her some books to read so she could understand better what it was like for a mother to give away a child. I gave her *Mansion on a Hill* and a couple other books of adoption stories that mainly talked about birth moms and what it was like for them to give up a baby. She read those to try and gain more understanding.

The next time Joanne saw Kim and me together was last November. She couldn't believe how connected and close we are. She could see we are really friends and trying to catch up on the seventy years we missed out on together. Joanne loved that and I believe it made Kim and her even closer.

Joanne still doesn't have much to say about her experience having me but she did tell me that when I was born, she and Allen named me Geri Thompson. They talked about me for sixty-nine years, each referring to me as Geri. *How is Geri? How did Geri celebrate her birthday this year? Wonder if Geri thinks of us on her birthday?* Joanne said, "We always just hoped and prayed that you had a loving family that was giving you really good care."

When I received my original birth certificate from the State of Missouri, the name on it was Geraldine Thompson. Joanne said that when she went to the office to do the paperwork, they told her that

Geri was not a name. The clerk was named Geraldine and she named me Geraldine Thompson. This is something that she does remember from her time at The Willows.

My adoptive family named me Janet. Allen's older sister was named, Janette. Allen and Joanne still think of me as Geri and have to stop to think about calling me Janet.

I told her that did happen and how much I was blessed with my family who raised me. I really think The Willows did a fabulous job placing me with a family. Other than their professions were very different, my father and birth father were very similar type men. My mother and birth mother were very similar type women. I do believe the four of them would have been very good friends.

I have wonderful adopted siblings and biological siblings and feel quite blessed. I feel very lucky that my birth parents are still living at their ages. My birth mother has some issues with glaucoma now and wears dark glasses because the light bothers her. My birth father has only had some farm accidents but no health issues. In fact, he just had a broken leg because he was out cutting firewood with a chainsaw. I said, "You're ninety. What are you doing with a chainsaw?"

The last time I was able to visit my birth parents was in February 2020. Because of the COVID-19 quarantine, I hate that I haven't been able to get back to visit them. This last visit was the first time I was able to stay at the farm. Always before I would stay in a hotel. It is always so much neater to stay with someone and see how they do life on a daily basis. We stayed up late talking every night. As I mentioned before, my birth parents were antique dealers. This last time I was up visiting them, we went to an antique show. We stopped at every single antique booth because they know everybody. They would introduce me and tell our story every time. It is wonderful that they are proud of me and want the world now to know I'm their daughter.

Chapter 10
Judi's Story
(1950)

S *ocial media has been so helpful in my meeting people with connections to The Willows. Judi is one of these people and I'm so glad we have been able to stay in contact through Facebook and The Willows Maternity Sanitarium group page. Judi and I have chatted for some time about her sharing her story. However, with moving and other commitments, she was afraid she wouldn't get her story written in time to be included in this book. She was able to finish her story last minute and I'm delighted to be able to include it.*

It must have been a long train ride from Bristol, Virginia, to Kansas City, Missouri, for an unmarried, pregnant twenty-year-old woman named Charmie. No one living knows whether she made the trip alone or if someone accompanied her.

My birth mother Charmie Nichols
Photo courtesy of Judi Askin Webb

She and my dad met at a church dance. He was tall, dark and handsome, fourteen years her senior. He had served in the Army during World War II and had been married briefly. His name was Dennis. As so often happens, they fell in love and were planning to be married. Then they found out that she was pregnant.

My birth father Dennis Hogan
Photo courtesy of Judi Askin Webb

My paternal grandfather was a minister in their town, so they discussed the situation with him. He was against the marriage; one reason was the age difference. The other for the obvious reason—me. How would it have looked in 1950 for a minister's son's wife to have a baby less than nine months after the wedding? That would have been a huge embarrassment. Perhaps the son of a minister was held to a higher standard and was not expected to give into temptations of the flesh.

I presume that they learned of The Willows through one of the brochures that the Haworths had mailed out. My aunt and uncles were young enough that they do not remember anything except her being gone and how sad she was when she came home.

My dad was working for the TVA (Tennessee Valley Authority) and covered her expenses at The Willows. I was born there on August 14, 1950. The little pink bracelet that I had worn in the nursery with the name Dorla on it and the crib card with my vital statistics were the only real information I had to connect me with my birth mother. I did have the general information on my birth parents that The Willows provided to my adoptive parents: mother's age, height, weight, education and religious background; same for Dad except, of course, no names for either of them.

I had been told that I was adopted before I even had any understanding of what it meant. I just knew that I was not "really theirs" (my thoughts when I was angry for some reason), but I was told that my parents had been selected to raise me because my mother had not been able to take care of me. My adoptive mother told me that they were lucky to get me since they were older than was normally considered acceptable for adoptive parents. They were thirty-nine and had been unable to have children of their own. I remember asking why I did not have a brother or sister because I did not like being an only child.

I have no clue how they heard about The Willows; I presume through a doctor in my hometown. I remember my adoptive mother showing me a telegram from The Willows Maternity Sanitarium and Mrs. Haworth saying they were holding a baby girl, and could they be there within two days.

She did mention the steps up to The Willows and how my dad was afraid he was going to drop me when he carried me down the stairs to the cab. I left The Willows in a cab bound for Union Station. This was the same place my birth mom had arrived, but I was headed to my adoptive home in Davenport, Iowa.

I did not have a particularly happy childhood. I was a very shy child, painfully thin, who would later become the subject of bullying because of being overweight. My mother was overly protective and domineering. She wanted control over every aspect of my life, even after I reached adulthood. She never was a warm, touchy-feely type person, and we never had a real bond.

In later years, she would display OCD (Obsessive-Compulsive Disorder) behaviors, something I think stemmed from her childhood. She was very much like her own mother, which made it difficult for her to show emotion. She never took much interest in my activities as a child. I do not really think she had the intuition to be a mother although she had stated that she wanted a child.

My dad was the one who attended my games and activities, took me fishing, and shared things of his childhood with me. He truly was my dad. I remember playing in the park with him and trying to jump for a trapeze swing. I missed and hit my head on the ground. He carried me to my grandparents' house across the street, went to the store, and bought me orange slices, my favorite candy. He felt so bad because he had been encouraging me to try to catch it and swing by my arms.

After I received my non-identifying information, it solidified my desire to find out more about my birth family. I had been wanting to try to find them for many years, but every time I tried, I came up with a dead end. I did not know if the name Dorla was my birth name, last name, or just something given to me by The Willows. With the adoption records sealed, there really wasn't anything to go on.

Once DNA testing became readily available, I decided to see what I might discover. With the encouragement of my husband and The Willows Maternity Support Group, I asked for a search angel to help me with my search. I was contacted by an individual and was asked to upload my information into the database. She said she had some work obligations that would keep her busy for a few days, but she would work on my search after that.

Judi and husband Mike on wedding day
Photo courtesy of Judi Askin Webb

It was not long after that she called to tell me she had located my birth family. She informed me that sadly both of my parents were deceased, but I had siblings, aunts, uncles, and cousins!

After my family tree was more complete, I started making contact via email and phone calls. My mother's youngest sister was the first one I heard back from. She was elated that I had located my mom's side. She said they had hoped to find me, but they did not know my name or exactly where I had been born.

My oldest brother on my dad's side was skeptical when I first contacted him. He did not know that Dad had a daughter before he and his brothers were born. My youngest brother, however, had been told about me by his mom. He had no clue where to start looking, having been told I was born in Arkansas and did not know my birthdate or name. He is a great brother whom I am looking forward to getting to know better. I have another brother on Dad's side that I have not met, and I doubt that I will. I have met none of his other relatives and have no idea if they are living or not.

I have met my siblings on my mom's side, a brother and a sister. My sister's middle name is Dorla. My brother Mark and I are remarkably close. My uncles and aunt are wonderful people who have helped me learn more about my mom. My aunt said Mom told her that giving me up was the hardest thing she ever did. She wondered where I was, if I was happy and had a good life.

Judi and her brother Mark
Photo courtesy of Judi Askin Webb

One day I will meet her. And him. My questions will be all answered. I am just grateful every day that I can now look in the mirror and know who I am.

Judi and her children
Photo courtesy of Judi Askin Webb

Judi with her daughter
Photo courtesy of Judi Askin Webb

Chapter 11
Patty's Story
(1951)

*P*atty *reached out to me shortly after* Mansion on a Hill *was published. It was fascinating to learn of Patty's connection to The Willows with her grandmother whose signature was on my grandmother's letter dated in 1925. Nelle McEwen's name was one my mother had read over and over as she looked at her adoption papers. I so wish my mother were still living to meet and talk to Patty. I am so appreciative for all the information Patty has shared with me over the years since getting to know her. I know you will enjoy her story.*

Prelude

I was born at The Willows on June 5, 1951. My adoptive grandmother was Nelle T. McEwen. Grandma started working at The Willows in 1921 at the age of thirty-three.

Patty's grandmother Nelle McEwen
Photo courtesy of Patty Brasel

The Willows closed in 1969, and this forced Grandma to retire at the age of eighty-one. I don't know how many years she was head of adoption, including social worker and matchmaker. (You can find her picture in KelLee Parr's book, *Mansion on a Hill*, on page 165).

Patty and her grandmother Nelle McEwen
Photo courtesy of Patty Brasel

With all this being said, she became acquainted with my birth mother and birth father, as well. They were in love and engaged to be married. On April 1, my birth mother and I (seven months in her womb) came to The Willows from Nebraska. She lived there until June 10. My birth father was very attentive with visits, bringing her flowers and taking her out for the afternoon.

This relationship was clearly the exception to the norm. Grandma became fond of my birth mom. She had good looks with a spunky and warm personality. Grandma's daughter, my adoptive mother, was married and they had a son of their own. They wanted another child to complete their family, but it wasn't happening. So, they looked to Grandma to help them select a baby girl, me. My brother is four and a half years older than me.

My adoptive parents' birth announcement
Photos courtesy of Patty Brasel

Patty's mother, Patty, her brother, and her father
Photo courtesy of Patty Brasel

Patty's brother (age 8) and Patty (age 4)
Photo courtesy of Patty Brasel

I recorded the events of my reunion shortly after it happened while I was swept up in the bubble of euphoria. Here is my reunion story.

An Enchanting Love Story

My first contact with my birth mother was four months after my fortieth birthday. Four years earlier she had been located through Juvenile Court. She was told my name and the city in which I lived. I learned she had, indeed, married my father and that I had three full-blooded sisters. She told the contact person she would have to think about a reunion, and that is as far as it went. Wanting to help her change her mind, I even wrote a letter to introduce myself. It was sent through Juvenile Court. She never replied.

Three-and-a-half years later, Ellen, a friend of my in-laws, called me and offered to try to find my birth parents. I had neither seen her since our wedding, nineteen years before, nor ever discussed with her my situation.

Patty's wedding day with father, mother and grandmother, 1972
Photos courtesy of Patty Brasel

Ellen had known about my adoption, and my mother-in-law had told her about not hearing back from my birth parents. She had felt the need to help me. I was so elated she had offered to help. This renewed my hope and brought a ray of sunshine. She was successful in finding their address, phone number, and dates of birth. Ellen sent a letter on my behalf, expressing my continuing desire for a reunion.

On October 3, 1991, one week after the letter was sent, I placed a long-distance phone call to my birth mother, age sixty-three, living in Wisconsin. We talked for fourteen minutes. Her name is Lou. This was our conversation:

Lou: Hello!
Me: Lou?
Lou: Yes?
Me: I am calling from Kansas City. This is Patty Brasel.
Lou: (an audible sigh)
Me: Will you talk to me?
Lou: You better believe it!
Me: You will???
Lou: Well, yes!
Me: That is great! Can you talk now?
Lou: Well, I'm on my way out the door to a meeting. It starts at 11:30, and I'm picking someone up.
Me: When would be a good time to call you back?
Lou: Talk now; I want to hear your voice.
Me: I want you to know I feel really good about this, and I have a lot of peace. I want you to have peace too.
Lou: Okay. (softly)

All obstacles and barriers seemed to be nonexistent. Some of the things I remember her saying were: "Meeting you has been my undying wish." "Giving you up was the worst thing that ever happened to me." "I was the first person who ever whispered in your ear, 'I love you.'" "Hearing your voice is like hearing from heaven."

I became very enchanted with her. She was so expressive and deeply sincere. Talking with her was natural and easy. Hearing her darling voice in my ear was something I couldn't believe! I was fascinated to recognize some similarities in our personalities. She said that at the time of my birth, she was engaged to my father, and they had married three months later. She said I had three sisters: Judy, Carol and Janet.

I asked her questions that most people have never asked their mother: "What color is your hair?" "How tall are you?" "What color are your eyes?" "Where did I get my red hair?" "What does my father do for a living?"

We agreed I would call her later in the day at 5:30. When she answered the phone this time, I said, "Lou?"

She said "Hi" in the sweetest voice.

"This is Patty," I said.

In the sweetest voice she said, "I know. I've been looking at the map, and it's about 500 miles to drive down there."

You could have knocked me over with a feather! She was already wanting to make plans to see me. We talked for an hour. Some of the things she said were: "When I got in my car, I was just flying along! I was on cloud nine! I am so damn excited! This is such a tremendous thing. I could get a headache over it if I let myself. I have suffered long enough! I am throwing all my guilt away right now. It has been nothing but baggage! When I see you, I will have a big hug for you; in fact, I'll kiss you all over."

One by one, Lou immediately began to tell her secret of over forty years to my sisters. None of her family or friends, at any time, had known about my birth except for my father. Of course, their reactions were shock and disbelief! However, they began to accept this remarkable opportunity with unconditional love and honor for their dear mother, and they were so touched by her elation and newly found freedom. Truly, God had prepared their hearts.

Judy, two years younger than me, called two days later to see if I was for real. We talked for two hours. We experienced a bonding from the start. She was so happy and excited about meeting me. She even sent me a card and pictures of what everyone looked like. She

signed it, "Lots of love from your sister." I also sent photos to her and Lou.

Lou and I talked three more times and made plans for our reunion. Our conversations were like rubies, diamonds and emeralds—all sparkly! Three weeks later on October 26, my adoptive parents drove me to the airport, and they paid for my flight. I arrived at the Milwaukee airport for a four-day visit. Lou, Judy, Carol and Janet (who came from Florida) welcomed me "home."

As I stepped off the plane and began walking down the jet bridge, my family was waiting at the exit. My sisters were standing in a row to my left. Then my gaze fell upon my birth mother. She grabbed me around the neck and began to sob, just a little. She hugged and held me, and the peace and joy of heaven saturated my soul. She was smiling as I kissed her right cheek. The very first thing anyone said was, "Look, she has Mom's hands."

Lou let go of me and Judy, a few steps away, walked up and said, "Hi, I'm Judy. I'm the one who called you." We hugged. Carol walked up and said, "I'm Carol." We hugged. Then Janet walked over and said, "And I'm Janet," and we hugged. Four pairs of blue eyes were checking me out. Everyone was smiling and looking just great!

We began to walk to the baggage claim. Lou's arm was locked on mine. Her comment was, "I'm just going to let the tears dry on my face." I was truly speechless for a time.

We drove a half hour to Judy's house. It was surreal. Almost immediately conversation began. The three weeks of anticipation for my arrival had absolutely wearied us. It had been like being caught in an unceasing mental and emotional avalanche and having nowhere to seek shelter for relief. We were so glad we didn't have to endure one more day of waiting. As we were riding along, Lou spoke up and said, "Well, let's have three cheers for Patty!" All of us chanted, "Hip, hip hooray!" three times.

As an icebreaker, we watched a video of my cousin David's recent wedding and reception. This meant I got to see two uncles, an aunt, two more cousins, etc. Oh my gosh, talk about overload! The day and evening were beyond my comprehension. By definition, these four ladies were strangers, but in reality, and in my heart, they were my roots, my very own flesh and blood. Everything and everyone flowed and blended in perfect harmony—our movements, picture-taking, conversations, our laughter, my chats with first one and then another.

They gave me presents. I found myself studying the facial features of each one, over and over again. I realized I was finally satisfying some lifelong insatiable curiosities. I reveled in discovering many of my own personality traits and likes and dislikes in each of them, but especially my mother.

At dinner, the table was beautiful, complete with candlelight and wine. Sitting down to dinner in my sister's home for the first time with my birth family was deeply special. The dinner music was very restful. After dinner, I gave Lou a present sent from my adoptive parents. It was a small box wrapped in pink with a pink bow. Inside was one bronzed baby shoe, which I had worn as a baby.

Here is the baby shoe
Photo courtesy of Patty Brasel

Mother had typed this note: "This little shoe is symbolic of our sharing a special and lovely daughter. We will always keep and treasure the other one! With love and gratitude." I'll never forget the expression on Lou's face.

The next morning, we worshipped at a historical Catholic church. The opening hymn was titled "The Gathering." Sitting in church for the first time with my family and receiving communion together was too good to be true. After Mass, we went into the bookstore. Lou bought each of us a Christmas ornament keepsake. We ate brunch at a buffet in a restaurant designed like an old rustic inn. It was filled with charming antiques. It had many dining rooms, each with its own wood-burning fireplace. My emotions were in a whirlwind. Nothing sounded good to eat.

**Patty (second from left) with her birth mother
and three sisters, October 1991**
Photo courtesy of Patty Brasel

After more picture-taking sessions, Lou drove me back to her house that evening, about a fifty-mile drive. I spent two nights with her. Sleeping in her home for the first time was strange and overwhelming, yet so much fun! We talked a lot about the past, including her family, her parents, three brothers, one sister and in-laws, etc. We looked at a lot of pictures. At times our hearts were aching, but a mutual sensitivity, understanding, and sense of humor eased our pain.

The next day, we drove to the adjacent town of about 15,000 people. She showed me the house where my sisters were raised, the school they attended, and the church where she and my father were married. I saw the house of my father's mother, where she also had owned a successful antique business with my dad's aunt. All of these places were within walking distance of each other. Nostalgia definitely tugged firmly at my heartstrings.

I marvel at God's power, love, wisdom, and His faithfulness to prayer. I believe He desires for families to be restored. My adoptive mother and dad's selfless love made this reunion possible. To begin searching for my birth parents had been their idea. They had felt my children and I deserved to know my roots and heritage. I blessed them with a never-ending bouquet of "thank yous."

When I returned home, my parents and my children, Ben, age thirteen, and Meryl, age eleven, were at the airport to greet me. My husband couldn't be there because of his job. My four days had been the epitome of perfection and a new beginning for us all.

On January 10, eleven weeks after our reunion, I returned to my sister's house in Milwaukee to meet Fred, my birth father. This four-day visit was also very heartwarming. The October reunion was planned at a time when Fred had out-of-town commitments. He had needed a little more time to prepare himself and accept my return into their lives. Lou had said in our first conversation that when they received the letter from Ellen, he had said, "We'll put this up on the top shelf and leave it alone." He placed it with the letter I had written and sent with the Juvenile Court. According to Lou, he had felt betrayed by the rules of the system. He had thought that the decision they had made about me was set in stone and would last forever. He said that the rules had changed.

As it turned out, Fred couldn't have been nicer and more attentive. He was delightful. The first night, just before we went to dinner, we were having happy hour. Sister Carol was also there. Sister Janet was in Florida. I had known Fred about twenty minutes, and Lou asked him to give a toast. Fred raised his glass and said with a smile, "to the family." The clinking of the glasses in response to the toast was music to my ears.

Patty with her birth parents, January 1992
Photo courtesy of Patty Brasel

After dinner we went dancing. The band played country and rock and roll. It was the kind of place where no one cared what you looked like, what you wore, how you danced, or with whom you danced. Shortly after we were seated and the band had slowed it down, Fred asked me to dance. I gave a nod, and I'm sure I must have stood up before he did! Moving rhythmically with him, arm-in-arm and hand-in-hand, was pleasure beyond measure. There were moments when I rested my head on his shoulder. My mother was right there with her polaroid camera, taking a picture. We danced many more times throughout the evening. I especially enjoyed watching him and mother dance. They looked so happy together.

Many days later, while reminiscing about the many diverse experiences that made my visit so gratifying, this thought crossed my mind: I wonder if Fred took us dancing (it was his idea) so that he would have the perfect excuse to touch and hold me close?

We all spent the night at Judy's house. It was wonderful to be with her again. The next day we went to a big antique show. Lou bought me a beautiful wooden box. Lou, Fred and I drove back to their house in the afternoon. It was a charming and picturesque route through the countryside. We ate leftovers for dinner by candlelight.

On Sunday we had a delicious home-cooked meal with prime rib as the main course. Sister Carol spent the day with us. Seeing her again was also wonderful. Feeling so at home in their house was an experience on a grand scale.

On Monday, Lou took me out to lunch and shopping. She bought three sweaters: two for me and one to take home to my daughter. She drove me to the airport late in the afternoon. With sweet sorrow and hugs, we said our "goodbyes for now," and went our separate ways, once again.

Truly, the Psalmist was right when he said, "The works of the Lord are great." Psalms 111:2.

Epilogue

It has been almost twenty-nine years since the reunion. My birth mother came by herself the first time she visited us in March 1992. She was overwhelmed and filled with gratitude to meet my two children, my adoptive parents, and my brother and his wife. My son was thirteen and my daughter was eleven when they met their birth grandmother. My two sets of parents became friends. My mothers became dear friends. My adoptive mother adored my birth mother. The whole family traveled from Wisconsin and Florida to attend my daughter's wedding in June 2006. My birth mother and I have taken trips together, including an Amadeus riverboat tour on the Danube River, and made visits back and forth.

**Patty's husband, Patty, birth parents
and adoptive parents**
Photo courtesy of Patty Brasel

Through the years, my birth mom has made many visits to Kansas City. She felt especially blessed to be able to meet four of her five great grandchildren. On her last trip we celebrated her eighty-fifth birthday. Our son has two girls and our daughter has two boys and a girl who is five. She won't get to meet the five-year-old. My birth mother is about to turn ninety-two. She is healthy, mobile, and enjoys quality of life, but air travel has not been an option for her in recent years.

My adoptive dad died in 2005 at the age of eighty-six. My adoptive mom died in 2009 at the age of almost ninety-one. They were married more than sixty-two years. My birth dad died in 2014 at age eighty-seven. He and my birth mom were also married more than sixty-two years.

Chapter 12
Linda's Story
(1951)

Back in 2018 after Mansion on a Hill *was released, Linda contacted me on Facebook and told me about her story. She shared if I ever were to write another book, she would love to have her story included. Her story is very special. It is heartwarming to know how life can lead us in different directions and then inexplicably bring people back together in time of need. Please enjoy Linda's story as much as I have.*

"Do you know why I named you Linda? That was the name your mother gave you and I kept it. It was the least I could do to thank her," my adoptive mother Frances told me in 2007 when I was fifty-five years old.

> *In all of us there is a hunger, marrow-deep, to know our heritage—to know who we are and where we have come from. Without this enriching knowledge, there is a hollow yearning ... and the most disquieting loneliness.*

—Alex Haley, author of *Roots: The Saga of an American Family.*

I understood this statement after I found my birth mother and discovered my roots. The next quote is also true, now that I have found my birth mother.

> *After search, an adoptee belongs in neither place, and in both.*

—LaVonne Harper, *Synchronicity and Reunion: The Genetic Connection of Adoptees and Birthparents*, 1992, p. 152

Finding my birth mother and meeting her was one of the most profound experiences of my life.

My story is similar to most of the other stories the birth mothers and children of The Willows have shared. My parents were unable to have children and sought out adoption options after thirteen years of marriage. They were middle-class, hard-working, upstanding citizens who met The Willows standards for adoptive parents.

I've always known I was adopted and felt very special because I was wanted and chosen. My parents gave me the little card they received from The Willows containing the minimal mother and father descriptions and the bracelet I was wearing when they picked me up.

Linda's bracelet from The Willows

I was curious about the genetics, medical history and ancestry of my birth family but knew the records for Missouri adoptions were sealed so I didn't spend much time wondering. I also thought it would be disloyal to my adoptive parents if I seemed to care too much about my birth parents.

After I had my first child, I realized what a traumatic event it must have been to give me up for adoption and I thought I would like to say "thank you" and "my life turned out well" to my birth mother. The law sealing the records was still in place in Missouri so I didn't try to search. I also considered that she might not want to hear from me, having put that part of her life behind her. I told myself it didn't matter and I didn't care.

My searching-and-finding story is a series of perfectly timed small miracles.

A Willows Facebook group member posted the passage of a new law in Missouri at the end of August 2011, enabling adoptees to access their adoption records. I deliberated about beginning a search. Why was I interested in finding my birth mother after all these years? I was curious about her but the compelling reason was to let her know I thought she had made the right decision for me. I assumed she would always wonder if she had.

On September 7, 2011, I mailed an application to the Missouri court to obtain my adoption records. Three months later, I received a notice from the court that, according to Social Security death records, my birth parents were still alive and I could hire a court approved searcher to continue gathering information.

I completed an agreement with a searcher named Laura on December 12, 2011. She received my records from the court on December 29, 2011, enabling her to locate both of my birth parents. On January 10, 2012, Laura sent a letter to my birth mother, asking if she could help locate a woman who gave birth to a daughter on January 18, 1951 in Kansas City, Missouri.

Upon receiving this letter, my birth mother immediately picked up the telephone and called Laura to confirm she was the woman Laura was looking for and would like to contact the daughter she had given up for adoption. (After we were reunited, my mother told me she was shocked when she opened the letter because she thought we would never find each other before she died.)

Laura recommended that I write a letter to my birth mother without any identifying information and she would send it to her along with the medical history questionnaire. She advised me that this letter should contain everything I would like to say to my mother as it might be the only contact I would ever have with her. A week later, on my sixty-first birthday, while shopping at Walgreens, I answered a call from Laura. My birth mother had just phoned her and asked if she would relay a message to me saying "Happy Birthday" for the first time. I dissolved into tears.

On the same birthday I received a card from my adoptive mother containing a newspaper story about a mother and daughter who had found each other after seventy-seven years. Because I hadn't told her about my search, I believe this was a sign that she approved. I had sought the advice of a counselor about telling my adoptive mother that I was searching for my birth mother. He advised me not to tell her because of her age. She was ninety-seven years old, had outlived my father and most of her friends and family, resided in assisted living, and was becoming a bit confused. The counselor thought if she knew I was searching, she might be afraid of losing me as well.

I read the medical information my birth mother had sent Laura and saw she had been treated for lung cancer five years earlier and it had returned. My husband, a pathologist, felt it was important to meet her soon, as she might not have much time left. Laura knew the courts were overwhelmed with cases requiring a judge's signature before mothers and children could be given names and contact information for reunions so she suggested we both register with International Soundex Reunion Registry (ISRR), which unites parents and children.

We both registered immediately and a volunteer with the agency called two weeks later to give me my mother's name and phone number. She had just finished talking to my mother who had asked that I call as soon as possible. I can't put my feelings into words ... it was the most amazing call of my life. She, of course, didn't know my adoptive mother had kept the name she gave me so she was shocked to learn my name was "Linda." She had three more children after giving birth to me and named the first girl Linda. So, I have a half-sister with the same name! We decided I should call her Mother Jane. She also signed her letters, "Love from your other Mother."

I live in Indiana and she was from Iowa but had been living in Texas for seventeen years. We talked on the telephone and exchanged a few letters before my husband and I arranged our in-person reunion four weeks later. Noting our enthusiasm about our growing relationship, Mother Jane cautioned me, "Don't forget your other mother."

I was able to visit Mother Jane three times before she died. One of my sons accompanied us on our second trip because he wanted to meet his grandmother. I met my half-brother, who was living with her as caregiver, and two of his four children. I have talked on the phone to my two half-sisters and a cousin for many hours learning our family history. I was able to meet my uncle, Jane's younger brother, in person when he came to visit her at the hospice facility on my last trip. He told me, "To her loved ones she gave all she had." I used this as the last line in her obituary.

I was very anxious about our first meeting, but as I walked into her home and gave her a big hug, I was instantly comfortable with her. We talked with no reservation, sharing extremely personal feelings and stories. More about her life than mine. She read the biography I wrote in the letter Laura sent before we met and that was enough information for her. She was content knowing I've had a wonderful life. Hers was not so good.

Mother Jane's pregnancy was kept secret from the family as well as the public. Her brother, who was still in high school, did not even know until sometime after she returned home. He thought she was going to Kansas City for a job as she was twenty-two years old. Secrecy was also maintained for the girls living at The Willows by having their personal mail delivered to the home address of Mr. and Mrs. Haworth, the owner/operators of The Willows.

While Jane was living at The Willows, some family friends stopped at the Haworth's home to visit Jane on their way through Kansas City while on vacation. They thought she was living with them because of her mailing address. The Haworths covered for her and told the visitors Jane had the weekend off and was out-of-town.

Highlights of what I learned about my birth mother and her family include the following.

- I don't look like any of them but I sound like my grandmother and youngest sister.
- Mother Jane and I both knit (she gave me an afghan and matching pillow covers she had knitted for me); we both have a cup of coffee by our side constantly, have identical handwriting, enjoy sports, have gray hair, alto voices, and like to keep busy. She told me she learned to knit at The Willows and she continued knitting the rest of her life.
- She married too soon after giving birth to me. She said she had made bad choices in men. (She had three husbands.) None of them treated her well.
- Mother Jane contacted a search company, The Adoptee's Liberty Movement Association (ALMA), in 1984 to look

for me.

- Mother Jane told her children about me when they were adults. They encouraged her to find me, but she didn't know if I would want to find her and she didn't want to interfere in my life.

- She wrote a letter to the Missouri court listing her current name and address to give permission to contact her if I ever needed medical assistance.

- She told me she remembered every one of my birthdays.

- She was an excellent seamstress. She gave me a shirt she had made for my brother when he was in a band.

- She had a lot of friends.

- She was given the option to keep me or give me up for adoption.

- She was asked if she wanted to hold me once. She checked me over and told me she didn't want to give away a "bad baby." She wanted me to know that I was very cute.

- Her friends at The Willows wrote to her after she left to let her know they saw the couple who picked me up and they looked like "nice people."

- Her life would have been *so* different if she hadn't gotten pregnant with me.

- Her family became very dysfunctional after I was born.

- My birth father didn't want to continue a relationship with my mother after she told him she was pregnant. She thought they were going to get married (before she became pregnant). Jane told me about him and gave me a picture of them together.

- My birth father did not want any contact with me.

- As she was dying, I truly loved and cared about her. The hospice personnel observed this and they called me first when she died and confirmed the arrangements with me.

I was the only one with her in hospice the last week of her life. I shared Mother's Day with her for the first time. Her last words as she held my hand and slipped out of consciousness were, "I love you." I wrote her obituary and received her ashes. There was no funeral.

I only knew my mother a year—nine months in her womb and three months before she died.

When she died, only a few people knew I had found her. I received four sympathy cards. I had to grieve in private. We were still keeping the secret.

> *We shall not cease from exploration*
> *And the end of all our exploring*
> *Will be to arrive where we started*
> *And know the place for the first time.*
> *Through the unknown, remembered gate*
> *When the last of earth left to discover*
> *Is that which was the beginning.*
> —T.S. Eliot (1963, Little Gidding, V)

She held my hand when I was born, and said "Goodbye."
I held her hand as she died, and said "Goodbye."

Chapter 13
Barbara's Story
(1952)

Barbara contacted me after attending my presentation at the Kansas City Public Library. She shared that she was not a Willows baby but was born at St. Vincent's Maternity Hospital in Kansas City. She asked if she could share her story and I was delighted to include it in this book. As I learn more about the different homes in Kansas City that led to the distinction of the "Adoption Hub of America," I think it is important for all to have a platform to document and share their stories for family and friends. Barbara's story, like all of the stories shared in my books, is unique in its own right but follows a similar theme of the desire to know. Please enjoy reading Barbara's story.

Bittersweet

In July of 1984, I located my birth mother, Elaine. I was thirty-two, married, living in Kansas City, Missouri, and had two young sons. Elaine was fifty-two, married, living in Little Rock, Arkansas, and had fourteen children – seven girls and seven boys, six of whom were still living at home. This is the story of my birth mother search, my reunion with my birth mother, and my friendship with her for over thirty-two years until her death in 2016.

I was adopted in February 1952 when I was seven months old. At the time, Kansas City was a midwestern adoption hub. A number of railroad lines ran through Kansas City's Union Station. St. Vincent's Maternity Hospital was one of several institutions in Kansas City where unmarried girls could travel to by train to hide away during pregnancy, deliver their babies, and move on with their lives.

Adoption in the 1950s was considered a win/win/win situation – the baby got a good home, the adoptive couple got a child to complete their family, and the birth mother got a fresh start. She could deliver her baby, leave the maternity home, and resume her life as if nothing had happened. At least that was the theory at the time.

I always knew I was adopted. My sister Cathy, who was adopted from St. Vincent's two-and-a-half years after I was, and I were told by our parents we were "chosen." We were assured that our birth mothers were good people and that we were a blessing to our parents, for which they were eternally grateful.

I accepted this interpretation of my situation without question. I thought being adopted was rather romantic, mysterious. My name Barbara means "foreigner" or "mysterious stranger." That is how I felt – a wanderer in a strange land.

My birth parent search began Memorial Day weekend in 1983 at a family gathering on the porch of my parents' 1950s three-bedroom ranch. Out of the blue, my dad blurted out, "You know, the reason you were so old when you were adopted is your birth mother tried to keep you?" I was stunned by this revelation. I promptly burst into tears and ran to my mother, sobbing. I asked why she had never told me my birth mother tried to keep me. She said that she didn't think I could handle it.

I now think the real reason she withheld that information was that she couldn't handle it. The idea that there was some woman out there, wanting me, grieving me, was too threatening. Just as I had my unspoken fears and imaginings about my origins, I think so too did my adoptive parents. When eventually I told my dad about finding my birth father, he said, "Does this mean I am not your real dad anymore?"

My parents married in 1946 after World War II. My dad worked as a salesman in the family-owned seat cover manufacturing business run by his mother. His dad, my grandfather, died of a heart attack in 1943, and my grandmother took over the business. Mom loved languages and had worked as a secretary for a Latin American import/export firm before her marriage. After she married, she quit her job and became a full-time homemaker. After trying unsuccessfully for five years to have children, Mom and Dad decided to adopt.

Two months after they adopted me, Mom and Dad moved into a bigger house so they could take in my mother's grandparents, who were in their eighties. Three years earlier, both of Mom's parents had died within a six-month period. Mom's grandparents had always lived with the extended family.

Barbara with parents in 1952
Photo courtesy of Barbara Cooke

After Mom's parents died, Mom and her three younger siblings took over the care of their grandparents. During the time my great-grandparents were living with us, my folks adopted Cathy.

Then, when the last of my great-grandparents died, my mother's youngest sister contracted polio at age twenty-six. She was nine months pregnant with her fourth child. We moved into a house across the street from my aunt and her family so that Mom could help out. This is where I grew up – on a quiet street across from my aunt, uncle and cousins.

While my adoptive status was never hidden from me, I knew intuitively that it was something I didn't talk about. I pushed any thoughts or fears about my origin story deep underground. I was very loyal to my parents, especially to my mom, and grateful she and Dad had adopted me. In college, I would blast "Love Child" sung by Diana Ross and the Supremes on the stereo in my dorm room, but I only told a few close friends I was adopted. While my sister had expressed curiosity about her birth parents from the time she was a young teenager, I was too loyal to my adoptive parents to even consider it. In reality, I think I was afraid of what I might discover.

My adoption became more of a conscious thought after my first son, Andy, was born. One night, sitting in the white wicker rocker that had been in my bedroom as a child, rocking him back to sleep, it suddenly occurred to me that Andy was the first blood relative I had ever known. This was a revelation to me – as my sister would say, "a wonderment." Now I had a genetic story going forward. I knew someone who had my skin, my hair, and my genetic history. But I was aware I had no genetic story going backward. All that was a mystery.

After Andy was born, I worked as a freelance writer for a suburban paper. I suggested to the editor that I do a story about women who had given children up for adoption. She agreed, so I set up a post office box to receive replies to an advertisement I ran in the personal column of the local newspaper. This was in the pre-internet days of 1978.

KELLEE PARR

WRITER wants to correspond with persons who have given up children for adoption. All names and information strictly confidential. Write PO Box 22394 KCMO.

It was exciting to go to the post office box every few days to see if anyone had written. I didn't get a huge number of replies – maybe twenty – and eventually I chose three women to feature. For all of them, giving a child up had been a painful and traumatic experience.

In psychology there is a concept called the Johari Window. It's the idea that we have some areas of our lives that are known to ourselves but not to others. We have other areas that are known to others but not ourselves. When my article was published, I think others saw that I was wrestling with my own adoption issues. I didn't see it. Writing that article was my way of exploring, from a detached, writer's vantage point, why a woman would give a child up for adoption. That was the burning question: why did my mother give me up? And what did her act of giving me up say about me – my value, my self-worth, my worthiness?

Adoption is a very rational, adult transaction. Adults – the birth mother, the adoptive parents, the agency social workers and the judge – make a decision that is supposedly in the best interest of the fifth party to adoption, the child. But children do not process what it means to be adopted with an adult, rational mind. In the absence of factual information, I created my own story.

As a child, when I asked my parents why I was so old when they adopted me, my folks said that in 1951, everyone wanted boys. They also said I had a heart murmur, but they didn't care. They loved me at first sight. All this was said in love and meant to convey how special I was to them. But in the silence of my child's mind, my suspicion grew that a series of people, starting with my birth mother, didn't want me. I was lucky to be adopted at all.

All this was out of my conscious awareness until I began my birth parent search. The way adoption worked in the 1950s, once an adoption took place, the past was over. It was sealed. Nature shouldn't be important to the adopted child. Nurture should be enough. Questioning the situation meant there was something wrong with the child, some ingratitude of the adoptee or some implied failure on the part of the adoptive parents to make the child feel securely their own. Love was supposed to conquer all. My job was to graft myself to my new family tree.

After I learned my birth mother had tried to keep me, I sat on this information for a few months before I worked up my courage to contact Catholic Charities, the agency that now housed my adoption records. I wanted my non-identifying information. This was information from my adoption file about each of my birth parents and the circumstances of my birth, edited to delete any information that might enable me to locate them.

The term non-identifying information refers to information an adult adoptee is allowed to see from the original adoption file in a closed adoption. A closed adoption is the process by which an infant is adopted, and the legal record is sealed by the court. My parents had a legal document, hidden in a drawer at home, saying they had adopted "Marie Elizabeth Crowley." But instead of my original birth certificate, I had an amended birth certificate that said my name was Barbara Ann Whelan, and that my adoptive parents, not my birth parents, were my legal parents. My original baptismal record was also sealed. This closed system was designed to protect the adoptee and adoptive parents from interference by the biological parents and to allow the birth mother to go on with her life as if nothing had happened. Closed adoption, where all records were sealed, was the norm in the 1950s.

I met with Catholic Charities. A social worker read from an old manila file folder that contained all the information about the circumstances of my birth – the names of my parents, which she was not allowed to reveal, their ages, their nationalities, some basic health information, the number of siblings for each, their interests and activities, and the fact that my birth mother converted to Catholicism while living at the maternity home. The social worker also said that my birth father had offered to pay for an abortion, but my birth mother refused. This information was another shock to me. I had assumed that because abortion was illegal at the time, my birth mother was forced to carry me to term.

I now had the following information to go on. My birth mother was born in 1931. She had two sisters. Her parents had both divorced and married other people. She attended college for one-half year. She had met my birth father while in high school and reconnected with him in college. She was interested in writing, journalism, dancing and music. They had met in Springfield, Missouri. She had converted to Catholicism while in the maternity home in 1951.

My birth father was born in 1930. He was an only child. He had attended college for two years. He was interested in art – painting and sculpture – as well as writing and debate. There was a note in the file that my birth father had been described by my birth mother as "very emotional and becoming nervous easily." My sister said, "I wonder if he was emotional and nervous before or after he found out she was pregnant."

With this information, I was off and running with my search. I was increasingly irritated that I was denied my own written history even though I was a thirty-three-year-old adult. I was determined to outmaneuver the system. It became a challenge and an adventure to see what I could find out.

I decided the first step was to look through copies of high school and college yearbooks from Springfield, Missouri. A good friend had a cousin who attended Southwest Missouri State College (later

Missouri State University) in Springfield. This young woman made photocopies of the Southwest Missouri State yearbooks and the Springfield Central High yearbooks for the target years I thought my birth mother would have attended high school and college.

I cross-referenced the last name Crowley with photos of club activities in drama, speech, journalism, and music, as well as with pictures of girls in other class years with the same last name. I identified a woman, now living in Arizona, who I thought could be my birth mother. A friend called her at her home. She denied having given birth to a child in 1951 or ever relinquishing a child for adoption. I was devastated. I thought I was emotionally prepared for what I might find in my search, but I wasn't. I felt like I was being rejected all over again.

I put my search on hold. A few months later it occurred to me that while my baptismal record was sealed, my birth mother's baptismal record might not be sealed, as she had been an adult when she was baptized. The Catholic church near the location of the shuttered maternity home was closed, but I tracked the sacramental records to a neighboring parish. I called the office and spoke to the nun in charge. She quizzed me at length about my motives, wanting to know if I knew who my "real" mother was – i.e. my adoptive mother. I assured her that I was not looking for another mother. I loved my adoptive parents very much.

She agreed to go through the baptismal records for January to July 1951. She told me that an Elaine Crowley, age nineteen, had been baptized at Holy Name Catholic Church in the spring of 1951. I recognized the name as one that had come up in my yearbook searches. The problem for me was that this Elaine had married less than a year after I was born – in May of 1952. It seemed too soon for a woman to marry who had relinquished a child at the end of November of 1951. I thought to myself, *Big loss.*

Again, I put my search on hold. Eventually friends convinced me that I had gone this far – I should see it through to the end regardless of what I found out. Elaine Crowley's baptismal record at the church also gave information about her marriage, including the name of her spouse, the church in New Orleans where she was married, the names of the best man and maid of honor, and the name of the priest that had married them. Using directory assistance, a friend rang the home of the best man, who was living in Louisiana. One of his teenage children answered and gave us the name and phone number of Michael and Elaine Foley in Little Rock, Arkansas.

At this point I talked to my pastor about whether to contact Elaine. Would she welcome me or not? Was I opening something I couldn't handle? After listening to me and giving it much thought, my pastor said, "If I were your mother, I would want to know you."

I asked Jane, an adoption social worker who was the sister of a close friend, to make the call to Elaine. It was July 14, 1984.

Elaine took the call at home in a back bedroom and broke down sobbing at the news that I had located her. She and Jane talked at length. Elaine said she had never expected that I would contact her, having been told at the time she relinquished me that the separation had to be permanent and absolute. After talking to Elaine, Jane called me and reported the conversation. Elaine had given her the name of my birth father, so in one phone call I had the names of both my birth parents.

Elaine told Jane the story of her pregnancy and her rejection by my birth father, who denied paternity. She said she had refused to sign the papers releasing me for adoption when she left the maternity home. She planned to go to New Orleans to be near her father and stepmother with the intent of getting a job and coming back for me when she could support me. She soon realized she could not afford to keep me as a single parent on a secretarial salary. She reluctantly signed the papers to release me at the end of November 1951. By this time, she was dating Michael Collins, the man she would eventually marry and with whom she would have fourteen more children.

When Jane told me about the fourteen children, I was aghast. I found myself taking two steps back emotionally from the whole thing. I wondered what on earth I had gotten myself into. I visualized the "Old Woman in the Shoe" in the cartoons, with children tumbling out the windows and sliding down the front of the shoe. At the same time, I was exhilarated to have succeeded in finding my birth mother and very excited about learning my roots. It was like landing in an airplane at night – one minute you are in complete darkness and the next minute you drop altitude to see a thousand twinkling lights.

After this initial contact, Elaine and I began writing extensively back and forth. It was as if a thin scab had been ripped open for both of us, and we were trying to clean out the wound so we could heal. In her first letter Elaine indicated that while she was glad this had happened – my reappearance – she was not ready to share the information with her husband and children. Her older sister, Jeanne, agreed to serve as courier. I would write Elaine and send it in an envelope to Jeanne who then forwarded my letter in a new envelope addressed to Elaine in Jeanne's handwriting so as not to arouse suspicion when the letter arrived at the house.

Elaine said she had planned a trip to Oklahoma City at the end of August to visit her mother, age seventy-nine, who was having health problems. Jeanne and her husband, John, lived on a farm about thirty miles outside of Springfield. Elaine invited me to meet her at Jeanne and John's farm. Elaine and Jeanne would drive to Springfield from Oklahoma City, and I would drive down from Kansas City to meet Elaine on Thursday. She would be alone at the farm.

I was in a complete daze driving the two-and-a-half hours to the farm, getting lost on unfamiliar country roads before finding the property. Elaine came out to meet me on the gravel driveway, and we hugged awkwardly. We then went inside to a back bedroom and sat across from each other by a window, knee to knee. I realized years later that it was like Elaine was going to confession. That seemed to be her primary need – to apologize for any pain her actions had caused me. My primary need was to find my roots – psychological, physical, historical, spiritual – although I didn't fully understand this at the time.

The best way to explain this is to quote from our first letters to each other. From Elaine:

July 19, 1984

The essential thing that has needed to be said so very long is – forgive me – please – for the pain it's caused you. I could never regret you – Over the years I have tried to make peace with what I do regret – the loss of you, my own weakness and helplessness at the time, etc.

Thank you for the gift of peace. I couldn't bear to think that anything terrible had happened to you or that you hadn't been cherished.

This letter is from me to my birth mother that I had been allowed to place in in my adoption file when I first met with Catholic Charities:

January 1984

I have to admit I have many questions about you, but if I could only ask one, it would be "Did you love one another when you made me?"

I am not afraid of a negative answer. I know who I am and don't need your reassurance of my goodness. It is just that it would be a nice feeling to know that the answer is "yes." No matter how deeply one is loved by others – and I am rich in such love – I think an adoptee always wrestles with the question "Am I someone's mistake, someone's regret?"

There would be a certain peace for me if you could tell me "No."

Elaine had met my birth father, Ed, in high school and reconnected with him when they were in college at Southwest Missouri State. They were acquaintances in high school, participating on the debate team together, but they didn't date until they met again in college. Elaine believed my birth father loved her. She later said that she mistook intensity for intimacy. When she realized she was pregnant, she assumed Ed would "do the right thing" and marry her. Instead, he denied paternity and suggested there had been other boys she had been intimate with who could have been the father of her child.

At the time, Ed was being inducted into the Army for the Korean War. He was being processed in Seattle. Elaine went to Seattle where they had another emotional confrontation, and she was rejected again. She went back to Springfield, approached his parents to intervene, but they too denied he was the father of her child.

Elaine was devastated by this abandonment. She contemplated suicide by jumping off a bridge. She realized she could not do that to her unborn child. Instead, she talked to a friend in Springfield who knew a priest who connected her to St. Vincent's Hospital, a maternity home in Kansas City. St. Vincent's was adjacent to St. Anthony's Home for Infants, which was where the babies were kept until they were adopted.

Barbara and Elaine in 1984
Photo courtesy of Barbara Cooke

When we first met, I did not think I looked a lot like Elaine, other than the shape of my eyes, the pronounced veins in my hands, and my big feet. As I looked at the family pictures she had brought to Jeanne's, I identified with the dark-haired Crowley features of her dad that I saw in some of my newly acquired half-siblings and in pictures of other relatives on her father's side. What most interested me was how I was psychologically like Elaine – in interests, in temperament, in values.

I had attended some adoptee groups in the months before I located Elaine. In those meetings, adoptees would share their reunion stories. It was uncanny how many adoptees found out they had similar interests and mannerisms to their birth mothers – a shared interest in quilting when no one in the adoptee's family could sew, a love of animals not shared by anyone in the adoptee's family, certain hand gestures used when talking, shared tastes in reading, art and music, etc. Both Elaine and I were good writers and enjoyed literature and the arts. Both of us were interested in religion.

It came as a shock to me that Elaine had not always been Catholic. I was raised in a very tight-knit, Catholic world. We attended Catholic schools, went to Catholic doctors, played with

Catholic friends, and patronized Catholic businesses. Our world was defined by parishes: you knew what part of the city a person lived in according to the parish name.

As an adult, I had remained Catholic despite my reservations about the church. One reason I knew I stayed was because I thought my religion was the one connecting link between me and my birth mother. She had given birth in a Catholic maternity home; therefore, she was Catholic. I was Catholic. If I let go of that, I let go of her. My faith gave me roots. To find out that I came from a long line of Protestants, some of whom fought in the Revolutionary War, was amazing to me.

Over the next few days, Elaine told me more of her life story. Her parents had a very tumultuous relationship. There were many moves, many schools, many uncertainties, including times when her dad was missing or in jail. Eventually her parents divorced and married other people. Elaine did not seem close to her mother. She was very fond of her stepmother, Marie, after whom she had named me.

Elaine said that after giving birth to me, she was never allowed to hold me. She could look at me through the nursery window in the days before she left the maternity home, but she could not touch me. She said she did not like the nun, Sister Margaret, who was the head of the maternity home. She had pressured Elaine to sign the papers before she left, intimating that by not signing, Elaine would make it difficult to place her baby later as most adoptive couples wanted infants. Ironically, the nun who was the administrator of St. Vincent's two-and-a-half years later when my parents adopted Cathy was a distant cousin of Michael Crowley. She was a grandmother figure to me and my sister over many years.

Elaine and I had a wonderful initial visit over three days. On Sunday Jeanne and I drove Elaine back to Oklahoma to catch her flight home. As we parted, again I completely dissolved into tears. It felt like I was experiencing a great abandonment a second time.

Elaine left and Jeanne comforted me. I told Jeanne I felt sorry for Elaine. It did not seem like she was living anything like the life she had hoped for as a young woman, that her dreams for herself had been sidelined by my birth. Jeanne assured me that Elaine did not feel sorry for herself and she would not want me to feel sorry for her. Elaine was living the life she chose.

It was almost another three years before Elaine felt it was the right time to tell her husband about my reappearance and introduce me to my fourteen half-siblings. In that time Elaine and I continued to write with both of us trying to figure out what this relationship would be in the present. It wasn't mother/daughter. I had a mother. I felt very protective of my mother, my dad and my sister, and I did not want them to feel I was abandoning them for my "real" family. I had to keep these loves separate.

Eight months after I met Elaine, I contacted my birth father in St. Louis, Missouri, where he lived with his wife in a Victorian townhouse near downtown. They had moved there after their three children were grown.

Ed, like Elaine, had married the year after I was born. He worked as a graphic designer in St. Louis, and he was also a fine artist and cartoonist. He did not seem surprised that he had been contacted. It was as if he expected this to come back to haunt him. His wife, a high school librarian, was gracious and welcoming.

Ed and I spent several days together wandering St. Louis and getting to know one another. Physically, I thought I looked a lot like his mother and her side of the family. I was interested to see that my handwriting was like his. That had been one of my curiosities. My handwriting was nothing like Elaine's and nothing like my mom's. I wondered if handwriting was a nature vs. nurture trait.

Ed was an only child. His dad had been a prison administrator in the federal prison system in Atlanta and New York City. He then reluctantly took a prison job in Springfield, Missouri, so his wife, my grandmother, could be near her mother and siblings. Ed and his father had a stormy, contentious relationship. His mother was caught in the middle.

It came as a shock to find out that Ed was a recovering alcoholic, sober for ten years when we met. This was medical history I did not want to hear. My adoptive dad had alcohol problems in addition to having mental health issues related to World War II. Finding out that there was so much alcoholism in my birth family – Elaine's father, mother, and stepmother were all alcoholics – and now my birth father was a recovering alcoholic – in addition to knowing the impact of growing up in an alcoholic home, I could no longer deny that my own drinking was something I needed to address. The genetic links were too strong. I quit drinking in March 1987, two months before I flew to Arkansas to meet my fourteen half-siblings.

In this period – after meeting Elaine and Ed but before meeting Elaine's husband and my newly acquired half-siblings – I told my mother, and then my father, about finding my birth parents. They both took it well, saying nothing could change our love for each other and the relationship we had formed.

I flew to Arkansas in May 1987. I had a wonderful "homecoming" with my newly acquired family, who all embraced me with love, curiosity and enthusiasm. Elaine said she knew that her children would welcome me, but she wasn't sure how they would handle the news about her past. For my part, I was especially intrigued to meet the boys, as I had grown up in a family dominated by women. There were more girls than boys in my extended family.

I would like to say that "we all lived happily ever after," but that wasn't the case, at least in the short run. I went through a tumultuous six-year period in which I was on again/off again about what kind of relationship I wanted with Elaine and Ed. At first, I romanticized them both, seeing only their good qualities and looking at how I was like them in these positive traits. Then I swung the other way, focusing only on their attributes I saw as negative and not wanting to see those qualities in myself. At the same time, I was trying to protect everyone's feelings. I did not want Elaine to know that anything bad had happened to me as a child, and I didn't want my mother to know that my relationship with Elaine was so important to me. It was overwhelming.

Eventually, I settled into a comfortable friendship with Elaine. We visited almost every year until her death. I would travel to Little Rock to visit or meet her in Springfield at Jeanne's. When I went to Little Rock, I enjoyed wonderful visits with the whole family, but Elaine always tried to arrange for us to have one or two days away by ourselves. These were special times for us both. We shared interests, ideas and perspectives. Elaine was a mirror in which I could see my strengths and weaknesses with more clarity.

Elaine and Barbara in 2013
Photo courtesy of Barbara Cooke

I think it is difficult for people who are not adopted to understand the disconnect of being raised with only nurture and no nature to reference. It's like trying to learn to walk with only one leg. Most people take for granted that they have both nature and nurture playing in the background as they grow up. They rely on this music to figure out who they are. They bounce themselves off real people

– parents, siblings, extended family – with whom they share both nature and nurture. "How am I like or unlike my mother or father or siblings?" Their answer references both environmental influences – nurture – and genetic influences – nature.

An adoptee does not have this balanced frame of reference. An adoptee only has nurture. How am I like and unlike these people to whom I am not genetically connected? It is "hit or miss." The mirror is foggy. It's like starting with one piece of a jigsaw puzzle and trying to match it to other pieces, which are part of a different jigsaw puzzle. Nothing ever fits completely right.

Add to this an unspoken cultural expectation that an adoptee should be grateful. Adoptees are seen as being rescued from a life of hardship, for which they should be grateful. This is part of the romantic narrative of adoption in the 1950s. In this narrative, the birth mother always makes an uncoerced, noble sacrifice for the good of her child. The adoptive parents fulfill their desire for a family while saving a child from a life of economic struggle and social stigma. The adoptee is given a better life, for which she will always be grateful and never need anything more. This is the win/win/win picture of adoption.

The truth is that every adoption, however positive and welcomed, is a bundle of joy wrapped in sorrow. There are losses before there are gains. The birth mother loses her child, and often her self-esteem and sense of power. The adoptive parents lose their dream of a biological child, one who mirrors their own traits and temperament and not those of someone else. The adoptee loses her biological parents and connection to her history. All these losses must be mourned.

As I write this story, I am approaching the thirty-sixth anniversary of my reunion with my birth mother. At the time of Elaine's death, I had known her for half my life.

Over the years, I have come to understand that we all have "sweet" and "bitter" parts of our lives. The challenge is to accept, rather than deny, the "bitter" so we can savor the "sweet."

I know I am very fortunate that both of my birth parents welcomed me back into their lives and answered all my questions with honesty and openness. Many adoptees never locate their birth parents or are rejected by them when they do find them. I have wonderful half-siblings with whom I continue to enjoy happy times. I have a genealogy. I have a history.

At the same time, finding my birth parents helped me to come full circle with my adoptive family. It made me realize how grateful I am to be adopted. I cannot imagine a life without my parents, my sister, and my extended family of aunts, uncles, cousins and friends who loved me and supported me over my lifetime. I would not be "me" without their love.

In the end it is all bittersweet, weaving in and out like the brown vines with orange blossoms that grace Missouri's woodlands in the fall.

Chapter 14
Cynthia's Story
(1955)

*C*yndi contacted me after participating in my online course about *The Willows the Osher Lifelong Learning Institute lecture series through the University of Kansas. I was so glad to hear from her and that she was wanting to share her story. Not all stories have the happy ending that my mother and others have had, but as Cyndi shares, just getting answers to her medical history and her birth family history is something many adoptees need.*

I was born at The Willows hospital in Kansas City, Missouri, in 1955. Although I have had my adoption papers with my birth name since 1992, I always wondered why I had been given up for adoption. As I got older, I wanted to know my medical history. The name of my birth mother was blocked out on those papers. The good news is that I found my birth mother's family in 2016. Following the Osher class, I was inspired to complete my story and I recently have contacted my birth father's daughter, my half-sister, and am waiting on a response.

At birth, I was given the name Kristi Mannino. In records I obtained in 1997 from Children's Mercy Hospital in Kansas City, my birth mother was listed as Carole Jeanne Mannino. She was twenty years old when I was born.

Shortly after birth I was adopted by John and Helen Drago of Leawood, Kansas, who are now both deceased. I was told that the adoption stipulated that I was to be adopted only by an Italian Catholic family. I am not sure if this was really true or if The Willows staff simply matched me with a family that matched my ethnicity. As it turns out, I am half Italian/Sicilian and the rest is Germanic Europe, French, English, Welsh and Northwestern Europe. This is the same combination that matches both my birth and my adoptive parents.

My adoptive mother gave me my adoption papers in 1992 and wrote a letter to me about what she knew about my birth family. She told me I was very ill shortly after I was born, and I was transferred to Children's Mercy Hospital in Kansas City. She stated that my birth grandfather was a doctor/surgeon and that my birth grandmother was an artist, and some of her art was displayed in their family home. She told me that she had always tried to provide opportunities like art lessons and encouraged my budding interest in science and biology. She firmly believed in nature and nurture.

In 1993, I was working in research administration of a pediatric cancer program at Texas Children's Hospital in Houston, Texas. I had a meeting in Kansas City at Children's Mercy Hospital and I told the chair of pediatrics and hospital chief of staff that the staff at Children's Mercy Hospital saved my life when I was a baby. I showed him the IV cutdown scar on my ankle that was made there as a lifesaving measure. He offered to locate my medical records. I gave him my birth name, Kristi Mannino, in case that is how my records were listed. And it was!

He called the next day and said he had sent a copy of my records. In those records was a page about my birth mother's pregnancy and stated she was twenty years old when I was born, thus she was born in 1935. There was a note that she was a student, the daughter of a doctor, and I was born out of wedlock. I recall that my adoptive mother told me my birth mother's father probably sent her there because she was a young student, not married and to have a baby out of wedlock in 1955 was not acceptable. The birth father's age was listed as twenty-four years old. The records describe the procedure of the IV cutdown on my right ankle in verification. The records, most importantly, contained a form regarding the transfer from The Willows to Children's Mercy and it was signed by my birth mother.

My adoptive mother passed away in 2007. Although she had given me my adoption papers, she expressed that she did not want me to look for my birth mother. Finally, in 2016, I figured it was now or never as I estimated my birth mother would be elderly if alive at all. I decided to order a DNA kit from Ancestry.com. I got a paid subscription service from Ancestry so I could do more extensive searches. I found a 1940 United States Census document that listed Joseph Dante Mannino, physician; wife Bessie; and four daughters, with the youngest identified as Carole, who was five in 1940 (thus she was born in 1935). They had lived in Cleveland, Ohio.

This last bit of data tied together the information I had, and therefore I believed that Carole Mannino listed in the 1940 census was my birth mother. I did more searches using Google and learned that she had been a student at Kent State University in Ohio. Unfortunately, I discovered that she had passed away in 2014. Her death notice listed all her daughters lived in the Cleveland area and included "the late Kristi." At first I thought the listing of Kristi was me because that is the exact spelling of my name on the medical records and adoption papers. Also, there is the fact that the last time she saw me I was deathly ill and was being transferred to an acute care hospital nearby to where she gave birth to me.

After speaking to one of my half-sisters, I found that my assumption was not the case. Carole named her third daughter Kristi, who was born in 1960, to hopefully avenge the memory that she gave away her first Kristi. Sadly, the second "Kristi" passed away in 1962 from a brain tumor. Apparently, my birth mother thought she was being punished for my adoption and told one of her other daughters that she feared her secret of giving a baby up for adoption would be found out due to the advent of DNA testing.

On her deathbed when asked by her youngest daughter if they should find me after she died, Carole said, "No." So, her oldest daughter I had found decided to heed her younger sister's warning and has ceased any communication. I was able to tell my half-sister (the oldest of five daughters) that her Mom went to Kent State and about the activities she participated in there. Her mother told her she went to a finishing school and had never discussed any details about going to college.

In 2017, I wrote the Jackson County Juvenile Court to release redacted caseworker notes they had on file, along with my original birth certificate. I found out about the possibility of getting these from an Ancestry bulletin board about The Willows. The caseworker's notes included this quote, "She said she has known the alleged father for one-and-a-half years and met him at college. She didn't tell him of her pregnancy as she said she wasn't interested in marriage at this point. Too, she said that she would not want to marry as a solution to this situation. She thought it might lead to much unhappiness. She said that she is confident that through adoption her child will have a good home and a legitimate status in a community."

Cynthia's mother (left) and Cynthia (right)
Photos courtesy of Cyndi Nelson-Weiner

In addition, from those notes I obtained information that although did not have names or locations, I figured out who my birth father was because he was a popular, active person who set swimming records at college. Since I found my birth mother went to Kent State, I searched through Kent State newspapers that were online and figured out his name.

My husband surprised me with Kent State yearbooks he found on eBay from the years my birth father attended. Now I have photos and articles that detail the organizations and sports my birth father was involved in while in college.

Cynthia's birth father
Photo courtesy of Cyndi Nelson-Weiner

His name is Robert G. Smith. Unfortunately, he passed away in 1997. Ancestry DNA pulled together my detective work as I started getting information on first and second cousins in the Smith family. I am proud of my detective work. If I can find someone named Bob Smith, I urge adoptees to search to find the information they want and need.

I had loving adoptive parents and I was given an ideal childhood. I grew up in Leawood, Kansas. My older brother was adopted too (he was born in Indiana) and we always knew we were "special and chosen."

Cynthia's adoptive parents and brother
Photo courtesy of Cyndi Nelson-Weiner

I spent over thirty years in Houston, Texas, working for Baylor College of Medicine. Now I live north of San Antonio, Texas, where I led a disease-related non-profit organization as CEO until I retired in April 2020. I have been in healthcare for my entire career. A year ago, I convinced my brother that I could find his birth family. And indeed, I did. He was lucky that his mother's family (she died in 2003) had been looking for him since just before his mother passed away. They are now in regular contact.

In 1997 my ex-husband had some time on his hands due to changes at his company and offered to use his time to see what he could find out about my birth mother. Although he claimed to be doing internet searches, he actually met someone online, for whom he later left me, and we were divorced. I always say that Children's Mercy Hospital saved my life twice: once when I was born and the second time due to the medical records sent to me that contained the full name of my birth mother who my ex claimed to be finding—and exited him from my life. On a very happy note, I remarried and it was my husband who encouraged me to get the Ancestry kit and try again to find my birth mother.

That's my story. Although it has not been the feel-good-story-of-the-year, I am very grateful that I know my background. I was able to get some medical history from my half-sister before she stopped talking to me. I now know some information about my birth parents, why I was given up for adoption, and know they both seemed like very good people. When I feel disappointed about the lack of interaction with my maternal half-sisters, I remind myself to feel happy about what I did find out. It is better than not knowing anything at all.

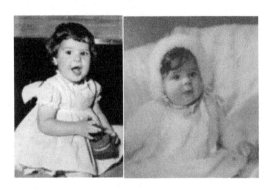

Cynthia (left) and her birth mother (right)
Photos courtesy of Cyndi Nelson-Weiner

Chapter 15
Joni and Susan's Story
(1955–1958)

*I*n March 2020, I gave a three-part lecture in Lawrence, Kansas, on *The Willows* as part of the Osher Lifelong Learning Institute. After the first of these classes, Joni Wilson and Susan Barnes motioned me over to their table. They shared that they were excited to find out about the class and thought I might be interested to know that they were sisters who had lived at *The Willows* as children. I am sure I had a shocked look on my face. They began sharing their story with me. They brought photos to the second class and shared more details about their time at the maternity home. I asked them if they would share their unique story. Thankfully they agreed and it is fascinating to get a totally different perspective of *The Willows* from their memories as little girls. Thank you, Joni and Susan, for sharing your experience with us.

Living at The Willows
Joni Wilson and Susan Barnes

This story begins with our mother, Virginia Zukowsky. Virginia worked at The Willows Maternity Sanitarium between 1955 and 1964 as a registered nurse to care for the young pregnant women and to help deliver their babies. We lived with our mother in an apartment at The Willows from 1955 until 1958.

Virginia was married and thirty-three years old when Joni was born in the spring of 1953. Susan was born at the end of the summer in 1954. In 1955, Virginia divorced her husband, our father, and became a single parent.

Virginia Zukowsky, registered nurse
Photo courtesy of Joni Wilson and Susan Barnes

We were not born at The Willows, but we were young children, between the ages of one and five, when we lived there. Our memories are pieced together from photos, anecdotes, and hazy remembrances. While our mother was alive, we didn't think to ask her specific questions about this time in our lives.

Virginia was licensed as a registered nurse in 1941. She served during World War II with the American Red Cross as a hospital nurse in Honolulu, Territory of Hawaii. In December 1945, Virginia returned to her hometown of Independence, Missouri. In February 1946, unmarried, she gave birth to a son in Kansas City, Missouri, however, there is no record that this happened at The Willows.

In April 1946, Virginia's parents adopted her baby and raised him as their son. David Kent Moorman was known as Virginia's brother and our uncle. We found out later that David was actually our half-brother, instead of our uncle, but we never asked him or our mother for details about his birth, his biological father, or the adoption.

David died in a small plane crash in 1975 at the age of twenty-nine. Our mother died in 1997 at the age of seventy-seven. We've asked relatives about the details surrounding his birth and adoption. However, no one has been able to provide any answers.

Working at The Willows, Virginia would have been empathetic and understanding with other young pregnant women, having been through a similar situation. Living at The Willows would have allowed her to see the residents on a daily basis and assist them when they went into labor and gave birth to their babies. Virginia said that she sometimes delivered babies at The Willows on her own, if the doctor couldn't get there in time, but that wasn't often.

The following table is a partial list that Virginia created about her work history and the money she earned annually.

Year	Virginia Worked	Earned
1955	Willows Hospital	$1,128
1956	Willows	$3,234
1957	Willows	$3,393
1958	Willows	$2,274
1958	Fairmount	$750
1959	Willows	$798
1960	Willows	$1,296
1961	Willows	$4,488
1962	Willows	$4,267
1964	Willows (Jan-May)	$1,734

The apartment at The Willows could have been part of her employment compensation during the time we lived there from 1955 to 1958, but there are no details other than these total dollar amounts earned.

The one mention of money earned from the Fairmount (a maternity hospital located in Kansas City) is a mystery. As a nurse, Virginia might have been loaned from The Willows for a brief period of time, or she might have worked there part-time during 1958.

Virginia's annual pay was in keeping with what nurses were earning at that time. In 1956–1957, the pay for a private hospital nurse was about $64 per week, or an annual salary of $3,328, which is comparable to the 1956 and 1957 salary that Virginia earned at The Willows. This amount would have been especially generous if it also included living at The Willows apartment.

In 1958, our family left The Willows apartment and moved to Independence, Missouri. Virginia continued to work at The Willows until 1964, but we no longer resided there.

Joni's Memories

As a toddler (two to five years old) growing up at The Willows, I have a few thoughts that I think really happened, but I realize that I'm also influenced by the photos, stories, and the way that memories can be affected over time.

I don't remember a lot about the apartment we lived in at The Willows. I think there was a small efficiency kitchen, a living room, a bathroom, and bedrooms.

I have fond memories of watching *The Lawrence Welk Show* on Saturday nights. This was also bath night to get ready to go to church on Sunday mornings. My mother would often put cloth rollers in my hair so it would be curly for Sunday.

Joni with hair in cloth rollers
The Willows apartment, c. 1956
Photo courtesy of Joni Wilson and Susan Barnes

The large kitchen downstairs at The Willows seems to play a significant part in my memory. I recollect helping Cecil (the cook) in the kitchen with food preparation. She would prepare toast, spreading it with melted butter from a large container kept on the stove.

Cecil appears in several family photos, accompanying us on outings, so it was likely that she and my mother were friends. I recall that she lived in a small apartment on the lower floor of The Willows near the back of the building.

I also oddly remember operating a commercial-style dishwasher—not washing dishes in a sink, but loading them into a large machine. This seems highly unlikely when I think about it now. There was a huge, vault-like room off the kitchen where food was stored, and I was familiar with getting food items from this area.

Joni, Cecil (The Willows cook), and Susan, c. 1956
Photo courtesy of Joni Wilson and Susan Barnes

In The Willows dining room, near the kitchen, I recall "playing" a piano—and specifically seeing Cole Porter sheet music. Later, in elementary school, I took piano lessons and often played for church, soloists, and the school chorus. The Willows might have been where I began my musical efforts!

Joni, Virginia, and Susan holiday meal,
The Willows' dining room, c. 1956
Photo courtesy of Joni Wilson and Susan Barnes

There was a grassy park-like area outside, near the apartment. While I have a few hazy memories of walking around there, it wasn't a playground.

Joni outside in yard, The Willows, c. 1955
Photo courtesy of Joni Wilson and Susan Barnes

I know I was in day care during this time, so I wasn't always at The Willows during the day. This outdoor area was likely reserved for times we could play when the young mothers weren't there.

I have one sad memory of sitting at the bottom of a long wooden stairway, which I think led to the delivery room. I was crying for my mother but knew I was not allowed to go upstairs to find her.

Overall, I remember this as a good time in my life. There are other remembrances that I can piece together from photos—celebrating birthdays and holidays in The Willows dining area, being asleep in a chair in the TV room, and wearing pretty dresses sewn by my mother. She often dressed my sister and me alike.

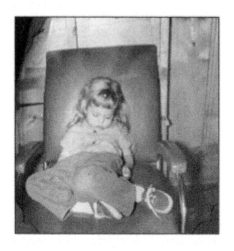

Joni in TV room, The Willows, 1957
Photo courtesy of Joni Wilson and Susan Barnes

While there are unanswered questions about this time in my life, as I learn more about The Willows and the people who were providing this quality service to unwed mothers, I feel fortunate to have lived there for these formative years.

Joni (right) celebrating five years old
The Willows dining room, March 1958
Photo courtesy of Joni Wilson and Susan Barnes

We moved from The Willows to Independence, Missouri, when I was going to start school in the fall of 1958. I was told that this was because Independence offered a better school district.

I'm appreciative of the years I spent at The Willows. As an adult, I realize that it was unusual for a nurse to live there with her two young daughters. But I felt accepted, loved, and part of an extended family.

Susan's Memories

My first birthday was celebrated in the dining room at The Willows, which means I was less than a year old when we moved there and nearly four when we left, so I have few recollections of living at The Willows. As with Joni's memories, many of my thoughts have been pieced together from photos and things we were told. But I have a few solid images in my mind about the building and some of the people who were there.

Susan (left) celebrating her first birthday,
The Willows dining room, September 1955
Photo courtesy of Joni Wilson and Susan Barnes

I can picture a dark TV room with paneled wood walls, a leather sofa, and chairs. Occasionally a few of the women would be in the TV room with Joni and me, but we never had a lot of contact with the residents. I don't recall any specific situations, but we liked being there to watch TV shows and maybe take a nap. It's likely that it was a good place for us to be when our mom was busy.

I'm not sure about the layout of the TV room. I believe there was an exit on one side that led to a hallway, perhaps to our apartment. On the other side, a door led to the area where the women lived.

I recall walking down a hallway that resembled a hospital corridor with private doors and rooms on each side. There was a large bathroom with several sinks and stalls that I used at least once, but I'm sure we were not supposed to be in the area where the women lived.

Susan, The Willows apartment, c. 1956
Photo courtesy of Joni Wilson and Susan Barnes

I have an unpleasant memory of eating the majority of a box of chocolates; I believe they were Reese's Peanut Butter Cups. One of the residents received them as a gift or bought them and didn't like them, so she gave them to my mother. I found the box, helped myself, and got sick.

I remember being in the main kitchen numerous times. I envision a big stove with burners on each side and a flat grill in the center. The cooks kept a small square metal container of butter at the back of the grill. They would fix us toast and use a brush to slather it with melted butter.

I know from photos that one of the cooks, Cecil, was a heavyset, Caucasian woman. She was a friend to our mother and probably helped keep an eye on my sister and me. I also recall a nice African American woman, Lottie, who worked in the kitchen and gave me buttered toast.

Joni and Susan, The Willows dining room, c. 1957
Photo courtesy of Joni Wilson and Susan Barnes

I remember a lovely formal area, which I believe was the front foyer of The Willows, the Main Street entrance. From this room, there was a doorway to a well-appointed office, possibly where the owners or the manager took care of business. At the time I think it was Mrs. Lowe's office; I'm not sure.

I don't remember what Mrs. Lowe looked like, but her name is familiar to me and perhaps I heard my mother speak of her. I recall being left alone in the foyer for brief periods; it might have been during a meeting with my mother and whoever's office was nearby.

In the foyer, there was a large mirror on the wall and a chest of some sort on which there was a large music box. It was wooden and about three feet wide and one foot deep with a lid that opened to view the internal mechanism. It was the kind of music box that was wound and played music with the cylinder circling across the prongs.

I don't recall any of the tunes, but I know I was mesmerized with the tinkling sounds that emanated from the box and the way the cylinder moved. I knew I couldn't touch it. I believe the person from the office came out and wound the music box for me to enjoy while I waited.

Besides a vague memory of others in the TV room with us, I do not recall being around the young women who were there, either while they were waiting to deliver or post-delivery. We were frequently in a dining room that had floral wallpaper but never while other people were there. I'm sure there was a nursery at The Willows but I have no memory of any time that babies were present. It's likely that the nursery and activities with babies were in areas of the hospital where we were not allowed to go.

Susan outside back door, 1955
Photo courtesy of Joni Wilson and Susan Barnes

The back entrance of The Willows ran along Walnut Street where I assume grocery deliveries and such were made. There was a half-circle driveway that went up an incline to the entrance, and we have several photos of us that were taken there. I don't ever remember using the front entrance with the long flight of steps from Main Street to the porch.

In later years, it seemed amusing to tell people that I once lived at a home for unwed mothers. That's how I viewed The Willows—an unconventional place I lived when I was a child without any real appreciation of its purpose. At some point I realized I had lived in a good home that served a specific need—a place that held a high standard and had a caring staff of good people. I recognize the unique opportunity the owners of The Willows gave my single-parent mother in the mid-1950s and I am thankful.

Joni and Susan
Back driveway at The Willows, c. 1956
Photo courtesy of Joni Wilson and Susan Barnes

Our Closing Thoughts

As adults, we've endeavored to discover more about our mother's past and the history she probably would have happily shared. Hers was a life full of interesting happenings. We're sure she would have had some great stories to tell us, if only we'd asked.

We are honored to contribute our memories about living at The Willows to this book. Our hope is that what we've shared can enlighten others about this period of history and The Willows Maternity Sanitarium, a special place that uniquely cared for young women and their babies.

Chapter 16
Sally's Story
(1958)

It has been a pleasure to talk to and get to know Sally over the past two years. She is a compassionate and loving soul. She has been a friend to others who have experienced the pain of placing a child through adoption. I appreciate her insight into what it was like living at The Willows and learning about the care she was given during her four months' stay there. Sally feels compelled to share her story and continues to reach out to help others who are searching or need support with reconnecting with a biological relative. This is her story.

Sally was sixteen years old when she and her mother took a train ride from Milwaukee, Wisconsin, to Kansas City, Missouri. Her mother was taking her young daughter to The Willows Maternity Sanitarium to spend the next four months of her life. It wasn't what Sally wanted but she wasn't really given any other option.

The year was 1958, Sally and her boyfriend were in love. They had been "going steady" since Sally was fourteen. Her mother never really approved of Sally's boyfriend but Sally didn't care. When Sally found out she was pregnant, life seemed to come to a roaring halt. Her parents were divorced and she was being raised by her mother and an aunt. Sally told her mother she was pregnant and wanted to marry her boyfriend. Because she was only sixteen, she had to have the consent of her parent. Sally said, "There was no way for us to get married and even if we had gone to another state, you had to show proof of our age or have parental consent."

Her mother wasn't about to let her marry "that boy." Her mother had gone over to the boy's home and didn't think he was good enough for her daughter. He was only seventeen and there was no way he could provide for a wife and a baby. "One must remember, that was pretty much the thinking in 1958," Sally said. "The only jobs a sixteen-year-old could get were babysitting or waitressing. Waitressing paid like thirty-five cents an hour and you were lucky if you got a dime tip. There was no way I could have supported a child and myself. I didn't really have a choice, I had to do what my mother said. I had to go away and have the baby and give her up for adoption. My boyfriend enlisted in the Marine Corps. He was a year older than I was, and I was sent to The Willows. I had no options."

Sally isn't quite sure how her mother found out about The Willows but assumes it was through her doctor. The arrangements were made and Sally and her mother headed for Kansas City on March 16. "I remember my mother and I taking the train and leaving Milwaukee after dark so we didn't have to worry about the neighbors seeing me," she said. "The train had yellow seats like the old streetcar seats. They weren't cushioned. It was bumpety-bump all night long until we arrived in Kansas City at eight or nine o'clock in the morning."

They arrived at Union Station train depot in Kansas City. They hailed a taxi and gave the address to the driver. "The driver never hesitated nor questioned where we were going," Sally said. "The taxi driver knew to go to the rear entrance of The Willows instead of the front with the many steps up to the front door," she shared. "It obviously wasn't his first trip there."

As they were getting out of the car, a nice older gentleman came up to the car and offered to carry Sally's suitcase. Later Sally was to find out there were two quite elderly men who lived in a small outbuilding next door to the mansion who were the caretakers, maintenance men, or handymen. Their names were Lyle and Ollie. They would carry suitcases in and out, do little repair jobs, and take care of cutting the grass. They were pleasant, quiet guys and didn't have much to say to the girls at The Willows other than "thank you" and "you're welcome." However, they were always there if something was needed.

Ollie carried Sally's bag into the building and showed the two women to the office where they were greeted by Mrs. Lowe and Mrs. Haworth. It was pretty overwhelming for Sally but they seemed like nice ladies. She and her mother were told that Sally could choose between two rooms that each had double occupancy. Mrs. Haworth said she could show Sally the rooms but her mother was not allowed to go where the girls were staying. The two of them went to look at the rooms.

One room had a wash basin and medicine cabinet, the other didn't. Sally said laughing, "In my sixteen-year-old rebellious mind, I wanted the one with the wash basin because it cost five dollars more a week. I wanted to stick it to my mother for making me come here and not allowing me to get married."

The room was very nice and decorated very contemporary for the time. "I am thinking it cost my mother sixty-five dollars per week but I'm not certain if that is accurate. The adoptive parents paid the nursery fees, which I believe were six dollars a day," Sally said. "My daughter showed me some paperwork her adoptive mother and dad had saved and it showed six dollars a day. I don't know if the doctor's fee was included."

"You'll get a laugh at the irony of this," Sally chuckled. "The doctor's name listed on my daughter's paperwork is Doctor Love. He was very nice to me. He was not judgmental at all. We were treated just as if we were respectable, married women," she said.

"We were seen by the doctor once a month until the ninth month and then once a week. He was always very nice and he made it for most of the deliveries," Sally shared. "They had labor and delivery right there, but they had an arrangement with a nearby hospital that if there were any complications, the woman would be transferred to the hospital. But during the time I was there, everyone gave birth at The Willows."

In addition to the doctor, there was a registered nurse who lived there. "I don't know if she was divorced or widowed, but she had two small children," Sally said. "They lived at The Willows and she was available twenty-four hours a day. Plus, there were always nurses in the nursery, taking care of the infants."

She found The Willows to be a very pleasant place to stay considering the circumstances. When asked about conditions of living at The Willows, Sally said, "As far as The Willows is concerned, I have nothing bad to say about the place. The doctor, the cook, the laundry people were all very nice. We never felt shamed there. Mrs. Haworth was extremely warm and accommodating."

Sally has an adoptee friend who was born at The Willows. They met one time in Kansas City at an American Adoption Congress conference. This friend had what she called her "Willows bible" that included every piece of paper she had accumulated over the years about The Willows. When Sally was looking through it, she saw a picture of Mrs. Haworth. "It brought tears to my eyes," Sally said. "It was like seeing the picture of a relative who had passed. She was so kind to me."

Sally shared one memory that wasn't pleasant, the first time she ever saw a cockroach. "Living in Wisconsin, we didn't have cockroaches except in extremely bad living conditions," she said. "I was sitting on the floor one night at The Willows and all of a sudden there was this cockroach crawling across the floor toward me." She laughed, "It was quite a traumatic experience."

"Here I was in my sixteen years, trying to be diplomatic when I went to Mrs. Haworth's office the next day. I said to her, 'Everything here has been very nice. Everyone has been very nice to me.' Mrs. Haworth said, 'What's wrong?' She knew right away something was bothering me."

After Sally shared with her the incident, Mrs. Haworth told her they had an exterminator come in on a regular basis, but she would have them come in for an extra call to take care of Sally's specific problem. "I never saw another bug again the four months I was there," Sally said.

"I had two roommates while I was there. When I first got there, the girl in the room I chose was also from Wisconsin. She was about my age or a year or two older," Sally said. "We got along but I didn't like her attitude toward her unborn baby, referring to him as 'it' or 'that thing.' She delivered a little boy in April or May."

"My second roommate was a college girl," she said. "I have forgotten where she was from. We got along but were not close; she 'hung around' with the other college girls. She was still there when I left."

"I would guess there were between thirty-five and forty girls who stayed there when I did," she said. "At that time, there were rooms on the first floor for four girls and private rooms and rooms for two girls on the second floor. The father of one of the college girls on my floor died unexpectedly. She lived in Nebraska and she was seven months pregnant when her father died. Fortunately, the weather was cool enough, she could wear a big heavy coat to conceal her pregnancy because she had to go home for his funeral. That stands out in my mind as one of the worst things that happened. On the other hand, there was a girl who delivered her baby about two weeks after I arrived. She got a going-home present of a brand-new Thunderbird car from her parents," Sally laughed.

They dined in the dining room in the basement. "The food was not served cafeteria style but the plates were all made up and you took your plate off a shelf," Sally said. "The food was really quite good, nutritious, and plenty to eat. The cook was quite talented. I read somewhere that some complained of having to eat liver at The Willows. I don't ever remember being served liver and I can't stand liver, even looking at it. Maybe we were given a choice, but I don't remember liver. So, I'm not sure if that was another era or just rumor. We were allowed to order out twice a week from what was like a frozen custard stand."

Some of the girls worked in the kitchen. Sally worked in the office. She stuffed envelopes with brochures that were sent to doctors all over the country. "I could work a couple afternoons a week," she said. "I could go down to work when I wanted, if I wanted. There was no pressure that I had to work. The girls who worked in the kitchen were on a more regimented schedule, of course, for preparation."

"I have heard that some girls worked in the nursery, but when I was there, no pregnant girls were working in the nursery," Sally shared.

During the day, the girls played games and had other activities they could do. "There were a lot of card games. I learned how to play solitaire half a dozen different ways," she said.

There were jigsaw puzzles. There were crafts for the girls who were interested. It was very social. There were TV rooms on both the first and second floors for the women to watch television. "The girls all seemed to get along well," Sally said. "Some of the older girls separated themselves from us younger girls, like they were superior to us. There was one woman that I heard was forty-two years old. She left her baby there for a month and she went out and got a job and an apartment and got established. I remember her coming back to get her baby. But she was the only one who kept her baby during the four months I was there."

Girls were allowed to go out once a week with another girl until their ninth month. Some went shopping downtown or to the Kansas City Plaza shopping center and others chose to eat lunch out and/or see a movie. In the ninth month, they had to go out with the nurse if they were to leave. Sally expressed that the nurse, Mrs. Zukowsky or just Mrs. Z, was a very sweet lady. "She was so accommodating to try and help if one wanted to leave and get away for a bit," she said.

There was also a place at The Willows where the girls could go outside to get some exercise and fresh air. Sally went on to say, "There was a big yard for the girls to get exercise. It had a sidewalk in a circle through the yard, and there was a lot of lawn furniture to sit on and enjoy the sunshine. There was always someone out there it seemed."

"A bit of excitement happened once at The Willows when I was there," Sally laughed. "We had a tornado warning. We all had to go down to the basement, which was the dining room. We had to stay there until the storm passed."

Sally's mother was able to come visit her twice during her stay there. She would come and get Sally and they would go to a hotel to spend a day or two. "I assume my mother made arrangements with Mrs. Haworth to allow me to leave," she said. "I really never paid much attention to that being just sixteen. It was nice to get away."

"Letters were a wonderful thing to receive from home," Sally said. "You could have your mail sent to Mrs. Haworth's home, which was residential, or you could have your mail sent directly to The Willows. It was a secret where I was staying. My mother told everyone I was suffering from a virus that was not responding to treatment and the doctor had suggested a "warmer climate," which was a bit of a joke because the climates in Milwaukee and Kansas City are not that different. That was one of the common stories that was told. When my mother would write to me, she would send the letters to Mrs. Haworth's home address rather than to The Willows. Mrs. Haworth would bring the letters over to me."

"The staff would call over the speaker system the names of the girls to come down and get their mail. We always got a chuckle when Mrs. Haworth brought the mail from her house and tried calling us girls over the intercom," Sally laughed. "She didn't really seem to know how to use the speaker system the same way that Mrs. Lowe who worked in the office every day did. Mrs. Lowe was very professional over the loudspeaker, but with Mrs. Haworth, there was always a lot of static and she just wasn't as tuned in to operating it."

"My mother worked at the newspaper in Milwaukee and current events were always dinner table topics around our house," Sally said. "When I was at The Willows, I got the paper sent directly to me under the name Carol Thomas, so nobody my mother worked with would know it was going to her daughter. However, I went by my name Sally when I was at The Willows. As far as I know, everybody used their own names. I know at different times people used different names. I have a friend who was there two years after me that used a different name."

Sally delivered her baby on July 4, 1958. "After delivery, the new mothers did not return to their prior rooms, but instead went to another area on the second floor known as convalescence," Sally said. "All of the rooms in convalescence were private rooms. It was recommended that one spend twelve days in convalescence before leaving, but not everyone did. I did."

"I only saw my baby one time," she shared. "I was able to see my baby for thirty minutes when she was eight days old. Up in the nursery I sat in a rocking chair and rocked her and gave her a bottle. The nurse didn't hover but I knew she was there. Seeing our babies was a choice thing. I would say half of the girls didn't want to see their babies. They felt it would be too hard. But I wanted to see my baby and have the memory of her. I named my baby Faith because as young as I was, only sixteen, I had a great deal of faith in the future. Faith spent thirty days in The Willows nursery."

"The social worker was nice who was from Jackson County," Sally said. "I only saw her twice. Once at a pre-birth interview and next to sign the relinquishment papers. She did impress upon me that I couldn't ever search for my child. That I was subject to imprisonment if I tried to, which is what they told the young women back then. She didn't say it in a punishment kind of way, more of a matter-of-fact way that I could go to prison and not to interfere in my child's life or in the life of her adoptive parents. I don't know if this was a law or what, or just something they said. I was only sixteen and I didn't know anything about assistance that could have been given to me."

"My mother came down twice to visit," Sally said. "She came down four times altogether. First time was when she took me, twice to visit, and then when she took me home after the birth of my baby. We stayed at the Hotel Muehlebach when she visited me. There was no problem with me leaving The Willows at that time. I guess my mother signed me out with the nurses."

Her mother again came back to Kansas City by train to pick her up. They went home on July 16, exactly four months to the day she arrived. She went back to her normal life. She corresponded on a regular basis with her old boyfriend who was in the military. When he came home on leave shortly after Sally returned from Kansas City, he wanted to get together again and be intimate. She just couldn't after having her baby and what she had gone through.

She wrote him a "Dear John" letter about a year after she got home and ended it. When she got married, she never told her husband about having had a baby until after they divorced. She was told at The Willows that it was better she didn't ever say anything, "because no decent man would want 'used merchandise.'"

Sally used to run a support group on the internet for reunited first mothers. This was a safe place for the women to communicate and open up. They often didn't have anyone else to talk to about the emotions and pain they dealt after giving their babies up for adoption.

"I learned a lot about some of the other facilities that these girls stayed in," Sally said. "Some of the religious facilities and Florence Crittenton facilities were pretty mean to the girls. They shamed them. I heard stories of girls having to scrub toilets, using toothbrushes as punishment, and asking for redemption. None of that went on at The Willows. I feel fortunate I was able to stay there. I've heard people call it the 'Ritz' or the 'Waldorf' of the maternity homes. From what I heard when running the support group, I would tend to agree with that. I personally can't say anything bad about the place. I had good nutrition and good medical care. There just wasn't anything bad."

A wonderful relationship came about for Sally through her reunited mothers' support group. "I was connecting with birth mothers all across America through the internet," she said. "One lady I met approximately forty-five years after my daughter was born was named Meryl. We discovered she too had stayed at The Willows. We started sharing about our experiences and I found how we had been at The Willows but ten years apart. Then we realized an incredible coincidence. We had stayed in the same room AND the same bed. What a very small world! We have remained friends all these years."

It took forty years for Sally to once again see her daughter. Sally never felt that her daughter would search for her. She wondered if she was still alive or if she even knew she was adopted. Sally shared, "I read in a Dear Abby column that there was an organization called the International Soundex Reunion Registry (ISRR) and I registered with it as soon as I found out about it."

Over the years, when I moved and bought a new house and changed jobs, I contacted the ISRR and updated my contact information. I always thought on my daughter's eighteenth birthday and again on her twenty-first birthday that, if she was going to search for me, those would be the times when she would. I just had that thought in my mind. The years went by and nothing happened. I didn't give up hope, but I pretty much reconciled myself to the fact we would never be reunited. I never had the funds to pay for a professional investigator."

One day Sally was at work. It was Monday, November 30, 1998. She was a legal secretary in a small office. One of her responsibilities was to answer the phone. "I answered the phone that day at 3:50 p.m. and a gentleman asked for me," she said. "He told me he was with the International Soundex Reunion Registry and I immediately knew why he was calling, even before he said, 'We have a match for you.' I got the chills. In fact, I just got the chills right now retelling this story again. Every time I mention it, it is like it just happened. It was one of the most beautiful moments of my life."

Sally went on to share how her daughter, named Jan by her adoptive parents, found her after forty years. Jan told Sally that she and her family had gone home to visit her parents for Thanksgiving. She talked to her parents and told them she wanted to see if she could find any blood relatives. Her mother left the room and came back with a folder with information she had saved for forty years and gave it all to her. Her mother and father gave her their blessing to search.

Jan sent for her non-identifying information and received it about a week before Thanksgiving. After she and her family returned home from their Thanksgiving visit to her parents' house, she contacted an organization in Washington, DC, and was told to get in touch with ISRR. Jan called and a man there told her he would send her an application form. He told her to keep in mind that a lot of times the birthdates are changed so ISRR staff would search a few days before and a few days after her birthday. He said, "But as long as I have you on the phone, when were you born?" She told him July 4, 1958. He said, "Well, nobody would change that date."

He put the information in his computer and asked what else she knew. From the non-identifying information from Jackson County, Missouri, she began telling him and he said, "We have a match for you."

Sally said, "Amazingly, I had waited forty years to find her and it took her less than two weeks and just two phone calls from the time she sent for her non-identifying information to find me. We talked on the telephone that night. A week from the following Friday, she and her family came to my home in Milwaukee where we met for the first time."

Susan and Jan, Reunion Weekend, September 1998
Photo courtesy of Sally Burke

Susan and Jan, First Hug, September 1998
Photos courtesy of Sally Burke

Sally still wants to help any birth mother who needs to share and talk to someone who had the same kind of experience she had. "Since I ran the support group and have some experience with reunited mothers," Sally said. "please share my email address sallyb1647@sbcglobal.net. I am open to having anyone contact me who might want to do so."

Two mothers and a daughter, 1998
Photo courtesy of Sally Burke

Sally celebrating her birthday, 2020
Photo courtesy of Sally Burke

Chapter 17
Amie's Story
(1961)

I am so happy Amie asked to share her story. She attended one of my presentations and got in contact with me. Amie was a Willows baby. Today she works for Zoe's House Adoption Agency in Overland Park, Kansas, working with adoptive families and expectant mothers who are making adoption plans for their babies. It is interesting how things have come full circle for her. I know you will enjoy her story.

My birth story began in the summer of 1960. My birth father and birth mother met that summer when she was a college student, and by the time she returned to school for the fall semester, she realized she was pregnant. The pregnancy was kept hidden until she returned home for Thanksgiving break, telling only my birth father. He actually asked her to marry him but they decided against it as he was Catholic and she was Protestant, making things challenging at that time. She never had met his family and said she was extremely mortified to meet them and share the news that she was pregnant. Together they made an adoption plan.

She told her parents she was returning to her private Presbyterian college for her second semester, but instead she traveled to Kansas City. I don't know if she traveled to Kansas City by train, bus, or car but many unwed mothers flocked to Kansas City by train because it was in the center of the United States and Missouri's laws were very favorable toward adoption. Kansas City was then known as the Adoption Hub of America. At first, she stayed with a friend she had known in college. While she lived with her friend, she was an outpatient at The Willows Maternity Sanitarium. As her due date approached, she moved into the facility. Finally, one of her friends visited her parents on her behalf and told them she was in Kansas City to deliver a baby.

My mother gave birth to me on May 20, 1961, and named me Jamie, after my birth father, James. I think that was a pretty common thing birth mothers did back then. My adoptive parents named me Amie, dropping the "J" and keeping the same spelling. I feel like they each had a part in naming me and I have always found that very heartwarming. My birth mom then returned home as if she had been at school the entire semester, hoping that no one would ever know. She had me in secret and placed me for adoption.

Amie's baby photo
Photo courtesy of Amie Kirby

My whole life I knew I was adopted. My adoptive mom ended up getting pregnant shortly after I was adopted and had my sister. My sister and I are just twenty months apart. We were always told how

213

much we looked alike, and people still say that to this day. My mom always said I was born in her heart and my sister was born in her stomach.

Amie and her sister
Photo courtesy of Amie Kirby

When I was seven, my parents adopted my brother in Ohio where we had moved. When I was ten, my mother was diagnosed with ovarian cancer and passed away months later. My dad moved us back to Kansas City where both sides of our extended family could be supportive. My dad remarried when I was twelve and I gained a new step-brother. We were now a blended family with four children and none of us were biologically related.

I got married at twenty-five and my adoptive father passed away that next year. I had lost both of my adoptive parents before I had my first baby at the age of twenty-eight. After my son was born, I began wondering about my birth parents more than ever. I kept thinking, *What in this baby looks like my biological mother or father?* I had no one to ask.

I did have some information about my adoption because my adoptive mom had made me an adopted baby book. It said in there that I was adopted through the Kansas City, Missouri Adoption Agency. I contacted them and they sent me a packet of non-identifying information. They then told me they could do a trace of my birth mother and if they were able to find her and if she wanted to meet me, they would arrange that. I said yes but I never heard back.

In the meantime, my husband looked at the information that was in front of us and said, "You know, we might be able to figure this out." This was back in the late 1980s, before the internet was available, so our search was challenging. Although the non-identifying information we received did not give us many specifics, it did tell me the time period that my birth mom was in college, her major, and the activities she was involved in. It did state that she was a student at a private Presbyterian women's college but didn't give the town or state. I assumed that since I was born in Kansas City, Missouri, that I should start my search in the state of Missouri.

The only all-women's private Presbyterian college I found in Missouri was Lindenwood College for Women in St. Louis. I called Lindenwood College and told them I was looking for a missing family member and they transferred me to the library. I spoke to an archivist and she pulled a yearbook off the shelf from the years listed in the information I was given.

The non-identifying information clincher for me was her being the runner up for May Queen. I read that information to the archivist and she looked it up. Sure enough, there she was. I had found my birth mother! The archivist photocopied the pictures from the yearbook and sent them to me. From the yearbook information, I was able to figure out that my birth mom was from Jasper, Missouri.

I only told two people, besides my husband, that I was looking for my birth mom—my sister and my best friend. My best friend lived close to me. In a bizarre twist, my friend was from Lamar,

Missouri, which is a town very close to Jasper, just to the north. I found out that my birth mom grew up on a farm and my friend's dad was a veterinarian in that area. His best friend, who was also a vet, was good friends with my birth grandparents.

After we figured out that my birth mom was from Jasper, my friend called her parents and was able to get my birth grandparents' phone number. My friend called my birth grandmother, saying she had heard of my birth mom through Lindenwood College and wanted to contact her. That's when we found out that my birth mom was then living in Kansas City.

My husband called my birth mom and she was willing to meet me for lunch. I was really nervous and excited all at the same time for this long-awaited meeting. Sitting at the table, and looking across at her for the first time, there was my biological mother. As I looked at her, I saw my eyes. I looked at her hands and saw my hands. It became a sacred, holy, and unexpected moment for me that I will always treasure.

When I was growing up in my adopted family, my sister was biological, and people would say, "Oh, she looks like so-and-so." Then they would get to me and not know what to say, "Oh, you look like your dad." But of course, I didn't because I was adopted. Meeting my birth mom that first time was so healing and reassuring for me that I could hardly handle all the emotions.

At my first meeting with my birth mother, she told the story of how she ended up at The Willows as an unwed mother and how mortified she was. She was the homecoming queen and valedictorian of her high school class. This pregnancy was devastating to her and she didn't want anyone to know. I did learn that my birth grandparents actually went to The Willows to visit my mother after they found out she was pregnant. According to my birth mother, after she had me, she came back home and saw my birth father only one more time.

She moved to Arizona with a friend to start life over. There she finished college and got married. She and her husband tried repeatedly to have a baby together, but she couldn't get pregnant. They decided to grow their family by adoption with their first child. As often happens, after thinking she could not have a baby, she then became pregnant and had a baby girl. She was able to have another baby fifteen months later and became a mother of three children, one adopted son and two biological daughters.

The very year I was trying to find her, she had moved back to Kansas City. At that time, she had not told her children about me. Her two girls were still in high school and she wasn't ready to tell them. Several years passed without my birth mom's children knowing about me. Then when her oldest daughter was getting married, the daughter asked her if she had ever been in love with anyone before their dad. She said yes and told her about her love for my birth father. She shared about having a baby girl and making an adoption plan.

She went on to tell her other children and that is when I ended up meeting everybody. Since we didn't live super close to each other in the Kansas City area, we did stay in touch but only got together maybe once or twice a year because of our busy schedules. I did get to meet her extended family and attended both of my half-sisters' weddings. She was always friendly and super kind to me.

A very important and life-impacting thing happened from meeting my birth mom's family as related to my health. I was involved in a fundraiser for cancer and went on a cancer run. When I got to the finish line, there was my birth mom's sister. She had lost her hair. I found out she had breast cancer and had recently had surgery and chemotherapy. After that, I found out that my birth mom had had breast cancer, though hers wasn't as severe, and she only had to have a lump removed. A few years later, when I was diagnosed with breast cancer, I called my birth mom, remembering the breast cancer in the family and wanting to get the full history.

She was just at the beginning stage of early onset Alzheimer's disease and told me to contact her sister. So, I called her sister and found out that their grandmother had had breast cancer also. She had two sons and these sons had four daughters. Three out of the four all had breast cancer. That was important information for me to know. They had all had the BRCA gene testing for breast cancer but were all negative. I had the BRCA test and it didn't show that I carried the gene either.

Before knowing my health history, the treatment suggested for my early stage breast cancer was a lumpectomy and radiation but after knowing this information, my surgeon suggested we do a double mastectomy. My breast cancer had been detected very early but the doctors were concerned my cancer could recur, given my family health history. I opted for the surgery. It was a very good decision because cells were found in the other breast that were changing and could have become cancerous. If I had not found out that information from my birth mom, I probably would have breast cancer now. God's providence led to meeting my birth mom and getting my health history, leading to a different direction in my handling of the cancer. This is a testimony to the importance of knowing one's medical history.

When I first met my birth mom, she told me my birth father's name. I knew he came from a large Catholic family and I knew the town he was from originally. I decided not to look for him right away. A couple of years went by before I started having any desire to look. Interestingly though, my oldest son was on a basketball team and I was talking to his coach and his coach's wife, thinking that they looked very familiar and that I might have known them from high school or somewhere else. I asked if they were from Kansas City and they said no. They were from another town in Missouri—the same town my birth father was from. I asked the wife if she had ever heard of my birth father. It turned out my birth father was the coach's father's best friend. I am sure we all had shocked looks on our faces.

My birth mom was around five feet five and she said several times that I must have gotten my height from my birth father's family. My son's coach confirmed that my birth father and his brothers were all tall, with my birth father standing around six feet three He also said my boys were probably going to be tall. My oldest and youngest sons are six feet one and my middle son, who looks the most like me, is now six feet four.

After this chance meeting, my birth mom gave me a newspaper article about my birth father's family, which included a family photograph. The birth father had four boys. My middle son looks exactly like his sons, including having the same body type and frame—tall, thin with narrow shoulders. He could pass for their fifth brother.

This next bit of information my birth mom shared really floored me. She told me that my birth father was a competitive swimmer in college. I was also a competitive swimmer growing up and even swam in the state meet in high school. I was the only one in my adoptive family who was a competitive swimmer. In addition, my third son was a very good competitive swimmer. When you are adopted, you usually don't get to know all of that biological information. Finding it out brought some clarity to me on what might have been passed on genetically.

In time, my husband called my birth father to try and make a connection. However, my birth father's wife was living at the time and he wasn't interested in meeting with me. I have thought about trying again as I found out his wife passed away a couple of years ago, but I don't know if he would be open to meeting me now or not.

Adoption has played a huge role in my family and who I am today. I feel like my life has come full circle, and I feel blessed to now be working as an adoption case worker for Zoe's House Adoption Agency in Kansas City. My love for birth mothers, and appreciation for their bravery, is immense. I long to carry on the legacy of love that The Willows provided my birth mother. But women will no longer have to go through the back door or receive a fake name prior to making an adoption plan for their babies. Zoe's House carries this mantle—this legacy of love.

My desire today is to help birth mothers choose life for their babies, give hope to families who want to adopt, and bring dignity and redemption to the brave birth mothers who Zoe's House serves. I feel like my personhood and destiny entwine around four parents, and I am forever grateful for this gift. I want to champion the profound joy that is adoption and be a voice for birth mothers and adoptive families. And in a recent delightful twist, my own nephew and his wife adopted Baby Laramie last fall—a beautiful Zoe's House baby girl! The Lord only does beautiful things!

Chapter 18
Norma and Dan's Story
(1962)

*N*orma and Dan have a very special story. I am so happy and appreciative that Norma contacted me about sharing her story. Giving up a baby for adoption is such a painful experience that doesn't ever completely go away. Norma sharing her story is so helpful for adoptees and friends to understand what a birth mother goes through. Her devotion to helping other birth mothers and being there to listen is commendable. It is also interesting to note that Norma and Sally (Chapter 16) have been friends for over twenty years. They have never met in person but have leaned on each other's friendship and camaraderie because of their similar shared experience of being birth mothers. They were both at The Willows but in different years. Norma gave birth to Dan in 1962. I'm so pleased that Dan wanted to share his story and tell of the reunion with his birth mother.

Norma's Story

I have been hesitant to share my story as it is still painful to me after all these years. After a failed first marriage at age eighteen, I met the guy I thought was the love of my life. We were together for about four months and then had a very painful breakup. I soon realized that I might be pregnant. A visit to my family doctor confirmed it. So I told my mother and she in turn told my father, which I was dreading. My father immediately took charge and made arrangements for me to be swiftly sent out of town to a home for unwed mothers, The Willows, in Kansas City, Missouri.

It was a step that would forever change my life. I arrived at The Willows shortly before Thanksgiving. At The Willows to hide my identity I was called "Sally." I was kind of slow to acclimate myself to my new reality and the first few weeks were so depressing that I actually wanted to die. I called my mom and dad shortly before Christmas and begged them to let me come home. Of course, they said no and that when this thing was all over, then I could come home and start anew.

My dad was concerned about me and flew to Kansas City near Christmas to visit me and get to know Mrs. Haworth. He was very impressed with everything about the home. I remember we went shopping so I could purchase some gifts for him to take back to family members.

Eventually I settled in and actually began to enjoy the company of the other girls, getting to know some of them very well. We would take a weekly trip by taxi to downtown and enjoy a restaurant meal and maybe a movie. I learned to crochet and knit. I also did some paint by number and embroidery. Lots of playing cards. I had two different roomies during my stay. The first one was from Florida. She managed somehow to leave The Willows and stay with a relative in Kansas City with plans to keep her child. Second one was not a good fit for me, constantly complaining so I did not spend a lot of time with her. I also worked in the office as a typist and sent out brochures to doctors throughout the country.

During the last weeks of our pregnancy, we were given a rubber sheet to put on our beds in case our water broke. Occasionally we would notice we were missing a girl at supper or in the TV room, and we were told that she "went upstairs." Upstairs is where the labor and delivery rooms were. I put a hand-drawn calendar on my wall each month and marked an X on each day that passed. My due date was

March 17. As it drew nearer, I had mixed emotions. I would be glad to be able to go home, yet I was torn about leaving a part of me.

I went into labor in the early morning hours of March 16 but went through the day until evening when it became so strong that I had to go upstairs. After a seemingly long labor, I delivered my first-born son at 8:30 p.m. My parents were called by Mrs. Haworth, who told them that the "package had arrived." We were required to stay ten days postpartum. Even though I had shots to prevent my milk from coming in, my breasts were so swollen and painful and I seeped milk for nearly a month.

On the ninth day, I was allowed to go to the nursery and hold my baby for the first and last time. This was so bittersweet, but I held him close, talked to him and even peeked in his diaper to confirm he was a boy. When the nurse came to take him, I went to my postpartum room and cried and sobbed like I never had before.

On day ten, Mrs. Haworth drove me to the airport. I was wearing the same black dress that I had worn on my flight to Kansas City. My father and younger sister came to the airport and picked me up. My sis was about thirteen or fourteen at the time, and she asked me if I had had a baby. I cannot remember what my answer was but of course she found out soon enough.

When we got home, my mom had fixed a terrific supper. I remember thinking how much older my mom looked. I think this took a tremendous toll on her, too. It was understood that we would not talk about where I had been or what I had been through. They wanted to pretend that it never happened, as if I could do that. In my family, in those days, we did not talk much about personal things and feelings. The days and weeks that followed were a blur. I could not sleep and I remember my mother coming to my bedside when she heard me crying at night.

After I returned home, I was very interested in getting back into my clothes so that I could go out and find a job. I had a couple of interviews and wound up working for a downtown loan company. It was a job, but not one that I enjoyed. I felt that we were taking advantage of unfortunate people with extreme interest rates. I soon got a call from a radio station that I had once worked for, and the station wanted me to come back. I jumped at the chance and spent several years working there.

I met my husband just a few months after returning home. Early in our relationship I told him of the son that I had lost to adoption. He was very understanding. We were married for forty-one years and had two sons. Sadly, my husband passed away in 2004 from a major stroke.

I knew in my heart that when my first born was eighteen, I would do all I could do to find him. I began my search for my birth son when he turned eighteen in 1980. I read every book and article that I could find about adoptees, birth mothers, and adoptive families. This was before the internet was available and all searching was by phone and/or mail. I joined every group I could find: CUB (Concerned United Birthparents), ALMA (The Adoptees' Liberty Movement Association), and KCAAO (Kansas City Adult Adoptees Organization), for example.

When my older son Mike graduated from high school and had enlisted in the Army, I told him about my son who I had given up for adoption. I was in the process of searching and wanted Mike to know. Turned out, after a three-year intensive search, I found him.

I began to write a lot of poetry about my loss and my search. One of my poems was submitted to one of the newsletters. That is how my search angel, Laura, came to contact me. She lived in Kansas City and said that she wanted to help me find my son. This was in March 1983.

My search angel Laura devised a plan that enabled her to ask the Bureau of Vital Statistics at the Jackson County Courthouse for a listing of all males born in early 1962 (January, February, and

March), who would be turning twenty-one and would be eligible to enter a St. Paddy's Day contest.

From that list, we chose a name. Laura did all the legwork in Kansas City to get the birth certificate. When I received the birth certificate for the first name submitted, I knew it was not him (wrong time of birth, wrong hospital, etc.). So, the next name submitted was for a young man named Dan. When I received that birth certificate, I was **sure** it was him. This would have been his amended birth certificate—not his original birth certificate. Due to sealed adoption records, I was unable to get his original birth certificate, the one with my name on it.

Laura followed up and contacted him. Dan was a student at a midwestern university and twenty-one years old at the time. He in turn contacted me. This was on April 19, 1983, a phone call that is forever etched in my memory.

I could not have been successful without Laura's help. Years later, Laura and her husband were passing through Tennessee. She called and I met them for lunch at a Cracker Barrel. I was so glad to be able to meet her in person. Sadly, a few years ago Laura passed away.

In April 1983, I told my other son Steve, three years younger than Mike, about Dan after I had located him and received a call from him. Both sons were accepting of Dan. My older son told me that he had always known that "something" from my past was bothering me, he just did not know what.

Dan was adopted as an infant, about one month old, from The Willows. He was very devoted to his adoptive mom because she raised him from age five by herself after she and his adoptive father divorced and he remarried. Dan never told her that he was in touch with me. We talked by phone and exchanged photos and mail. In a few months I was able to fly to Kansas and visit him at his school. My son Mike was at Fort Sill, Oklahoma, in the Army at the time. I notified him that I was flying to Wichita to meet Dan. Mike took a weekend leave and drove to Hays, Kansas, and actually met Dan before I did!

When I arrived at the airport, Mike was there along with Dan. Mike snapped a photo of Dan and me. My surprised look was because I didn't know that Mike would be there. He rode down to the Wichita airport with Dan to meet my flight.

Norma and Dan at airport in 1983
Photo courtesy of Norma Samsel

Mike went back with us on the trip to Hays and we stayed in the dorm for a couple nights. We all went out with Dan's friends to a bar/restaurant. Mike had to return to Fort Sill on Sunday. My flight was on Monday and Dan drove me back to Wichita for the flight home.

In 1987, I wrote to Judge Donald L. Mason and requested our adoption file. The judge responded with a letter and enclosing the "totality of information found in the court adoption file concerning the birth and placement of your son." It had a copy of the Baby's Health Report from The Willows and a copy of the Consent to Adoption of Child that I signed at The Willows. I never did have to go to a courtroom as it was all taken care of at The Willows.

My husband and I visited him once when we drove to Kansas in 1992 and met his wife. I got to meet and play with my first grandson, who was two at that time. That was the only time I have seen my grandson. I have been blessed with three other grandsons and two granddaughters from my other two sons. My son visited me and met my extended family on one occasion. He was in Nashville on business and at the end of his trip he drove to eastern Tennessee for a two-day visit. I invited all our local kin, cousins, etc. for a "party" at my house and a chance to meet Dan. He and I had a good visit with time to ourselves to get to know each other better.

Sadly, my husband passed away in 2004 and Dan lost his wife to cancer a few years later. He remarried, and he and his wife visited in August 2017 on their way to the mountains of Virginia. At that time, they got to meet my friend and companion since 2006. It was a wonderful visit. Dan and I have stayed in touch thanks to the computer.

Norma and Dan, 2017 in Tennessee
Photo courtesy of Norma Samsel

After I found him, I "came out" as a birth mother and no longer felt the shame I had been forced to feel for being an unwed mother. I was active in CUB for a few years and even established a support group for birth moms and adoptees in my area.

Dan's Story

From my earliest childhood memories, I knew I was adopted. In fact, it was one of my favorite bedtime stories from my mom, as she recounted the trip to Kansas City to pick me up. As I grew, the story became more detailed with the information that my birth mother had given me up for adoption because her husband was killed while serving in the armed forces. She couldn't properly care for me as a single mother.

In 1962 adoption was a complicated event. My parents started the adoption process before I was even born. My dad had been married prior to marrying my mom and had two daughters (Diana Sue and Becky) with his first wife. My mom was incapable of bearing children and he wanted a son to carry on the family name as he was an only child. Thus, I became the adopted or "chosen child," as my mom liked to put it.

She said that when they visited the facility to choose a child, which was a hospital in Kansas City, I reached up from my cradle and grabbed her thumb. The nurse in attendance said, "Well, there you go. There's your son." And, so it came to be, that I was born on March 16, 1962, and adopted in May 1962.

I found out some details much later in life from an entry in my grandmother's diary, provided to me by my little sister. It said that on the return trip to southwest Kansas from Kansas City, my parents stopped in at my dad's parents' farm to show me off. I was named after my paternal grandfather—George Daniel and my grandmother's father—James. I was still unsure of the hospital from which I was adopted or where I was housed from birth to adoption.

My dad worked at a gas plant south of Ulysses, Kansas, and my mom was a housewife. We lived in a company-owned house at the plant, along with my sister Diana Sue, whom my mom had adopted prior to my arrival. When my dad's first marriage dissolved, Becky had gone to live with her mother in Colorado and Diana Sue stayed with my dad. A situation/decision that I have never understood even to this day.

My mom was diagnosed with a brain tumor in 1965 when I was three years old. The doctors in Wichita told her that if she lived through surgery, she would probably be blind. I recall her story of thinking that she would be seeing me for the last time at the hospital. However, the surgery was successful and she retained her sight, much to the amazement of her doctors.

I believe the surgery and my mom's overall health had an impact on my parent's marriage, however, as they divorced two years later in 1967. My mother and I moved to town (Ulysses), where I attended kindergarten. We lived on welfare checks and food stamps, as well as child support from my dad. We then moved to Torrington, Wyoming, to be closer to my mom's family in the LaGrange/Cheyenne area, where I attended first grade.

While living in Torrington, my dad and his new wife Shirley came to get me in order to go on vacation in Colorado with them. I remember being amazed at now having three stepbrothers—Terry, Ronnie and Mike—as well as a stepsister—Carla—and Shirley had a baby on the way. That baby turned out to be Jalene, my youngest half-sister, whom I have been the closest to for most of my adult life.

After that vacation, I found that my mom had moved to Garden City, Kansas, because Wyoming was not what she thought it would be as she had been gone for many years. I attended the first half of second grade in Garden City and the second half of second grade in Ulysses. Mom decided Garden City was too big and she desired to be back in a smaller town where she knew more people. Being disabled from her surgery, she did not drive (never had) and relied on friends for transportation.

Second grade was a strange time in my life as coming back to Ulysses and reuniting with school friends didn't go well. Evidently, the curriculum in Wyoming was ahead of Kansas because I was relearning the same things in second grade in Kansas that I learned in first grade in Wyoming. The teacher caught me missing answers on a test on purpose, and it was recommended that I see a counselor. Because my mom was a single parent, on disability/welfare, I already had to appear at the county health nurse's office every month for inspection. This ended about fourth grade and I am not certain what changed.

Anyway, at the counselor's office, I remember he was very concerned about my thoughts on being adopted, which I remember as being strange, and was not certain what that had to do with my missing answers on purpose. I explained that I missed some of them on purpose because only the girls got 100 percent correct. I wanted to fit in with my friends, who did not get 100 percent on the tests.

It was also about this time that I recall going to a family reunion with my dad's new family. While I spent every fourth weekend at my dad's house at the gas plant, I spent very little time with him without my step brothers included. I remember feeling like an outsider. The family reunion reinforced that when I was referred to as the "adopted son." This continued at family reunions on my dad's side until I took my first wife to one. She was furious that as a grown man, over forty with a son of my own, my dad's cousins still referred to me as the "adopted son." I was used to it, but she was so irate that she vowed never to attend another reunion. I have not been back to one since.

By the fifth grade, I started to wonder more and more about where I had come from. My dad and I really never had a father/son relationship. I used to joke about being an only child, living alone with Mom. However, I had three stepbrothers, one stepsister, two half-sisters, and a sister. Also, it was at this time that being from a divorced family and single parent household in Ulysses became less of an unusual occurrence. I was still thinking more and more about my true heritage, and I don't recall knowing of any other adopted kids.

My father figures were fathers of my friends. One specifically was a man named Richard Dudley. He owned and ran the Ulysses Drive-In movie theater and The Movies downtown theater. He hired me as a fifteen-year-old kid and treated me as a son. He had four daughters and once told me that if I ever felt left out, let him know as he had "a wife, four daughters, two female dogs, and a female cat." Since I did feel alone quite often, I became a part of the Dudley family at the theaters.

In high school, I often thought of attempting to research and try and find my birth mother. But I never mentioned this to my mom. By high school, I was taking care of her as much as she was taking care of me. I feared that my searching would hurt her and/or make her feel like I wasn't satisfied. Due to the divorce years before, my mom became estranged from my sister Diana Sue. I realized at an early age that I was all she had.

I also feared researching and finding my birth mother would ruin her life by me showing up to say, "Hello, I am your bouncing baby boy." This thought bothered me as I had become pretty independent from family and on my own. I was able to go to college at Fort Hays State University (FHSU) on an industrial education scholarship and various grants and loans, based on my mom's income and my income.

It was during my junior year in college that my roommate received a call from Laura, a girl who said that she was in touch with my birth mother. Laura had called my mom in Ulysses, saying that she was a friend from high school and was trying to get in touch with me. My mom's phone number in Ulysses was in my name and that is how she found me. My mom gave her my phone number at college.

After receiving the message from my roommate, I immediately called Laura back. She told me that my birth mother—Norma—had tracked me down and just wanted to make sure I was alive and doing okay. If I wanted to be in contact with her, Laura would give me her phone number. And if I didn't, that it was okay.

I jumped at the chance and that evening went to my office in the Memorial Union on campus. I was the Film Director for the Activities Board at FHSU and knew that I couldn't afford the long-distance call that would occur, so I billed it to my office phone.

I called the number and the first thing I remember is Norma's Tennessee accent when she answered the phone! I asked for Norma and she said, "This is she." I said, "This is Dan." The rest of the conversation was about describing ourselves to each other, our likes and dislikes, etc. It was one of the most memorable events in my life to that point.

We exchanged letters and found that our handwriting was similar in style as we both tend to insert and mix cursive and printed letters in our sentences and over use capital letters. Over the years, we've found other heredity versus environment factors in common that we share. But we have also found that we disagree completely on politics, as she is a liberal democrat and I am a conservative republican.

I remember when Norma flew to Wichita, Kansas, to come and visit. I drove from Hays to pick her up. When she got off of the plane, I somehow recognized her immediately although we had yet to exchange photos. She stopped and appeared a little stunned, later telling me how much I looked like my birth father at that age.

During her stay, we visited a lot and I introduced her to my friends and co-workers at the Residence Hall where I served as Resident Manager. I was able to set her up with a dorm room for her stay. Her son, Mike, came up from Fort Sill, Oklahoma, where he was stationed in the Army.

Dan, Norma, and Mike, 1983
Photo courtesy of Norma Samsel

I didn't get to meet her younger son Steve at that time but we exchanged a few letters. During her visit, I added two new half-brothers to my family. I liked Mike and enjoyed visiting with him, but I also remember that he was seeming to be there in protection of his mother. I admired him for this. After I met Norma, she asked if she could meet my mom, but I explained to her that there was just too much risk for any gain. Thus, this meeting never occurred. I guess I was a little protective as well.

Shortly after her visit, Norma called me and told me that my birth father—Gene—had found out that she had found me thanks to some mutual high school connections. He had asked for my name, address and phone number. Norma asked me if it was okay to pass it along. I gave it some thought, knowing he had left her during her pregnancy, but decided that the man had a right to know who his son was, so I said yes.

I never ever heard from him. As the years passed and email became a thing, I would get jokes from Norma's sister—Peggy—and I saw that Gene's name/email was next to mine in the address line. I would respond to "All" with comments and/or jokes of my own and still never heard back from him.

I always felt that it was his place to reach out to me if he had any interest in getting to know me. Because I was never that close to my own family, other than my mom, and again being independent enough on my own, I didn't really need him in my life. I was elated to know the real story behind my birth and meeting Norma and her family. Figuring he was just like my dad, Gene had his own family going on. Years later, Norma told me that Gene had been very ill and he passed away. His daughter called me after his death, as evidently, he told her about me on his deathbed. The call was brief, as I really didn't have anything to say, and in fact, don't even remember her name.

I believe that my independence frustrated Norma as I was not the best at staying in touch. She once told me that after she had found me, she was "afraid of losing me again." I tried to assure her that this would not happen and we have stayed in touch for over thirty-seven years.

The first time I visited her home in Tennessee, I was overwhelmed by the turn out of relatives that she had invited to meet me. I met Steve in person for the first time, and I think that we kind of freaked each other out as we shared a lot of the same interests in terms of sports, sports betting, and occasionally, found ourselves completing each other's sentences. I also met Ben, Norma's husband, who I respected immensely for supporting her in her search for me—her son from another man. I felt as if Ben, as Norma's husband, was somehow closer to being my birth father than Gene was. I was very sad when Ben passed away.

Steve, Dan, Norma, and Mike in 1994
Photo courtesy of Norma Samsel

During this visit to Tennessee, I felt like I was some sort of celebrity, and yet, I was very hesitant. I feared the disappointment that I knew would follow. They were all family, cousins, nieces, nephews, etc., and I was the newly found son, Mike and Steve's older brother. And yet, a stranger. I knew that I would never fit into the whole family thing due to the distance from my home in Kansas. Plus, a lot of time had elapsed in being a part of this family as well as my own independence from my adopted family. I prayed that Norma would understand this. My "family" had become my wife and son, plus in-laws in Hays, Kansas. And yet, I never wanted to lose the connection to Norma that I had made and the bond that we had developed as mother and son.

I had moved my mom to Hays in 1989 to be closer to me and my family and to be able to help her out. She passed away in 1999 and my dad died in 2017 with Shirley following him in 2019.

I always wanted to return and visit Norma again in Tennessee, as she and her husband Ben had come out to Kansas after my son was born to meet her first grandson. But, when I had the money, I didn't have time, and when I had time, I didn't have the money.

235

After my first wife passed away and I had remarried, the opportunity presented itself. I jumped at the chance to stop in to see Norma at her home while I was in Tennessee on vacation with my wife and her daughter's family.

We had a great visit and it was like we had not been apart as long as it had actually been. It had been almost twenty years since my last visit. This time it was just Norma and her friend Bob, who Norma refers to as "not a bad guy, for a Yankee," and my wife Tammey and me. Norma and I also share a similar sense of humor.

Over the last couple years, we are in touch daily via a game called Words with Friends, where we play each other on a pretty equal basis. Although the last time I checked, she was up on me in wins. This game has a chat feature, so between that and email, we are staying in touch now more than ever.

I have wondered from time to time, what my life would have been like if I would have grown up differently as a Tennessee boy. But then I realize that I wouldn't be me. I wouldn't have experienced all of the things that make me who I am. Norma wouldn't be who she is and she is a wonderful person and the most understanding birth mother that there could ever be. Therefore, I have no regrets and I'm happy to be Norma's son.

Chapter 19
Kathy's Story
(1964)

K *athy and I met at a presentation I did at the Kansas City Public*
Library. She shared with me that she would like to tell her story of
finding her birth mother. What a wonderful story it is! Kathy has built
a very special relationship with her biological mother's family. I know
you will enjoy her story as much as I did.

December 14, 1998 is a date that will forever be in my memory.
That was the first time I spoke to my birth mother and started a
wonderful relationship with her and her family. I was born on March
9, 1964, at The Willows. I was adopted through the Jackson County
courts to a family in Kansas City. I had a wonderful adoptive family
and a great upbringing.

As most adoptees understand, I had a desire to know about my
birth parents and family information. I went to my parents when
I turned eighteen and asked if I could have permission or if they
would mind if I searched for my birth mother. At that time, they
said they didn't have any trouble with me finding her one day. They
were apprehensive of letting me do it right then. They felt I was
too immature and maybe not ready to handle it. I told my parents
I would wait. I think they were concerned and maybe scared that
if I found her, I would want to go live with her. I wasn't married
or grounded or doing much with my life yet being so young. They

might have been afraid I would abandon them, which I never ever would have done because I loved them so much, but I understood and waited to search.

My parents had a biological son who was eight-and-a-half at the time of my adoption. My brother was the greatest big brother growing up and is still an awesome person. I love him dearly and we have a very close relationship. He was always there to protect me and watch out for me. When our mom passed away in 2009 and our dad in 2013, he was there for support with everything. We don't talk as much now as I'd like though as he has a very demanding job.

When I turned twenty-eight, I decided to begin searching for my birth mother. It was at the time I had my daughter. I felt I needed to find out more about my own health history for my daughter's sake in case there was some medical issue that I needed to know. I started doing a little searching just before my daughter was born. I would get a little momentum searching and then I would back off, get a little going again and back off. I think I was a little anxious and scared of rejection.

This went on several years without making much headway until I was thirty-three and I had my son. At that time is when I really got focused and decided to look more seriously. My husband spent many hours researching and trying his best to help me find my birth family. In September or October 1998, I found out about a group in Kansas City called the Adoption Triad Support Network KC started by Carolyn Pooler. The Adoption Triad helped me by telling me to contact the county court to get my non-identifying information, which I did.

In this information, it stated my birth mother was from a northern state and that she looked forward to going back to work at The Swiss Colony *(a food gifts company specializing in Wisconsin cheese)* house. I didn't know exactly what that meant at first. Also, my adoptive mother had shared what information she remembered.

My mother was pretty sure she had seen that the birth mother was from a mid-northern state, thinking maybe Michigan, Wisconsin, or possibly Minnesota. She also had seen a document when she and my dad signed the adoption papers and thought she had seen my birth mother's last name.

When I read The Swiss Colony house, I figured out after a while that she must be from Wisconsin. Later I was to find out the spelling of her last name was actually a little different, and if I had called The Swiss Colony company, the staff would have known the name. My birth grandmother retired there after thirty-five years.

My next step, however, was to contact a group called the International Soundex Reunion Registry (ISRR). I submitted my application to the ISRR and received a letter back stating they had received my application and were entering my name and information into their database. If they found any connections, they would then contact me. This was somewhere near the end of October 1998. My son had just turned a year old and I was staying at home for a while to take care of him before I went back to work. I received a phone call on the fourteenth of December and they told me they had a match. I was jumping around and so excited. They asked if it was okay for them to call and give my birth mother my phone number and I said, "Absolutely!"

They called me back and shared they had called my birth mother on her home phone but there was no answer so they left a recorded message without too much information on her answering machine. It was just that they wanted her to call them back. Well, my birth mother came home and heard the message and thought it was some kind of telemarketing call. She deleted it without calling them back!

When ISRR didn't hear back from her, they called her again a little later that day and reached her in person. They told her that her daughter had a Christmas present for her. But my birth mother was a Jehovah's Witness and didn't celebrate Christmas and couldn't figure out why her daughter would have a Christmas present for her. As it turned out, I have a sister and my birth mom was wondering why the heck her daughter would be giving her a present when they didn't celebrate Christmas.

So, the ISRR representative then said to my birth mom, "Does Kansas City ring any bells?" She started crying because she knew right away it was me. My birth mom called me soon after and we talked for two hours. Then she called again a little later that same night and we talked for five more hours. Of course, it was long distance back in those days and was kind of costly but so worth every penny.

Kathy's birth mother
Photo courtesy of Kathy Dayberry

There was so much new information to take in. I found out my new family is from a small town near Madison, Wisconsin, where The Swiss Colony has its home offices. Close by is a little town called New Glarus known as Little Switzerland. Many Swiss migrated to this area and became dairy farmers and made cheese. My great grandparents both migrated from Switzerland and became dairy farmers and cheesemakers. My grandmother was one of fourteen children. She was third to the youngest. I was able to get photos of all of my family and eventually was able to meet my grandmother's surviving siblings.

Kathy's birth grandmother and birth mother
Photo courtesy of Kathy Dayberry

After we established the connection, my birth mother decided to meet. We agreed to meet halfway in St. Louis. On the weekend in January we planned to meet, Chicago had a huge snow storm. The bus station, train station and airports were all closed. There was no way for my birth mother to get to Chicago in order to get to St. Louis. We called and were both on the phone crying that we weren't going to be able to meet. We figured we would just have to wait. But my husband, bless his heart, told me to get my clothes packed, we were driving all the way to Wisconsin! I thought he was kidding. But he said, "Nope, we are going up." So, a trip that normally would have taken us seven to seven-and-a-half hours took us ten-and-a-half hours because of the weather.

We drove all the way to Wisconsin and got there and checked into a motel. We went to my birth mother's apartment and met her in the hallway at 10:00 p.m. at night. We stayed up until about 3:00 a.m. in the morning before we went back to the motel. My poor husband had driven all day and then we were up so late. I found out my birth mom was only nineteen when she had me and she was fifty-three when we met thirty-four years later. We were just trying to make up for lost time. It was a wonderful experience.

All those questions that I had over the years were finally answered. I asked about her family and health history. I asked how I came to be and why the decision was made for placing me for adoption. My birth mother shared what happened and about my birth father. She said he was from a small town close by and they only met a couple of times. They had gone to a bonfire together and one thing led to another and I was conceived. It wasn't like they had dated but it was consensual. Weeks went by and she realized she was pregnant. She never talked to him much after that during her pregnancy or after my birth.

My birth mother went to her parents and told them she thought she was pregnant. They took her to their doctor and he told them about The Willows. My mom told me that she came to Kansas City by train to the Union Station. She got into a taxi with a few other people. The taxi driver took her first to The Willows and dropped her off, which was only a mile away. She said the passengers gave her dirty looks. She didn't go to The Willows until right after New Year's and I was born in March, so she would have been showing quite a lot.

At The Willows, my birth mom worked quite a bit to help pay for her stay. She worked in the office doing some paperwork and also helped in the kitchen, serving meals and such. She became friends with a couple girls and her roommate. That was about all the information I had been told about her stay at The Willows.

After giving birth, my birth mother returned home to Wisconsin. At this point, she still didn't think the birth father's family knew she had been pregnant. It was a pretty small town back then but my birth mother had worked at a previous job with my uncle, my birth father's brother. When my mom got back from Kansas City from having me, she ran into him one time. He started singing, "Kansas City, Kansas City, here I come!" She just looked at him and thought, *Yeah, he knows. What a jerk!* Later my mom learned that my birth father dropped out of college to get a job to help pay for her stay at The Willows. My grandfather must have confronted him.

I not only met my birth mom but also met my extended family and was greeted with open arms. My birth mother had gotten married, had a daughter, and divorced. A few years later, she met another man, married again, and had two sons. I would have been three when my sister was born and about nine and ten years old when my brothers were born. Unfortunately, one brother passed away about fifteen months after meeting him. I also got to meet my grandparents and my only aunt.

My grandfather was in the latter stages of Parkinson's disease but his mind was sharp and he knew exactly who I was. I developed a very special bond in the short time I had with him. He passed away in August 2000, soon after we found each other. We didn't get to spend a lot of time together, but the time we did have was very precious to me. My grandmother passed away in April 2012. I had fourteen years with her. She taught me a lot about our Swiss heritage and how to cook Swiss dishes.

After we met, I realized my mother and I had the same body shape and physique. I also found other similarities to my new family. One thing was that they all liked cats. My grandpa had a garage with all these cats. They called it his "Cat House." My sister loves cats and had four cats. Both my mom and my aunt each had two cats. And I had a couple and have always loved cats.

Kathy's birth grandparents
Photo courtesy of Kathy Dayberry

Another similarity was that my mother, sister, and I all had jobs in the accounting field. They lived in the cheese capital of Wisconsin and I had grown up loving cheese. I love macaroni and cheese, Cheetos, and just anything with cheese. I always wondered why I loved cheese so much and I came to find out why. I guess it was inevitable.

I was never able to meet my birth father. One time when I was visiting my birth mom, I had found information about my birth father's five brothers and one sister. I found the phone number of one of the brothers and called him. It was the same brother who had confronted my birth mother after my birth. He basically claimed I wasn't his brother's child and he didn't want to have anything to do with me. So, I said, "How come he quit college to get a job to help pay for my mother's stay at The Willows in Kansas City?" He said, "Leave him alone. He doesn't want to talk to you anyway."

I never had any desire then to contact them again after that and my mother asked me to not search any further for him until my grandmother passed away. When I did start looking again, I found out he passed away in 2010, two years prior to my grandmother's passing. I have found my birth father's family on Facebook but have not contacted them yet. I've thought about it, mainly out of curiosity about my heritage on the paternal side but just not followed up and not sure I will.

As with many adoptees, the lack of medical information has been a big deal to me my whole life. Prior to 1998, I didn't have any medical history to tell doctors. The medical information I gleaned from my birth mother was very beneficial because there have been several health issues in the family. My grandmother died from kidney failure and my birth mom also suffered from kidney disease. My birth mother passed away in June 2018 at the very young age of seventy-one.

One of the best things I experienced when I found my birth mother was that my adoptive parents were still alive at the time. Though they hadn't wanted me to search when I was eighteen, they were very supportive of my search when I did find her. One time my birth mom came down with some friends, who were visiting others in Kansas City, just to meet my parents. That was a fabulous time with the four of us together.

Both of my moms were thanking each other for their unselfish acts, one for giving me up and the other for wanting to raise me. I will never forget that moment and was so blessed in having them both and my father in my life. I wouldn't have changed anything about my adoption and finding my birth mother other than I wish I had searched and found her sooner and had been able to have more time with her, her family and my adoptive parents. I continue to keep in contact with my extended family and visit them as often as possible.

Kathy and her birth mom and parents
Photo courtesy of Kathy Dayberry

Chapter 20
Peggy's Story
(1965)

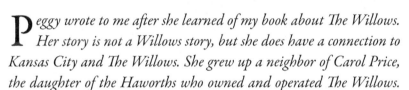

*P*eggy *wrote to me after she learned of my book about The Willows.* *Her story is not a Willows story, but she does have a connection to* *Kansas City and The Willows. She grew up a neighbor of Carol Price,* *the daughter of the Haworths who owned and operated The Willows.* *They have remained lifelong friends.*

Peggy's father was a traveling salesman who traveled all over. She said he always went where he thought the grass was greener. In 1964, he took a job in Kansas City, Missouri, when she was sixteen years old, almost seventeen. The family moved to Kansas City from Nashville. While living in Nashville, Peggy had a boyfriend. He was actually her best friend's cousin who was visiting from Virginia. She said when she told the boyfriend (Cliff) she was pregnant, he didn't act the least bit interested.

Later Peggy was to find out that he had gotten another girl pregnant back in Virginia at the same time and left her too. She had heard he passed away at an early age (around twenty-five years old) but not sure what was the cause. Her friend told Peggy that Cliff and his siblings had a horrible childhood. They lived in poverty and their parents were alcoholics and abusive. Jim (Peggy's son) also had a half sibling about a month older than him. Cliff was definitely not parent material.

Peggy had just turned seventeen, so of course she had to tell her parents she was pregnant. Her father was furious. He threw her photo into the fireplace and wanted to kick her out of the house. After things calmed down, her parents, being Catholic, found out about Catholic Charities and a home for unwed mothers where Peggy was sent. She really didn't want to give her baby up for adoption but in her young heart she knew that this child deserved a lot more than what she could offer him. He needed a family who could take care of him. She was only a junior in high school and had nothing to offer him. She said, "It was so, so, so hard."

Peggy went to stay at St. Anthony's Home in November. The nuns lived on the third floor and the girls stayed on the second floor. The basement was the dining room, kitchen, and laundry. The first floor was the chapel and the offices. She went to St. Mary's Hospital to deliver. She thinks she went by cab alone and was pretty sure the St. Mary's staff knew what to do with the girls when they arrived. Dr. King was the obstetrician. Her son was born on April 1.

She held him every single day for a week and named him. "They would bring him to me and a nurse would stand over me," Peggy said. "I don't know if they were afraid that I was going to take him and run. They would hand him to me (for about an hour) and I would cry the whole time and of course many tears later. It was terribly hard. I loved him and wanted him to have more than me. I just never had a choice. My parents didn't give me a choice and I had nowhere to go. I hadn't even finished school."

She believes the babies went immediately to a foster home or directly to adoptive families.

Peggy later married and had two sons and a daughter. When her firstborn son would have turned eighteen, she told her other children that she had given birth to another boy. She had hoped that when her son turned eighteen, he would look for her and didn't want her other children to be shocked to find out they had a brother. She felt they deserved to know.

Come to find out, her son had been looking for her and wondered why his birth mother hadn't looked for him. However, being born in Missouri, the birth records were sealed and she couldn't have looked for him. She had just hoped he would find her. "He was always, always, always welcome in my life," Peggy said. "I wanted him in my life."

They both had written to the state asking for their records to be open in case the other came looking. Peggy wrote to the Catholic Charities early on, stating she wanted her records to be open in case her son wanted to find her. That didn't seem to matter. She even went to the Office of Vital Statistics in Jackson County, Missouri, and asked if she could pay to open her records in case her son came looking. That didn't work either. So, her information sat on a desk in someone's office for six years.

The day came when they did find each other. At the end of March 2010, Peggy got a call from her son. She was thrilled. "I told him I would love to know him and be a part of his life," Peggy said. "I sent him an email with all the vital information on the whole family that he might like to know. I told him about my other children and about my life."

Peggy told him how much she always loved him and wanted him in her life. She found out her son had grown up with wonderful parents and he was one of four adopted children. His parents adopted twin girls and another girl. He told Peggy he was always the apple of his mother's eye. He did well in school and was quite athletic. He went on to college and played on a hockey team and competed in bodybuilding. After leaving college, he coached a high school hockey team. He had married and divorced but never had any children.

Finally, Peggy got to meet her son in May 2010. He was forty-five years old and he raced motorcycles on oval race tracks. He asked Peggy if she would like to go with him to one of his races. She said sure. At this time Peggy was living in Kansas City so she flew to Chicago where her son picked her up at the airport. "I just wanted to hug him a lot but I was afraid I would scare him," Peggy said.

Peggy and her son, 2010
Photo courtesy of Peggy Arthurs

They headed to the track and her son pitched a tent for them to stay in at the track. He had a trailer with his bikes. "It was amazing to see how close the genetics were," Peggy said. "Very much a perfectionist. It was really funny because my other boys were like that." They spent the weekend together and later on it started to rain so everything inside the tent got wet; they had to go to a motel. But not even rain could dampen their meeting. It was a wonderful weekend.

She had wanted to meet him again at one of his high school hockey games that he was coaching in Michigan. Peggy had a sister not too far from there and so she said it would be easy for her to go stay with her sister and watch the hockey game. But he didn't respond to that. She never really knew why. She sent him cards and she would hear from him once in a while back with texts or emails. She still sends him cards, emails, and texts. He even sent her a Mother's Day card once.

One time her son was in Florida, where Peggy was living, and said he would stop to see her. Unfortunately, she was in Kansas City visiting and missing him broke her heart. He has drifted away though and they have not been in touch in some time. Peggy never knew quite what happened. She felt that he might have felt guilty as if betraying his mother. Peggy didn't think he had ever told his adoptive mother about finding his birth mother. She thinks he told one of his sisters and that was all. However, Peggy was so happy she got to meet him. She knew he was okay and learned what a fine man he turned out to be.

Peggy's children, especially her daughter, would love to meet Peggy's first-born son. But so far that hasn't happened. They have each other's information and hopefully one day they will meet. Peggy said one of the things most fascinating to her is the genetics and how similar her son is to her father in looks and personality. She can just see her father in him and in her other sons.

Another interesting part of Peggy's story is her friendship with Carol Price. Carol's grandparents started The Willows and Carol's mother ran it until it closed in 1969. Peggy lived next door to Carol and her husband Bud. Peggy's father worked for Carol's husband. Bud owned the company Aunt Martha's, which was an embroidery pattern company. Peggy said they always teased her father he was Aunt Martha. She and Carol have been great friends for years. They have the connection in Peggy having given up a child for adoption and Carol being adopted. Plus, Carol's grandparents and parents spent their entire lives helping other young women like Peggy.

One final comment from Peggy was that she was so appreciative of her son's adoptive parents and how they had raised him to be a good man. His adoptive father is no longer living but she wished she could meet his mother in person to express her thanks and did actually write her a short note one time to tell her what a great job she did raising him and loving him.

Chapter 21
Jane and Peter's Story
(1966)

Jane and I were connected through her son Peter. He attended my presentation in Kansas City and shared with me about his birth mother and their reunion. He said Jane might like to share her story. I am so thrilled she did. It has been a delight to get to know them both and to hear her story. Peter also shared letters that Jane wrote to his birth father during her time at The Willows. His birth father had kept these letters all these years. They were tied with a ribbon and he gave these letters to Peter after they met. What an interesting look back in time and getting a glimpse into the mindset of a young woman who was so in love and dealing with such a trying time. I appreciate Jane and Peter's willingness to share their stories and know you will, too.

Jane's Story

I was a young graduate just out of high school in 1966 and living in Wichita, Kansas, when I started dating a young man who was from Iowa. He was twenty years old and in Wichita to go to college. He went home for the summer and I realized I was pregnant. Being young and naïve, I just couldn't believe it. I tried to hide it with my clothing. Thank goodness sack dresses were in.

Throughout the early part of my pregnancy, I had a job working as a secretary for an oil company and went to work every day. I had my own little apartment in Wichita. Each day I would go to work on the city bus, work from eight to five, and come home again on the city bus. When I got to my own apartment, I would fix chicken noodle soup and go to bed. Often, I would run a fever and wasn't taking care of myself. I laugh now realizing just how naïve I was at the time. I started smoking at the age of fifteen and had heard that smoking would cause a baby to come early and it would be small. The thought of giving birth scared me. Life was like this over the summer until I told my parents. It got to the point only one dress fit me.

Jane in tent dress at friend's wedding reception, 1966
Photo courtesy of Jane Ervin

It wasn't until August of that summer that I started to realize my situation. That summer I still couldn't believe I was pregnant and at one point my boyfriend talked me into going to this doctor in El Dorado (less than an hour from Wichita), who was well known to the college guys to provide a "backdoor solution" to an unplanned pregnancy. I was willing to go because I wanted it to be over and hadn't told my folks.

I went there by myself and was scared. It was at night. I walked into this old house. This man told me I needed to take off my clothes.

I was so uncomfortable and thought, *I don't want to be here. What am I doing here?* He told me I was due in six weeks (which turned out to be wrong) and there was nothing he could do for me and that I needed to tell my parents. It freaked me out to think I could be due so soon and what was I going to do now. I was relieved to get dressed and get out of there and go back to my apartment in Wichita.

Not too long after that, I called my sister who lived in California and told her I was pregnant. My sister, who was six years older and married (and pregnant with her second child), told me there was no choice but to tell our parents. She told me if I didn't do it that day, she was going to call and tell them. With dread I went over to my parents' house to tell them the news.

My parents had recently been on a trip to California and they brought with them crates of oranges and lemons. It was the oddest thing. I just craved those lemons and started eating them when I would go to their house. Chicken noodle soup and lemons, I just had a craving for those two things while I was pregnant. That evening my mom made us dinner and then I told my parents I had something to tell them. My dad said, "It doesn't have anything to do with lemons does it?"

I told my parents about my pregnancy and cried. They said for me to move home and they would take care of things. I had a twin brother and two younger brothers living at home and my parents didn't want them to find out I was pregnant. They had a lot of discussions. My mother said she thought I should have the baby. We could go to Oklahoma (she was from Tulsa) and I could have the baby there. Then when we returned, Mom would say she had or adopted a baby. I didn't like that idea at all. (Coincidentally, my mother was born in 1917 to an unwed mother and also was adopted as an infant in Tulsa. She never knew anything about her biological parents and never even had a desire to know.)

My folks had me move back home and out of my apartment. I remember one morning after I had been back home, I woke up and I was huge. I guess I could finally breathe. My parents saw how much I was showing and told me to get back in bed so my brothers wouldn't see me. They called the family doctor. He came over to the house to check me out and said I was about six months pregnant. He told my parents he would help make arrangements for me to go to The Willows, which was a place in Kansas City, Missouri, for unwed mothers.

After the decision was made, things were just a whirlwind for us. My parents told me I would be leaving Monday morning, which was a shock it was happening so fast. I hadn't even quit my job yet, but Dad knew my boss and everything got worked out. They told everyone I was going to go to airline school.

My folks didn't want me to have anything to do with my boyfriend. My dad didn't think he had proven himself to be a man since he had never once talked to my dad about the situation and avoided all responsibility for it. But I went to see my boyfriend anyway after he returned to Wichita for college. I pulled up to the house where he lived with his college buddies and he came out to the car to see me. I told him I would be leaving for Kansas City, and he couldn't believe how much the baby had grown in my belly. I had only seen him one time that summer in early July when I went to see him in Iowa and I still wasn't showing too much then.

Dad drove me to Kansas City around the second week of September. It was just the two of us. I was dressed in my best and only dress I could fit into and high heels. When we got to Kansas City, Dad drove by The Willows and he goes, "There it is." I was in shock because it looked kind of big and scary to me. My reply was, "You're going to drop me off there?"

My dad hadn't ever seen The Willows before either so he suggested we get a room at a hotel (it was the Glenwood Manor) and spend the night. He told me he would take us out for dinner and then the next morning go over to The Willows to check it out. I was quite happy to stall a little longer. We had a nice night out and went back to the hotel.

The next morning Dad called The Willows first and then we drove over. We parked in back and went in the back entrance and into the office. There I met Mrs. Haworth and some other ladies. I had two girdles on, my sack dress and "spiked heels" (as we called them back then). Mrs. Haworth said the first thing I needed to do was get out of those shoes and those clothes. I said okay and then I looked like everybody else and felt so much better.

One lady (I think it might have been Mrs. Haworth) took me to the room where I was going to be staying on the first floor. It was actually like a little studio apartment. I had a sitting room with a TV. It had a small couch and chair. In the other room was a bed and my dresser. I felt really comfortable there and loved the room. I think it was probably a little more expensive. I remember my dad paid her cash. No check or credit card then. Mine cost me $3000 and I was there from about the second week of September until just before Thanksgiving. *(This was actually the apartment that was Cora May Haworth's apartment on the first floor where she stayed when she ran The Willows until 1953. After she passed away, one of the nurses stayed there with her two daughters for a time and then it was rented out to girls.)*

While being given the tour, I saw my dad walking to the car. Mrs. Haworth had told Dad that he could go and she would take care of me. I told the lady showing me around that I thought we were going to talk about it. It was at this moment I broke down. I saw my dad drive off and I knew it crushed him and it crushed me. I didn't get to see him before he left to tell him goodbye or give him a hug. So that's how we were separated. After that, I didn't want anyone coming to Kansas City to see me. I was going to do this on my own.

If my boyfriend would have wanted to keep our baby, I would have married him. But he didn't want to keep the baby. He said we were too young. He was a real jerk, but I still loved him. You know how it is at that age.

While I was at The Willows, I pretty much stayed by myself and didn't meet too many other girls. Often, I stayed in my room and played solitaire. They called me Jane unlike other girls who changed their names while at The Willows to hide their identity. There were a few friends I made and they would come to my room. We would sit on the floor and play cards. Those couple girls and I just stuck together. After my baby was born and I went home, I would call and write to them. I would ask them if they knew if my baby had been adopted out.

The girls staying at The Willows were from all over. I heard when I was there that a married lady was also a resident. She was thirty-four years old and pregnant with twins. She already had children. She gave up her twins for adoption because she didn't want to have any more children. That story stuck in my head as I couldn't figure that out.

Though I had a TV in my room, I don't remember watching it that much. I spent a great deal of time writing in the "bullpen." This was the outdoor area with a small circle where the women could walk and spend time getting fresh air. It was here that I would sit at a picnic table and write love letters to my boyfriend. I don't remember if I wrote home because I didn't want my brothers to know where I was and what was going on. All the letters I received went to Mrs. Haworth's home address.

I will never forget Mrs. Haworth. She was such a nice lady. She was so pleasant and treated me so well. She reminds me of the actress Doris Roberts, who plays Marie on the TV show *Everybody Loves Raymond*. I laugh every time I see that show and think of Mrs. Haworth. She would take a few girls out once in a while to the

Kansas City Plaza. She would drive her big car. I think it was a Cadillac. We would walk around, go to the drugstore or any other place we wanted to shop. I remember I was afraid to get out of the car because I was scared, but it was so nice to get out for a drive. I always thought that was so nice of her to take the time out to take us shopping.

There was a routine that we would go through at The Willows. I think we got weighed every day but I can't quite remember for sure. At least it seemed we got weighed all the time. Then we would have breakfast. We had to go down this narrow hallway and it was kind of crooked and scary to me where it would lead to the dining room. I remember the food was pretty good. I couldn't complain about that. I remember the elderly maintenance guy named Ollie. He was scary because he had this bad limp and I could hear him shuffling down the hall.

The rest of the day was free time. We could do pretty much what we wanted to do. Usually the women went back to their rooms. Most of my time though I was out in the bullpen. I don't remember many of the girls being outside. It was fall and so pretty. I was in love and I was going to have his baby. I knew I was going to adopt my baby out but I still wasn't for sure in my mind. I would talk to my boyfriend and he would say we'll decide what we're going to do and just put me off. So, I still had my hopes up to keep the baby.

I remember going into labor. I was in my room by myself late afternoon and we had played cards earlier. I didn't know what labor was and I was uncomfortable on the floor. Then it was night and I mentioned to one girl I was uncomfortable but she's the only one I told. I was so shy and embarrassed. I went through the night and it started getting worse and worse. Then the next morning I told the nurse when I was being weighed at about eight or nine o'clock that I was having backaches and my stomach hurts. She had the doctor check me out and by noon I had a baby. So, I went through the first part of labor all by myself because I didn't have any idea what labor was like.

My baby was born on November 16, 1966, which was a Wednesday. The doctor had been there that morning, but I can't recall if it was him or a midwife who actually delivered my baby. (I had forgotten this until seeing the letters I sent to my boyfriend, which my son now has. The doctor at The Willows estimated my due date to be October 28 so I ended up delivering him almost three weeks later!) I named my son Robbie. (I had to pick a name for the birth certificate and so I just picked the name "Robbie" because there was a guy back in high school named Robbie whom I had a crush on and so I liked the name.)

I only got to see Robbie for a minute. They took him away immediately when he was born. I knew he was in the building, but I can't say what I was feeling back then. It was almost like I was in a daze. I didn't think to ask to see him because I was so shy. However, on that fifth day, I was taken to this little room that had a rocking chair. A nurse brought my baby to me and put him in my arms. I had thirty minutes with him. I rocked him and barely remember it as the time went so quickly. Again, it was like in a daze. I remember being in my apartment and watching couples come up the steps to adopt their babies. After I had my son, I always wondered if one of the couples leaving had taken him. But later I found out he was six weeks old when he was adopted, so he was still there when I left to go home.

Tuesday was court day and I had to wait until the next week to go. I went with the social worker Mrs. Nichols and signed the papers for the adoption. My dad came and picked me up the next day on Wednesday and I was home for Thanksgiving. I remember when I got in the car, I asked my dad if I had done the right thing. He said, "Yes, you did."

After I went home, I put all of that experience behind me and tried not to think about The Willows. My sister was pregnant at the same time I was. She was due in December but she had her baby girl about five weeks premature in October. I was so upset because she had the baby early. I thought, *Why couldn't that have been me?* Her baby was so tiny though. She brought her baby back home to visit my folks in Wichita for the holidays that year and I would hold her. It made me very sentimental for my son who was nearly the exact same age.

Jane holding her niece
Photo courtesy of Jane Ervin

But I was glad I did what I did for my son. I never forgot my son or his birthday. In fact, my parents didn't forget his birthday either and whenever his birthday or the holidays came around, I would privately ask my parents if they were thinking of somebody today and they said, "Yes, we always think about him." It was the only time we would mention my baby. I always felt that if my son wanted to find me, I would let him find me rather than for me to interfere in his life.

My tale with my boyfriend didn't end with The Willows and having our son. I was forbidden to see my boyfriend when I got back home, but you can guess what I did. I still loved him and wanted to be with him. Despite my parents' disapproval, we continued to date for six more years. I still loved him and he made me feel like we were still going to have a life together.

Jane's photo taken for her boyfriend, 1967
Photo courtesy of Jane Ervin

Toward the end of our relationship, he finally asked me to marry him one night and I was so excited. The next morning, he had this scared look on his face and he said he couldn't do it. His mom would kill him. She wanted him to marry a nice Lebanese girl because they were of Lebanese heritage. I always had the impression his family didn't approve of him dating me, a blonde-haired American girl, or that was the impression he always gave me. That was it. I said I was done and left. I never dated him again after that and all those years of promises.

Years passed and then one day in August 1991 after my parents had both passed (Dad died in 1984 and Mom died the next year in 1985, both of cancer), I went to the mausoleum to see my folks' grave. The lady in charge of the mausoleum said, "Oh, Jane, there was somebody here to see your folks." I asked her, "What did he look like?" The lady said he was a nice-looking young man. I thought it probably was my nephew, but the lady told me he wanted to know where my folks were located. I thought that was kind of strange but it was really nice he wanted to visit them. Little did I know it was my now-adult son who had located me and his grandparents.

Then on my birthday in October that same year, I got a dozen yellow roses. There was no card attached. I thought I must have had a secret admirer and I was quite flattered. Then it was about three months later when I got the call from a lady and she asked, "Does the date November 16, 1966, ring a bell with you? Was that a special date?" I didn't have to think about it and quickly said, "Well, yes!" The lady said she had a young man who wanted to call me that night. I asked if his name was Robbie. She said, "Yes, but his name now is Peter and he would like to talk to you." I said, "Sure!" I was just ecstatic.

Peter called me that night and we talked and talked. We made an instant connection. When I met him, I asked him about the flowers. He said, "Oh yes, that was me." I told him, "Here I thought I had a secret admirer," and we both laughed.

Peter sent me photos from when he was growing up. I always imagined what he would look like as he got older. When my son sent me a picture of himself when he was three or four years old, it was the same image I always had in my head of what my son would look like, what he was wearing, everything! It was amazing that was the image I had carried in my head all those years. The other coincidence is that I always liked the name Peter and even wanted to name my child that but wanted to wait and use the name on a future baby that I would be keeping.

I just thank God that Peter was healthy and okay. When I met Peter a couple of weeks after that first call, I told him I used to hide him by wearing tight girdles and dresses. I asked him if his head was stretched in any way or if there were defects from all the girdles I had worn. He laughed and said no. I also asked him if he liked lemons because I ate like a dozen a day when I was pregnant with him. He laughed again and said he did.

Jane and Peter's reunion in 1992
Photo courtesy of Jane Ervin

Peter never told his adoptive parents that he had searched and found me. He never felt comfortable telling them. He was protective of them and didn't want to hurt their feelings and I understood. I never did get to meet them and they have now both passed away. I wish I could have met them and thanked them for raising Peter to be the fine man that he became.

When Peter reached out to me, it couldn't have come at a better time in my life. I only married once, in 1974, and never had any more children. I did tell my husband about the baby I gave up for adoption. He was very understanding and even wanted to help me find my baby, but we didn't even know where to start. Plus, I thought it was better to let him find me.

After being married for five years, my husband was in a terrible car accident in 1979 and had brain stem injuries. For thirty years I had my husband at home to take care of him with some nurses who came in and helped me. It was at this time that I met Peter when he was twenty-five years old. I had my son back in my life in a time I really needed family. With both my parents gone and as I had no other children, Peter was my family now.

The night Peter first called me, I found a phone number for my old boyfriend (now in his forties). He was living in California and had only been married a couple of years and had a baby. I called and told him the shocking news that "Robbie" had found me and was going to be calling me that night. He was stunned and excited and said he would call me back. He called back later that night and his demeanor had completely changed. He sternly and coldly said not to call him again and didn't want to be contacted ever again about this.

I was shocked and hurt. Later I learned that in between the calls, he told his wife about the baby he had during his college years that was given up for adoption. His wife had a very bad reaction to the news and said she didn't want him to have anything to do with this son or me. So, he felt he had no choice but to reject any contact from his now-grown son.

About six months after meeting me, Peter decided to reach out to his birth father, who did end up wanting to get to know Peter and meet him. But he felt he couldn't tell his wife, so it was limited contact. Eventually during the following year, Peter was able to meet his birth father's three siblings and mother, who was still living.

I told Peter that several years after he was born when I was still dating his birth father, he showed me he had kept all my love letters I had written to him during the time I was pregnant at The Willows. They were bundled with a ribbon. So I told Peter he should ask his birth father about the letters. After Peter and his birth father had met, Peter told me that his birth father still had them! He had saved them in a sack at his brother's place. He felt it was only right that Peter should have them now. I figured he must have cared for me a little if he kept those letters all those years even if he was a jerk back then.

I'm just sorry that Peter didn't get to meet my parents. They would have been so happy with their arms open to meet him. The one thing I know after meeting Peter, I did the right thing. And I am so blessed to have him in my life now.

Peter's Story

I was born in Kansas City, Missouri, at The Willows in 1966 and brought home by my adoptive parents when I was just three-and-a-half weeks old. The adoption was done through the Jackson County Juvenile Court. My parents lived in Kansas City where I was raised. My parents were in their mid-30s when they married; it was the second marriage for my mom and she had a daughter who was already seventeen years old by the time I was adopted. I was pretty much raised as an only child because she was already grown and out of the house as I grew up.

My adoption was a 100% success story. I couldn't have asked for better parents. I was 100% theirs and they never made me feel anything less. They loved being parents and were my number one cheerleaders in anything I did, taking pride in any of my accomplishments in life. I also had two maternal grandparents who lived two hours away in Pittsburg, Kansas, and my dad's mother, a widow, lived here in Kansas City.

I seemed to always know I was adopted but as a young child I didn't know what it meant. When I would ask, my parents would simply tell me it meant that I was special. I can't recall my exact age, but sometime around age seven or eight, the kids next door asked their mom why they weren't "special" like I was. She told them that being adopted means these aren't the adoptee's "real parents." They couldn't wait to run over and tell me that. So that's how I found out what adopted really meant. I remember being devastated and just crying, trying to understand. My parents were so good and gently explained how someone else gave birth to me but I was theirs. The reason I was upset was more because my mom and dad weren't my "real parents" and not because I was yearning to know about the birth parents.

MORE VOICES OF THE WILLOWS

I asked my mom if I also had a baby book the way my next-door neighbors did and she showed me. There was one thing from The Willows in there—a set of my footprints that said "Robbie" on it. Mom told me that's the name my biological mother had named me when I was born. My parents told me what they were told by the court that the birth mother was nineteen when I was born and had sandy-colored hair and was of Scottish and English heritage. All they knew about the biological father was that he was twenty-one and of Lebanese heritage. They said the social worker at the court felt like we were just a great match because my mom's parents were both born in Lebanon and my dad's parents were both from Greece. My mom was raised Catholic and converted to the Greek church when she married my dad.

Over the years, whenever we would be driving past 30th and Main Street, my parents would point out, "That's where we got you." At the time in the 1970s, there was just this vacant lot atop a hill where The Willows once stood. I never saw The Willows, only the concrete steps still there which led up to The Willows. I remember Mom and Dad telling me that they picked me up from The Willows when I was three-and-a-half weeks old. They remembered those steep steps and worried with the weather outside that they would slip while carrying me down those steps.

As I got into my teenage years, I don't actively remember thinking about my adoption or searching one day. I guess every once in a while, because I didn't have any siblings my age, I wondered if I had any siblings out there. It wasn't anything I focused on though. But as an adoptee, I believe the curiosity is always in the back of one's mind.

The next thing I remember is during my freshman year at college here at UMKC (University of Missouri Kansas City), the assignment for a research paper had to be a topic about Kansas City history. I decided I would do mine on The Willows. I was starting to get very curious about it. This was all pre-internet in the mid-1980s so I went to the downtown library and they had a folder of articles about The Willows in their Missouri Valley Room. The articles were mostly about its closing in 1969.

Although I had on occasion in the past driven by The Willows location when I was with my parents, I had never gone there by myself or stopped there. I clearly remember deciding to do that. I drove there, parking on the street in front of where The Willows had once been. I walked up those steps and stood atop the hill on that empty lot, taking it all in and thinking about being born there and trying to picture what once stood there. It's too bad we didn't have cell phones then because I would have taken a few pictures I'm sure. I wish I had a picture of what it looked like that day—the concrete steps leading up to the empty lot.

When I did my paper for my English class, I had made photocopies of what was in that file folder at the library. I remember they also had information about a group called the Kansas City Adult Adoptees Organization. I made a copy of that too, which showed when they met. I believe it was every third Saturday at that downtown library. It took me two more years, while still in college, to get up the courage to actually go to one of those meetings one Saturday. I didn't tell anyone; it was something I had to do by myself.

I remember a sign-in sheet went around the large conference table. One of the columns asked who were you searching for. It's strange how my heart skipped a beat because I remember thinking to myself, *Wait! I'm not looking for anyone yet! I'm just here to listen and get some information.* I was actually a little nervous going there. I felt some guilt as well because I didn't want to do anything which would hurt my parents. They were always open about the fact that I was adopted, but we had never talked about the possibility of actually searching for my biological parents one day.

So I felt like this was a journey I had to take by myself. It was something I had to do on my own. I would occasionally attend the meetings over the next couple of years. When I did decide to dip my toe in the water with learning more about my biological past, the research director of the group, June, told me the first thing to do would be to send my name and info to the ISRR (International Soundex Reunion Registry) to see if I would get a match (only if the birth mother had also signed up with ISRR, which she had not). The other thing to do was to request non-identifying information from Jackson County Juvenile Court. All my dad had in his personal files was just correspondence with the juvenile court, which was of course interesting to read but there wasn't anything about my biological background in there since Missouri was a closed adoption state and everything is sealed. Original birth certificates were sealed at that point. I remember the group telling me it was much easier for Kansas adoptees because they could get a copy of their original birth certificates at age eighteen. Missouri adoptees could not.

I remember when I finally received that big manila envelope from the court. All names had been whited out on the copy sent to me but this was so huge to be able to read more about my birth parents! I pored over every sentence. The information included a paragraph about the birth mother, her age (nineteen) and a bit about each of her family members, including her parents and each sibling. It was then that I first learned she had a twin brother, along with an older sister and two younger brothers. The same kind of information was included about my birth father (age twenty-one) with information about each of his parents (his father had died of a heart attack the previous year) and his siblings (an older brother and sister and a younger brother). So the limited information my parents had been given, which they had told me about, matched the non-identifying information from the court.

When I did finally learn the names of my birth parents and where they were from (she was from Wichita and he was from Iowa but went to college in Wichita), it was a whirlwind. For a little more than a year, I spent the time just basically trying to do things like find their yearbook pictures and basically do good old-fashioned genealogical research to learn more about my roots. It was a safe place to be because I had not committed to any decision to make contact; all I was doing was learning as much as I could about my roots without actually meeting them. It was also a safe place to be because I didn't want in any way to hurt my parents.

I went through the process on my own except for telling my closest friend all the steps I was going through with each discovery. I remember at one point driving to Wichita to do some research after figuring out which high school she attended. I went to the high school library and had them pull the yearbooks. I can't remember if I started with her sophomore year or her senior year (class of '65), but I do remember what a big step it was. From this point on, that image I had conjured up in my head all those years would be gone forever and would be replaced by the reality of seeing a picture of the real person.

As I turned to the correct yearbook page, I put my hand over the pictures to cover them up as I scrolled down to find "Jane" and her twin brother. Then I took a deep breath and saw her picture for the first time. Luckily it wasn't too far off the vague image I had in my head all those years. I made photocopies of the pages from all three yearbooks for her three years in high school.

Sadly, I discovered that her parents had both died (of cancer) about a year apart around six years earlier. Her father was only seventy and her mother was sixty-eight. I was so disappointed that I would never get to meet them. I did visit the cemetery; they were in the indoor mausoleum part of the cemetery. For some reason, I just felt more "connected" to her family instead of my birth father's family in terms of wanting to know more about them. I also drove by her condo when I found out where she lived. At the time, I had no idea if she even had other children. I caught a glimpse of her but knew I just wasn't ready to make contact. What if her family didn't know anything about her teenage pregnancy? I didn't want to intrude or cause any problems for her if people didn't know she'd had a baby.

Also that same year, I made the same kind of trip up to Cedar Rapids, Iowa, to look up the yearbook pictures of my birth father from the class of '63. I did the same thing I did with Jane. I covered the pictures with one hand as I scrolled to his name on the page and then slowly revealed his pictures. It's funny how I never really had any kind of image in my head of what he may have looked like. At first glance, I could see how people would say I look so much like him, but I didn't see it as much. I definitely had his coloring with the dark hair and brown eyes but my facial features seemed more like hers in my opinion.

I already knew his father had died before I was ever born; my birth father was nineteen when his father died of a massive heart attack at age fifty-three. I then discovered that his mother was still living and was seventy-five at the time I was there that spring. She even still lived in the house where he and his siblings grew up. I had a dilemma. How much longer might she be alive and would this be my only chance to ever see my only living biological grandparent? I definitely knew if I met her in passing, I couldn't say anything to her about who I was without making contact with my birth father first as a courtesy. So, I picked a middle ground.

I parked and spotted her taking something outside. I summoned up my courage to go up to the door. I thought about asking for directions but that sounded lame. So, I came up with a story that I was doing family research on that last name and the man at the mausoleum told me about her and that she might be helpful. I was so nervous as I rang the doorbell. I thought worst case scenario that she would be leery of this stranger at the door. Luckily, she didn't ask too many questions and seemed willing to chat and after a few minutes she actually invited me in! I couldn't believe it. I was there in my birth father's boyhood home!

We visited for quite a bit and she showed me pictures of her four grown children and then showed me a picture of my birth father with his new baby. My head was swimming; I thought how can it be that he's forty-five and just now has his first child. The crazy thing I later discovered was that his daughter was born on my birthday, except twenty-four years later than me. What were the odds! Apparently, he had remained single all those years and finally married at the age of forty-four. She said he was now living in California along with her other children. I thanked her for the hospitality. As I left with my heart racing, finding it incredulous that I'd just been talking to my biological grandmother. I couldn't help thinking of my grandparents I had growing up and how I wouldn't have traded that for anything.

Throughout the year, I deeply delved into doing genealogy and loved going back generation after generation especially on my birth mother's side since her side had deeper American roots. I loved finding the obituaries on newspaper microfilm and reading about my great-grandfather or a great-great-grandfather and seeing those graves. It was such an exhilarating process of discovery! An exciting nugget I learned was that my great-great-grandfather was named Dr. P. J. Morrison, who came from Canada (with Scottish ancestry). He settled in the small town of Hillsdale, Kansas, and his first and middle names happened to be the name my adoptive parents gave me! It was purely a neat magical coincidence.

Later that year, I decided to anonymously send my birth mother some yellow roses on her birthday in October. I felt like I was getting closer to that decision of whether to make contact. Once I opened that door, I knew there was no going back and I didn't know if I was ready for that. But there were so many other questions I had that I couldn't get from obituaries, marriage records, and city directories that only she could answer. It was a tough decision and I still was very apprehensive about telling my parents.

I had also seen a story on TV on 20/20 about a pro football player who was an adult adoptee. He did tell his parents he wanted to search for his birth mother. The adoptive parents were understanding but said something to the effect that in their heads they understood why he was doing it (searching) but in their hearts they felt like there was something they were not giving him that made him want to search for his birth mother.

I was so protective of my parents and didn't want in any way for them to feel one bit of hurt as I met and got to know my birth family. It was a very personal decision that only I could make at that particular moment in time.

A few months after sending the birthday roses, I was twenty-five and finally ready to make contact. I consulted June from the group I had been a part of these last few years. She told me it was preferable to have an intermediary make contact; that way if the woman didn't want contact she could say so. It was winter time and I braced myself for this momentous day. I gave June my birth mother Jane's phone number to make contact. June called me back and told me what happened. She said when Jane answered, June (the intermediary) said something like, "I'm looking for Jane (and gave her full maiden name) who gave birth to a boy at The Willows Maternity Hospital in Kansas City in November 1966. Are you that person?"

I can't recall if June told her I was looking for her but June told me that Jane said something like, "You don't have any idea how many years I've waited for a call like this!" June was so happy to tell me this! She said that Jane asked that I wait to call her later that night at a certain time. I couldn't believe all of this was happening.

In the meantime, my birth mother Jane was calling people to tell them about her long-lost son "Robbie" finding her. What I didn't know was that she called around to find the phone number of my birth father in California to tell him I was going to be calling her later that night. He was stunned and said he'd call her back. He later called her back and said he didn't want to be contacted and for her not to call again. (I would later learn that after telling his wife about this, the reaction was not good and that's why he said what he did to Jane.)

I called Jane at the appointed time and she was so easy to talk to. We spoke for the longest time. I told her about my life (and what my name was since all she knew was Robbie) and she answered so many of my questions about my origins. She told me she had dated my birth father for about seven years, which stunned me, and that I happened at the very beginning of their relationship. She had met him at age eighteen during her first year out of high school. She told me the story of going to The Willows and answered my many questions.

Jane told me she never had any other children; I was her only child. She had met her husband in 1974 and gotten married. They had not yet had children when five years into their marriage, he had suffered brain stem injuries from a car accident in 1979 and she had been caring for him in the home ever since. Her whole life revolved around that. She told me how my birth father did not want to be contacted and I could tell she was kind of hurt by that. I told her it was okay and I didn't take it personally. I told her I was the one who sent the yellow roses on her birthday!

We made arrangements to meet within the next two weeks. I drove to Wichita and decided to stay at a Fairfield Inn even though she said she'd be glad to have me stay there. She came that night to pick me up to go to dinner just the two of us. When she came to my door, I opened it slightly and handed her one yellow rose. Then

I opened the door and we came face-to-face for the first time in twenty-five years!

She was so easy to be around and we felt very comfortable around each other. She had been such a young mother that she and my birth father were virtually a generation apart from my parents who were older. The next night she arranged for a family dinner (with her siblings and her uncle) at a restaurant. It was such a neat experience and I enjoyed meeting them all. Her uncle (her father's brother) and I really hit it off. He was a judge and keenly interested in genealogy so we had a great time sharing information. I was finally able to see pictures of some of these ancestors I'd been researching the past year. One important piece of information I never would have learned had I not met Jane was that her own mother was adopted as an infant in 1917! Her mother apparently did not even know she was adopted until she was an adult and according to Jane, she didn't have a desire to know about her biological roots.

At one point during that first year of knowing Jane, she came up to Kansas City. I wanted to bring her to meet the adoptee group and especially June during one of those monthly Saturday meetings at the downtown library and they shared a hug. June got a real kick that I had Jane stay at "The Willows." Let me explain. By this point in the early 1990s the vacant lot where The Willows once stood was finally developed by the Marriott and a Residence Inn was built there. So I had Jane stay there!

Also that year, about six months after first contacting Jane, I did reach out to my birth father and told him he could accept or reject this, but I at least wanted him to know where I was coming from. I told him I was grown and twenty-five and wasn't looking for a mom and dad; I already had a mom and dad and that ideally it would be cool just to get to know one another and have a friendship as adults. He seemed very open to that but he couldn't tell his wife we were communicating because she had a bad reaction to his telling her about his having a child with a girlfriend during his college days. I told him I understood and whatever he was comfortable with was fine. We did meet in person later that summer in California and had lunch.

The following year I did get to meet his siblings and his mother—as myself this time! His mother of course recalled that I had come to her door nearly two years earlier and she understood why I couldn't say anything at the time. I also was able to meet several of his aunts, uncles and cousins who lived in Wichita (which is why he had gone to college down there). Around that time, when his mother was in Wichita visiting her relatives, I arranged for her to have lunch with me and Jane; it was the first time they had seen one another since Jane dated my birth father. I always thought at least back then it would be a neat moment to get together briefly with both birth parents at the same time and take a picture together, but it never happened. I also have never met nor spoken with his wife and now-grown daughter, which would be my only biological half-sibling; I learned that he did tell her about my existence when she was grown.

I'm so glad I was able to find my roots when I was still young and in my 20s. Otherwise I would have missed out on meeting some of the older relatives who were still left (my biological grandmother and the great-aunts and great-uncles who are now no longer living). It has been so rewarding learning about my biological side and seeing pictures of them, present and past. I do wish that I had gotten to meet Jane's parents, my maternal grandparents, since they knew about me from the start.

I always told Jane I've never held any resentment about being given up for adoption. Instead I told her she absolutely did the right thing at that age and how grateful I was that she did because her unselfish act of coming to The Willows to have the baby resulted in me being paired with the most wonderful mom and dad who couldn't have loved or cared for me more. As glad as I am to know my biological roots, I can't imagine growing up any other way than I did and with the family that I had, and I thank Jane and The Willows for that.

Jane's Letters

Jane and Peter wanted to share a few excerpts from Jane's letters to her boyfriend from when she was at The Willows. This will give you a firsthand look at what it was like living at The Willows. This will also give insight to the mindset of a young woman in love and in a terrible predicament. Peter first explains how he got the letters.

Sometime after meeting Jane, she told me she recalled during the time she and my birth father had been dating that he showed her he still had all the letters she had written him from The Willows. She said he had tied a ribbon around them and she couldn't believe he still had them after several years. So after I had met him, Jane wanted me to ask if he still had the letters. I thought chances were between slim and none that he would have kept them after twenty-five years, especially since he was married now. Imagine my shock when he told me that he indeed still had the letters!

When he had gotten married several years before, he packed them in a sack, taped it up, and kept them at his brother's apartment. He told me that he felt I should be the one to have them now. I told him how surprised I was that he had the letters and asked him why he had saved them. He replied, "There was so much love in those letters. How could I throw something like that away?"

It took about a year and a half to finally get the letters. My birth father said he wanted to give them to me in person rather than shipping them to me. We had to coordinate him getting them from his brother and then meeting with me to transfer this time capsule. He handed them over still in the sack in which he'd stored them in all those years earlier. What was inside surprised me even more.

Almost all of the letters were still in their original envelopes and the letters weren't just from The Willows during Jane's final months of pregnancy. The letters actually started with the summer months from Wichita when he had gone home to Iowa for the summer. She wrote him several times a week throughout the summer and fall of 1966. There were letters from the following summer of 1967 and then a few sporadic letters after that with the latest being in 1973, which even included a few references to the child she'd given up for adoption years ago.

I couldn't believe there were nearly one hundred letters in the sack, virtually chronicling their relationship. Before delving into them, I sorted out and put them into chronological order, which wasn't too difficult because of the postmarks and Jane having dated most all of her letters. I never dreamed I'd actually be able to read a contemporaneous account of her pregnancy months of her time at The Willows! I got to know the young Jane, my birth mother, through all of her letters written over a seven-year span.

One of Jane's first letters before going to
The Willows
Dated August 25, 1966
Letter courtesy of Jane Ervin

September 14, 1966

Well, here I am at last. It's really more like a sanitarium. At the present I'm rooming by myself, until Sunday. When my father and I drove by it at first, believe me we both burst out with laughter. That night I stayed all night with my daddy at the "Glenwood Manor."

My letters from now on won't be so long and newsy. For one thing there are no planned activities. You just have to entertain yourself. I have done some painting, playing cards and T.V. watching. The exercise area is really terrible. It's about the size of one-fourth of my parents' driveway. It really was great to hear your silly voice tonight. Remember, Sam, when you call me – make it before 9 o'clock because everyone still is up. When you call, ask for "Jane" only! You don't give out last names. Please do write me, Sam – and tell me what's going on in Wichita. Are you being a good "D-D"? I hope so!

I asked her about visitors – I can see people and go out with them for a couple of hours. It's wise to be alone. If you do decide to come, call first, because I have to get special permission beforehand. Okay? I really do miss you, Sam. Please be good until I get home. Can you wait for me, honey? You better!! "I love you." Love Jane.

September 15, 1966

This is one of those nights when I can't get any sleep. Today has been a little exciting. I had blood taken from my arm for the first time in my entire life. I got weighed today plus my blood pressure checked. Tomorrow I have a complete physical. Have you been good? Never mind, don't answer that. I have, that's for darn sure. I really miss you, Sam. We have really been split up. I hope it's good in the long run. Just think when I'm home, we won't have any problems whatsoever, except maybe my parents.

September 16, 1966

Today all I did was talk with the girls and everything. Late this afternoon the "Doc" came to see us. Would you believe the date is now set for October 28 – three days before Halloween. He said he was sure it was a "boy-type spook." Are you happy?

September 20, 1966

It seems like I haven't seen you for ages, but it has only been eight days. I really wish I was home right now. I miss my family and most of all – you. I hope you are finding some time to think about me. You really are making me worry about you. I hope you can stick it out for six more weeks.

September 21, 1966

Well, I feel great tonight. I don't know why. I guess because it's already Sept. 21. "Butch" has settled down quite a bit today. He'll probably gang up on me tomorrow. He says hello and that he loves you. Wasn't that sweet?

September 23, 1966

Well, Friday night and all I've done is watch this darn T.V. I swear when I get home, I never want to look at another deck of cards, paints, or T.V. I just found out that I wouldn't be able to see you here without their having my parents' permission. I really would rather wait and have you see me when I get home. That way maybe you'll want me more. I have lost 1½ lbs. and my blood pressure has gone way down. Now I have to start taking vitamins twice daily. Well, that's my medical news for today.

September 29, 1966

I can't wait to get home and start fresh. It will be like my first date with you in my life. I don't know what it will feel like to go out after being closed in for six to eight weeks. I have only been outside once since I have been here. Well, at least there is one load off my mind, you are not going to be drafted. If you were, Sam, I think I would go crazy worrying about you all the time.

October 3, 1966

Only 25 more days left until the day. Have you been a good boy? I am trying to figure out what I am going to do when I get home. I don't know whether to go to school or find another job. Sam, are you going home for Thanksgiving? I hope not, because that means by the time I get home (if "it" is late) you will be leaving.

It is pretty out tonight. It is a typical fall evening. What am I doing, but sitting in an old stuffy hallway typing you this sweet note. At least you know that I am thinking of you. I just wonder what you are thinking about now. I do love and miss you, Sam. I will try to come to your rescue as soon as I am able.

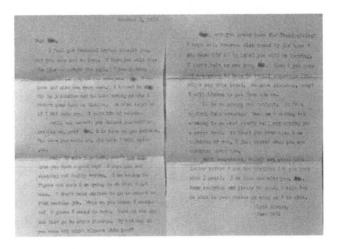

Jane's letter typed at The Willows to boyfriend
Dated October 3, 1966
Letter courtesy of Jane Ervin

October 4, 1966

Today Mrs. Nichols, our social director, talked to me about us. I'm sending you a paper for you to answer. Answer all they ask, okay? Sam, I feel so funny filling out all these papers. I wish you were here with me. I just thought – do you realize what we're doing, honey? It's for the best, I guess. Maybe we'll have our chance again, at the right time.

Right now I'm sitting here listening to records. I'd give anything to come home right now. If only I could leave and see people besides these stupid-looking girls. Well, I guess maybe I shouldn't be talking. Do you have any desire for finding someone else? Sam, when I come home, I want to know what to expect. It's really funny, but I don't want you to see me until I get home. If you saw me now, I'll probably not have a chance at all, right?

October 6, 1966

Sam, how have you been behaving? You sounded awful devilish on the phone tonight. I know I'm just nervous now. Everything seems to bother me. So don't think anything about it. Well, honey, I feel like "it" is ready for me to retire for the evening. Be good.

October 10, 1966

I'm going to try my best to hurry this thing on. Sam, I'm getting so I can't wait to come home and see you. I'm so scared that I'll be acting like a frigid ole nut. Wouldn't you love that – you'd probably go crazy, right? Well, I'm sure you'll be able to straighten me out.

Well, you're probably dying to find out what I had for dinner and supper. Dinner: roast beef, cabbage – cooked, peas, corn bread, and ½ pear. Supper: hamburger patty, baked beans, jello, tomatoes. Now you can't tell me that that really sounds appetizing. The food here really has gotten me down. I can't even walk up one flight of stairs without gasping for breath. It's really going to take a lot to regain my energy. I just hope I have enough energy to go through all this. It just seems funny that I'll be going through all this by myself. But I hope you'll be thinking and praying about me even though you can't be here.

Would you believe my hair is 13½ inches long? Do you like that? Right now it looks almost two-toned. It's time for my monthly retouch. Yesterday I went outside and painted. It felt great to be out in the fresh air. This is my favorite season of the year. Everything is so beautiful. I only wish I could go walking miles and miles.

October 11, 1966

These past few nights I haven't been able to sleep. Maybe it's because it's coming so close to the 28th. Today we had a total of 1,125 calories for all three meals. Could you live on that? I doubt it!

October 13, 1966

This morning I was on my way upstairs and I fell. I just froze after hitting the floor. I thought maybe I could have been hurt. Well, that shows you how graceful I have gotten. Another thing that happened was by the time I reached the top of the stairs, I was panting like a tired horse. I hope I'll be home within three or four weeks if not sooner. If you've waited this long, I'm sure you can give me a few more weeks. Right now I'd give anything to be home with you.

I got your letter today. It made my day a happy one. Thank you, Sam, for being so prompt in returning your history. Now it wasn't so bad writing me a letter, was it? I about died when you wrote me about your uncle finding out about me. Now I <u>know</u> I won't have a chance with your family.

October 16, 1966

Well, it's now Sunday night and I am sitting here listening to records. I wonder what you're doing now and what you're thinking about. Guess what, honey, only 12 more days left (maybe)! I can't wait to go out on a real live date with you. I wonder what we'll do, Sam. We'll probably just talk all night (ha). I'm afraid I forgot how to kiss you. You'll probably have to teach me all over again. Are you willing to put up with me, Sam?

Just think, we can keep on dating – pretending like none of this happened. To me it will seem too unreal to have been true. I'm going to try and put it all in back of my mind. But I won't ever forget this. I'm afraid I'll keep on wondering where it is. I wish you could be here with me when I see him(?). I 'll need you, Sam.

I haven't seen you or the family for over a month. When I get home, I'll have to go out and find me another job. As of now, my parents have decided not to let me fly home. My dad wants to drive me home – sweet thing! Honey, about your sweater, I'll have to wait until I get home. Is that okay?

October 25, 1966

Only three more days (I hope). Then it'll be all over and I'll be home – then we can go from there, okay? Happy belated anniversary! October 21 – "9 months"! Do you still love me? Miss me? I hope so.

October 28, 1966

Thanks so much for calling me today. It really did something wonderful to me and on this particular day. I'm so tired and very much excited. I have a funny feeling that it may still be another week. But I know it has to come soon!! Love you "D-D"

November 4, 1966

Honey, it looks like I'm going to be here a little while longer. I really can't understand what's holding things up. Believe me – I can't stand being here much longer. I'm getting at the point where I'm beginning to go out of my mind. It's terrible not being able to breathe fresh air and see people, in other words, the outside world. Sam, I do miss you and I can't wait to come home and be with you. Pray that I'll go pretty soon. I hope I'm home at least by Thanksgiving!!

November 6, 1966

Things here are still as boring as ever. I can't seem to get interested in anything. Honey, nothing has happened yet! I hate this waiting, but I pray it won't be much longer. I can't wait to come home and start living again. I really feel like I'm just existing and not really living. If you were only in my place, you'd know exactly what I mean. Love always.

Jane finally gave birth on Wednesday, November 16, 1966, at 11:55 a.m. and was able to leave The Willows and return home to Wichita with her father on Tuesday, November 22, just in time for Thanksgiving.

December 22, 1966

Just a little note wishing you a Merry Christmas. I talked to my dad about seeing each other. I think with a little more talking, that things may work out. I love you, Sam. Love always.

Chapter 22
Carol's Story
(1969)

I am so glad to have gotten to know Carol. Though Carol's story did not take place at The Willows, she is one of the thousands of women who were part of Kansas City being known as the Adoption Hub of America. Carol's experience is quite different from many of The Willows stories I've heard. I appreciate her sharing her story and so happy she has developed a special relationship with her son.

The topic of homes for unwed mothers has been at the forefront of my life. Every time I see a story in the paper, or an article in a magazine, I have to read every word. Every other young woman's story is also mine—we have all shared the same emotions that carry us through the years, and the memories never go away.

My story begins in the summer of 1967 at the Jewish Community Center pool where I met my boyfriend "Jack." It was a popular place to meet and hang out with friends, enjoy the pool, and talk about the coming school year. At the time I was fourteen and Jack was sixteen. My parents had already told me I was not allowed to date until I turned sixteen. He and I spent summer days at the pool or at my family's home after school where we did homework. Occasionally he stayed for dinner. There were dances sponsored by Center High School, where he attended, as well as at my school, Loretto Academy. Sometimes Jack would pick me up after school in his orange Mustang and we would head for The Plaza to Winstead's Drive-In for fries and a cherry Coke. We were still seeing each other the following summer of 1968, looking forward to my sixteenth birthday that fall; I was looking forward to going out on a "for real date." Jack and I had been officially dating for several months when I learned that I was pregnant.

I was full of fear about the unknown. I told my mom first—she was devastated. I still remember her ironing in the kitchen and slumping against the wall. We shared a lot of girl-talk and she was encouraging, helping me to understand what my body was going through. I was so afraid to tell my dad, so Mom told him one morning as he was leaving for work. Mom later told me he had the most heartbreaking look on his face. Later that evening, he knocked on my bedroom door and told me not to worry, he and Mom would talk about the best way to "handle it."

My parents counseled with one of our parish priests who recommended Catholic Charities. From there, my parents learned about St. Anthony's Home and my fate was sealed. I was able to finish my sophomore year at Loretto Academy, then packed my personal things, and moved to 27th Street and The Paseo in Kansas City, Missouri.

Of note, it's important to share that my dad was elected the Jackson County assessor in fall 1968 but wouldn't take office until September 1, 1969. My dad came from a very shame-based family, and he wasn't about to let this scandal be the first topic of his new position in the courthouse. He devised a plan where I would supposedly become a foreign exchange student in Toronto, Canada. I had taken French during my first two years of high school, so it was plausible.

He arranged, with the help of Catholic Charities, for a young couple in Toronto to receive my mail from family and friends as well as send it all back to me in Kansas City. This was the first way to isolate me from calling my friends. I was strictly forbidden to call anyone other than my parents. Because my dad wanted to protect his name politically, I was not allowed to see the doctors and deliver at St. Mary's Hospital on 27th and Main in Kansas City, but instead, I was set up at Kansas University Medical Center (KUMC) for all appointments.

When I first went in the door of St. Anthony's, my mom and I were greeted by one of the Sisters of Charity who ran the home. As time went on, I found that these nuns were anything but charitable. Every week, the other girls and I were reminded, "Remember, you're not guests here!" We were also told that we had sinned and would be punished by God, and because of that sin, we were told that we were never to see or hold our babies.

We had to work various chores. My first assignment was working in the kitchen, right after breakfast until lunch. At least the morning hours were not too uncomfortable as it was very hot—no air conditioning and minimal fans. After the kitchen for the months of June and July, I was assigned to the laundry for August, then back to the kitchen for September before being retired from chores as my due date was October 10.

Occasionally I would play board games or work puzzles in the main living room, but we were not allowed to share any personal information about ourselves. Likewise, my dad insisted that I change my name and instructed the staff at St. Anthony's to strictly adhere to that rule, even when going to medical appointments. The only times I was allowed out of the building were to see the doctors, always taking a cab, or enjoying Saturdays with my mom at the movie theater in North Kansas City with an awesome lunch of cheeseburger, fries and cherry Coke. The nuns were very strict about our diets. They told us girls that adoptive parents were expecting perfect healthy babies, so we were never allowed to gain over a total of twenty pounds. But if we did, our diets were drastically cut, and many of us were hungry, sneaking pieces of fruit to our rooms.

Everyone dreaded complaining of a headache or an upset stomach, for the nuns insisted on giving a young woman a rectal exam. It was very humiliating and served no purpose at all! During my off time, I stayed caught up with my schoolwork. One of the teachers from my school visited me every week. The most enjoyable moments for me were spent in the upstairs library where it was cool and warm at the same time with so many books to keep my mind occupied, and I loved it!

When it was time to deliver my baby, I was sent to KUMC in a cab by myself, and I was frightened. A nun had promised to call my parents, and I prayed they would meet me at the hospital. I was taken to a large room with shower stalls and told I had to be clean, but I wasn't prepared for the staff to have me strip in front of them so they could hose me down. I wasn't even allowed the privacy of taking a shower by myself.

Taken to a private labor room, I was left alone without pain medication, crying, and sometimes screaming when contractions were too intense. When a nurse finally checked on me, she found that I was almost ready for delivery. Being taken to a sterile suite and strapped down was not my idea of what should be normal. Both ankles and wrists were secured and I was powerless to do anything but cry and scream (we had not received much information about childbirth, how to breathe with contractions, etc.). I was given a form of gas and don't remember much of anything until I was in recovery, but my parents were there finally and I cried with relief. They had already seen my son. A son! I was so excited and wanted to see him but was told that would not be a good idea; after all, he was going to be someone else's child.

There were three days in the hospital and Day 1 was spent in a "ward" with other women and young girls. My bed was against a wall with a pulled curtain and no windows. Nurses were politely ignoring me, only caring for my health needs and bringing trays of food. Day 2, I got out of bed and walked to the nurses' station, telling them I wanted to see my son. I was told they had orders not to allow that because I was giving him up for adoption. I was so angry! I reminded them that I was still his birth mother, had not signed any papers giving him up yet, and I was entitled to see him! A head nurse was brought to see me, same story, same excuses.

But when evening shift came on, there were nurses willing to help me see him, except I was shoved into a linen closet with a chair and his bassinet holding bottles of water and formula, and one diaper. I reminded them that my aunt had lots of children and I was capable of changing a diaper, so they brought more. Day 3 was another argument with the nursing staff but they relented because I was being discharged that afternoon and the papers would be signed before leaving.

The time I spent with my baby boy was incredible. Lots of joy, and lots of sorrow. My time with him was short, only those couple of days. I did what every other woman does—I unwrapped his blankets and checked his fingers and toes, rubbed his back, and snuggled with him, especially after he was circumcised and whimpered sadly from the discomfort. I held him for hours. I talked to him and saw a look of concentration on his face, his eyes looking serious, and of course, he didn't know I would soon be leaving him, but he knew I loved him. He knew my heartbeat and always stilled when I held him close to my heart. So, when I said that every woman's story was my story, yes! We all shared so much through our pregnancies and felt that joy at seeing our babies and felt that sorrow at signing them away.

I was returned to St. Anthony's Home, alone and in a cab, my heart breaking at never seeing my son again. My parents had informed the staff that I was to stay there for two weeks to recuperate before going home and back to school. I was more isolated than ever.

My belongings had been taken from my room. I had to stay in a small infirmary-style room and take my meals alone. I just wanted to go home but my parents wanted to avoid having me seen until I could fit into my school uniform again.

Back in my school environment, I felt very out of place. I had just given birth three weeks before. I had been forced to sign adoption papers. Nothing was ever going to feel the same for a long time. I went through the motions of everyday life, smiled when I was supposed to, but never let my family see me cry. There followed many years of living a life the best way I could. I never forgot, even though the nuns said, "You must forget this and go on with your life as if it never happened." That's exactly what they said, but guess it's easy for a nun to say that.

Five years later I was married and went on to have four more children. Each pregnancy and birth reminded me of my first son. I loved and cherished my children but they didn't know about their brother until they were about ten to twelve years of age. My husband was an abusive alcoholic and I filed for divorce eight years after marrying. He chose to use the birth of my first son against me, telling our children I was not a good mother because I gave one away. My children believed him and despite what I shared with them, they continued to grow up but became more distant as the years went by.

I always celebrated my first son's birthday each year. Those around me were not aware of it but in my mind and heart I was loving him and celebrating the milestones of his growth. When he was about to turn twenty years old, I began to hope that he might want to find me one day. I held onto that hope until he turned thirty-five. I felt by that time he would have married and started a family, and would want to know me, know about my life and other siblings he may have. But he never did, so I had my own private "farewell" and prayed that he would always be safe and happy throughout his life.

In May 2007, just before Mother's Day, I received a letter from Des Moines, Iowa. I didn't recognize the address, and I didn't know anyone in Iowa! When I opened the letter, I read the first line "born on October 8, 1969" and was in shock. I was standing in the kitchen and slid to the floor, laughing and crying all at the same time. He found me! His adoptive parents told him about me when he was five years old.

When he was a teenager, he became interested in music—guitars in particular—and played bass with several bands during his twenties. He never married, telling me later that he couldn't marry anyone until he had met the woman who gave birth to him. Two weeks after receiving that letter I drove to Des Moines to meet him. I was so excited! We spent a weekend looking at all of his pictures through the years, having pizza for every meal, and he took me to meet his parents, who were awesome. I couldn't have selected a better set of parents than God did.

Several months after we met, he joined a dating site and found "the one!" In 2012 they were married and I was so blessed to attend, welcomed by his parents and entire family. I felt as if I were a member of this huge family who loved me and thanked me for choosing life instead of abortion.

Now it's a little over thirteen-and-a-half years later and we, my son and I, are as close as ever. With social media so popular, we stay in touch through Facebook and occasionally talk on the phone, and our conversations through Messenger are so treasured, full of information, and just so much fun. On his fiftieth birthday, my cousin and I drove to Des Moines to help him celebrate.

Carol and Rob on his 50th birthday, 2019
Photo courtesy of Carol Sweeney Fletcher

I am now sixty-seven years old and my son is about to turn fifty-one this October, and though I missed the first thirty-seven years of his life, I have him now! His adoptive mom even said it was "time to share him with you."

Sadly, my dad passed away in 1987. He never met my son, who was named Robert but goes by Rob (and that's my brother's name, too). But my mom was blessed to see my son a number of times before she passed three years ago. Rob was one of her pallbearers (and she was the first to hold him as a baby). Also sad is that my other children don't want me in their lives, and they aren't interested in Rob either. I'm always praying for healing in these relationships for they are the only things that last.

Even though I don't have any good memories of St. Anthony's Home or my treatment at KUMC, I look at what I went through in order to have a beautiful baby son. He has become an amazing and handsome man, who's lamenting getting old. Oh, how I love him.

My son Rob has such a positive outlook on life. One thing that shows the man he has become can be seen on his Facebook page called *COSMO The Man, The Myth, The Mower.* Rob's motto is that if you can't make people smile, at least don't make them frown. He basically dresses in costume every week while riding his mower, a different character each time. A few years ago, a TV news crew in Des Moines, Iowa, visited Rob and his wife, Amanda, after hearing about the "crazy characters" showing up in their neighborhood. It's a delight for me every time I see it. If you have the chance, check out his Facebook page, I believe you'll enjoy it too!

Yes, I have had a very happy ending to my birth story. There are many who never do, and for them I feel overwhelming sadness and continue to pray that someday they will have their happy ending, too.

Rob as StormTrooper (*Star Wars*)

Rob as Thing 1 (*The Cat in the Hat*)

Rob as Woody (*Toy Story*)
Photos courtesy of Rob McGrath

Yes, I have had a very happy ending to my birth story. There are many who never do, and for them I feel overwhelming sadness and continue to pray that someday they will have their happy ending, too.

Chapter 23
Letters to the Social Worker

O ver the years since I started this journey learning about The Willows, I have talked to many women who spent time there. Each one has shared how difficult the experience was that she went through, but she felt The Willows staff treated her well and with respect. I would imagine out of thousands of women who lived at The Willows, there would be a few who would have negative things to say about the place and their stay. The memories have to be haunting, no matter what kind of care the women were given. But more than one of the women I spoke to told me if they had to be sent to some place, they are glad it was The Willows.

The following are ten letters that Carol Price shared with me. They are from women who stayed at The Willows. After returning home they wrote letters to the social worker who worked with The Willows staff. The social worker gave these letters to Carol's mother after The Willows closed to show what appreciation the women had for Mrs. Haworth and The Willows. Carol inherited and kept the letters, cherishing them all these years. I asked Carol if I could include some of the letters in this book to share more voices of The Willows. Names and dates have been redacted.

I believe you will find it interesting to read the appreciation the young women showed to the social worker for the care given during this stressful time. The letters give a look into how the young women perceived their stay and how The Willows staff treated them. They show their continued love and concern for their babies left behind. They also shed light on a new term I had not heard before, which was R. P. (responsible party). This was commonly used at The Willows when referring to the birth father rather than give his name. Finally, the letters show the women's need to share what their lives were like after leaving The Willows and open up about trying to forge ahead with future plans after such a trying experience.

Letter 1

Dear [Social Worker],

I received your very wonderful letter Thursday. I have been waiting so long to hear that [baby's name] *has a home with two parents that will love her as deeply as I do. From your letter I can take comfort in knowing she will have a life full of opportunity and happiness.*

When I received your letter, a feeling of relief came over me and also one of great sadness in knowing I can never share any part of life with my little girl. However, the family you describe is very much like my own. I think it is best when a family "grows up" doing things together. It gives a certain closeness. I am also happy the parents are Jewish and religiously active.

I thank you too for your kindness and friendship while I was at The Willows. It was not an easy period of my life but you made it much less painful.

My stay there was not one of joy because of the circumstances. However, I gained so much in learning about life and people. The friendships I will always cherish, even though we will probably never meet again. You, The Willows, the girls, Kansas City, and many other things will always have a place in my heart.

I was even sad in leaving my friends and most of all my baby. I think it is only natural to try to hold on to your child as long as possible, now with your letter I know she is no longer mine. She is part of another very happy family. I know she is much better off with two parents and that she will have all the things I would want her to have.

As I told you, I am finishing up my last six audits and will receive my degree in January. I am also working part time in a department store. I hope to go into the advertising department when I get my art degree. I have a studio apartment and I really enjoy it. I've done quite a bit of sewing, since I learned there. When I came home, I even bought a sewing machine.

When I went for my six-week checkup, the doctor said I was fine.

Last night it turned cooler and today is the first sunny and cool day since all the rain from the hurricane.

I will write a note to Mrs. Haworth, too, this week.

If you don't mind, I would like to keep your address and write from time to time just to keep you posted.

Best wishes to you and yours. With love.

Letter 2

Dear [Social Worker],

Hi! First of all, I want to thank you (a little bit late) for the letter you sent me. It was everything I had hoped for. Thank you for ALL your help!

[She shared about her work she is now doing and loving and about dating her boyfriend before she got into her situation. They plan to get married.]

Now for my problem, one of my closest friends is in trouble and is going to go away. I have talked to her about that home in Texas and the one in Wisconsin, but I am not sure how to write to them. She knew all along where I was and I just wish there was some way she could go there [The Willows] *but I suppose you are getting letters like this all the time from girls who feel the same way I do! I hate to ask this of you, because you have already done so much, but if it wouldn't be too much trouble, let me know how she can get information about these places (or any others as close to what The Willows was like as possible, which I know doesn't exist!) She will appreciate any advice or information she can get.*

How is Mrs. Haworth doing? Hope everything has worked out alright for her. Thanks again for everything!!! Love,

Letter 3

Dear [Social Worker],

I want to take this opportunity to thank you for all the wonderful help you gave me while I was in K.C. It is good to have someone believe in you. Love,

Letter 4

Dear [Social Worker],

Wanted you to know the happy news. I'm very happy and am really looking forward to starting a new home with my husband-to-be. He is a wonderful guy.

Hope you and your family are all fine. Thank you again for being such a wonderful person. Love,

Letter 5

Dear [Social Worker],

I want to thank you for taking the time to visit with a stranger about The Willows. It was gratifying to me to talk for the first time with someone who had first-hand information and knowledge of my birthplace. When I was in K.C. ten years ago, I didn't think about taking the address from the stationery. This time I was able to spot the location. I can visualize it from the picture and your description.

My adoption from The Willows was a planned situation. It reads like a story. Thanks to both you and your gracious husband for returning my call. You are most gracious. Sincerely,

Letter 6

Dear [Social Worker],

Well, we've been home a couple of weeks now. Everything has been so busy and hectic. I'm exhausted, but feeling fine. I've started to write to my friends that I disappeared from and explain my absence without too many lies. I try to ignore any questions on the <u>past</u> 6 months so I don't *get involved in too many stories. Do people ever stop making confusion and hurt and problems for themselves and others?*

I'm being my carefree, fun-loving, old self as much as I can, putting on my usual mask for people. But I'm as full of thoughts and questions and emptiness. I hope I can someday find a self-contentment and peace somewhere in this old world.

Enough pitiful ramblings. I pray [Willow's friend] *is well and home soon. Let me know as much as you can whenever you can.*

Say hello to your husband. Take care of yourself and keep in touch when you have a minute (I know how few of those you have free!).

Love,

Letter 7

Dear [Social Worker],

Since people come to you so often with their problems, I thought you might enjoy hearing about all my good "unproblems." I wrote to you last fall (after leaving The Willows in July because my R. P. (responsible party) wanted to get in touch with me. You gently reminded me of his disinterest before my baby's birth but when I got his first letter, I was ecstatic. As an unusual coincidence, the day I received that letter, I had a blind date with a very nice guy. My correspondence with my R. P. continued until Christmas, but my frequent dates with my new friend were showing me how really wonderful some guys can be. To my great happiness in January I had to write to my R. P. and tell him I could never really love him again and on February 1, my boyfriend presented me with a gorgeous diamond. I can't begin to tell you how wonderful everything is. He knows all about my baby (I told him when I was first realizing that I loved him) and he is understanding as I knew he would be. We talked about it sometimes but always end up talking about our own future children.

I would never have believed it six months ago, but my whole experience at K.C. has brought far more happiness to me than sorrow. I know now that my husband and I will be sure of each other's love and my parents like him so much. I know that some family too has a lot of joy in their little daughter and so, though I regret making everyone sad for a while, the long-term effects that made me a little wiser and more mature are worth it.

When I left K.C., I was sure I could never find anyone to love again, but actually it all made me more capable of loving. If you could put this letter on the bulletin board, (by the dining room) someone might get the hope from it that I have found. A letter like this would have been an assurance to me last year at this time. Thank you always,

Love,

Letter 8

Dear [Social Worker],

Remember me? I'm writing to find out about the parents of [baby's name]. *I hope you will find the time to write and tell us about them. The "us" means my husband and me. Surprise! This is why there has been such a delay in writing to you...the wedding and honeymoon, not to mention writing all the thank you notes!*

When my husband and I fell madly head over heels in love, I told him everything that happened. He tried to find out where I had gone to have my baby so that we could get her back again. When I found out about this, we sat down and talked about it for a while. All I really could say to him was that it was best for her that she had two parents that loved her very much and would do all they could for her. We as her parents would be complete failures because I would probably take out some vengeance on her for everything that happened to me and would always resent her as the child of another man. I hope my reasoning here is sound!

My husband and I are both concerned about [baby's name] *and want to know all you can tell us about her new parents. I'm sure they are wonderful people but please confirm this for us so that we may feel that she is in a fine family with a good life ahead of her!*

And please assure all the girls there that there is a future to live for with many promises of a happy, good, and wonderful life. I was so depressed once I was on my own again that I honestly could see nothing to live for since I had such a personal failure.

We are anxiously awaiting your letter!! So please write soon. Cordially yours,

Letter 9

Dear [Social Worker],

My dear friend, I feel so inadequate. I can't seem to fully express how I feel. I am so relieved and thankful that [baby's name] *now has a home; and yet I am sad. Now, I know she is gone from me forever. However, that is something I must learn to live with.*

I can't begin to tell you how grateful I am to you. I want to thank you ever so much for all you have done for [baby's name] *and me.*

I am so happy for her sake and thankful that she was placed with such a fine family. Thank you for telling me what you could about her family; that really meant a lot to me. I have no doubt that she will have a wonderful home and life. As you said, this placement was well worth waiting for.

Thank you again for all you have done for me and please forgive me if I caused you any trouble.

May God bless you for all the good work you are doing. I'm sure God loves you dearly.

With love and appreciation,

Letter 10

Dear [Social Worker],

It was good to hear from you and I want to thank you ever so much for telling me the good news. It took a big load off my parents, as well as mine, and I was so happy to hear she's in a good home with parents who will love and care for her, believe me! I'm sure she'll be as happy with her new parents as they are to have her.

Thank you so much again for everything. I can't begin to express the deep thankfulness and appreciation I feel towards everyone at the hospital. You all were so very dear and understanding. I shall never forget. Take care and my sincere and best wishes for the Holidays! Love,

Author's Notes

It has been an amazing journey in compiling the stories and information for this book. I appreciate everyone who helped bring this to fruition and those who have opened up their lives and stories for us all to enjoy. I am still stunned at how the stories seem to interweave together and the connections that are made throughout the years. I don't know if there will be another book about The Willows, but I do know I enjoy hearing the stories and helping others to document their history for family and friends. One wish would be that my mother and grandmother could have been a part of this while they were living. I know they would be thrilled to have read the stories and met the wonderful people I have in the past four years. Again, thank you and I am looking forward as the journey continues.

Don't miss out!

Visit the website below and you can sign up to receive emails whenever KelLee Parr publishes a new book. There's no charge and no obligation.

https://books2read.com/r/B-A-HBG-LVBJB

BOOKS 2 READ

Connecting independent readers to independent writers.

Did you love *More Voices of The Willows*? Then you should read
Mansion on a Hill[1] by KelLee Parr!

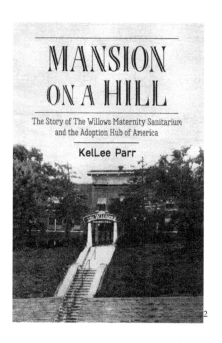

The Story of the Willows Maternity Sanitarium and the Adoption
Hub of America.

For the readers of *Orphan Train* comes the true story of a second
wave of humanity that traveled to the Midwest by train. Not well
documented in American history, over 100,000 pregnant, unwed
young women traveled mostly by train to Kansas City – known as
the Adoption Hub of America – in the early- to mid-1900s.They
would live in one of several maternity facilities before giving birth,
signing their babies over for adoption and returning home empty
handed and heartbroken.

1. https://books2read.com/u/31x8qr

2. https://books2read.com/u/31x8qr

One of these facilities was The Willows Maternity Sanitarium, known as the "Ritz" or "Waldorf" of the maternity hospitals. It truly was a *Mansion on a Hill* and one of the largest of such facilities in America, this is the incredible, true story of The Willows and the compassionate family, yet savvy business owners, who started and operated the seclusion "home" from 1905 until its closing in 1969. With over 35,000 girls passing through its doorway, tales abound of Willows' children questioning the "who" and "why" as they search for answers to their separation. Changed laws and DNA testing are sparking reunions to happen more and more every day. The second part of the book "Voices of The Willows" includes moving stories of those whose lives were touched and changed forever by The Willows.

Read more at www.mylittlevalentinebook.com.

Also by KelLee Parr

My Little Valentine
Mansion on a Hill
More Voices of The Willows

Watch for more at www.mylittlevalentinebook.com.

About the Author

KelLee has enjoyed many different careers. He is a former agricultural and literacy missionary in Guatemala, county extension agricultural and 4-H agent, third grade teacher, and adjunct professor. He has worked for publishers of academic materials in mathematics and science in both management and sales. Currently he helps with writing science curriculum for elementary students. KelLee is a graduate of Kansas State University and is an ardent K-State sports fan. From his rural roots, he loves the beauty of the Flint Hills and resides in Manhattan, Kansas. He is co-chair for the Manhattan Walk to End Alzheimer's Disease in honor of his grandmother Emma and father Lee who both passed from this terrible disease.

Read more at www.mylittlevalentinebook.com.

Made in the USA
Monee, IL
04 November 2020